Augsburg Commentary on the New Testament
MARK
·
Donald H. Juel

Augsburg

Minneapolis

For my Teacher,
Roy A. Harrisville

AUGSBURG COMMENTARY ON THE NEW TESTAMENT
Mark

Library of Congress Cataloging-in-Publication Data
Juel, Donald.
    Mark / Donald H. Juel.
      p. cm.—(Augsburg commentary on the New Testament)
    Includes bibliographical references.
    ISBN 0-8066-8856-4
    1. Bible. N.T. Mark—Commentaries.   I. Title. II. Series.
BS2585.3.J84   1990
226.3'07—dc20   90-32876
                                                 CIP

Manufactured in the U.S.A.   AF 10-9014

00   5   6   7   8   9   10   11   12

CONTENTS

FOREWORD

The AUGSBURG COMMENTARY ON THE NEW TESTA-MENT is written for laypeople, students, and pastors. Laypeople will use it as a resource for Bible study at home and at church. Students and instructors will read it to probe the basic message of the books of the New Testament. And pastors will find it to be a valuable aid for sermon and lesson preparation.

The plan for each commentary is designed to enhance its usefulness. The Introduction presents a topical overview of the biblical book to be discussed and provides information on the historical circumstances in which that book was written. It also contains a summary of the biblical writer's thought. In the body of the commentary, the interpreter sets forth in brief compass the meaning of the biblical text. The procedure is to explain the text section by section. Attempts have been made to avoid scholarly jargon and the heavy use of technical terms. Because the readers of the commentary will have their Bibles at hand, the biblical text itself has not been printed out. In general, the editors recommend the use of the Revised Standard Version of the Bible.

The authors of this commentary series are professors at seminaries and universities and are themselves ordained. They have been selected both because of their expertise and because they worship in the same congregations as the people for whom they are writing. In elucidating the text of Scripture, therefore, they attest to their belief that central to the faith and life of the church of God is the Word of God.

The Editorial Committee
    Roy A. Harrisville
    Luther Northwestern Theological Seminary
    St. Paul, Minnesota

    Jack Dean Kingsbury
    Union Theological Seminary
    Richmond, Virginia

    Gerhard A. Krodel
    Lutheran Theological Seminary
    Gettysburg, Pennsylvania

ABBREVIATIONS

JB	Jerusalem Bible
JBL	Journal of Biblical Literature
NIV	New International Version
RSV	Revised Standard Version
ZNW	Zeitschrift für die neutestamentlichen Wissenschaft

INTRODUCTION

The commentary is a difficult form. It developed out of rather different notions about how truth was to be extracted from texts. From New Testament times, meaning was understood to be located in words and sentences. Despite the fact that Paul wrote letters to congregations that dealt with specific problems, and regardless of the intentions of the evangelists who produced whole narratives, interpreters tended to work with words and sentences rather than with larger units of the Scriptures. Further, interpretation was not restricted to the literal meaning of the text. By the Middle Ages, the science of interpretation had identified four different levels of a text, all of which were fair game to the exegete: the literal, the allegorical, the tropological, and the anagogical. In addition to the literal meaning, every passage of Scripture said something about "faith, hope, and love." Interpreters were trained in the secrets of extracting these hidden truths from the words and sentences of the texts. The wholeness of scriptural truth was sought not within the world of the text but in the dogmatic world constructed by the theologian. The commentary was thus an appropriate form of scriptural interpretation.

Modern interpretation, at least as practiced among learned exegetes, is the result of many changes that have occurred since the Reformation and the Enlightenment. The "modern era," one might say, began with the collapse of the dogmatic structure that provided wholeness and coherence for interpreters. Without the structuring of dogma, piecemeal exegesis does not necessarily generate interpretive stability or coherence. Proof-texting could no longer suffice, but it was unclear what approach could replace it.

At least one proposal was that "history" ought to be the goal of interpretation, by which interpreters meant the world behind the text which had been obscured to an extent by tradition and which, with the proper approach, would yield a coherent picture. Others insisted that the goal of interpretation was the personality of the community that remembered stories about Jesus, or the genius of the author who wrote them down. Students of hermeneutics have analyzed such developments in exquisite detail elsewhere.

The problem is that throughout the last century and a half of such major shifts in perspective, the commentary format has remained relatively unchanged. Consider our present situation. In the past twenty years, students of the Gospels have come to appreciate the artful dimensions of scriptural narrative, taking seriously the literary forms the Gospels assumed. Such appreciation marks a considerable change in exegetical agenda from the previous century. Such shifts imply not simply that the Bible is now fair game for literature teachers but that the "truth" of the Scriptures must be understood in terms of whole stories as well as in terms of words and sentences. Yet commentaries still appear in a form that suggests meaning will be extracted from words and sentences. Format has become problematic, and it is hardly surprising that there is considerable confusion about what form a good commentary ought to assume. My own attempt should be understood as a compromise with traditional standards. That seems appropriate in view of the series in which this volume is placed. I hope that the expository style has not proved to be overly incapacitating with respect to larger—and perhaps more interesting—dimensions of interpretation. I hope also that there will be other occasions for more bold experimentation in writing commentaries.

Introduction

1. Methods of Approach to Mark

Anyone writing a commentary on a biblical work must acknowledge how great a debt is owed to prior scholarship. The tradition stretches back almost two thousand years, and, however different our approaches, one cannot help but appreciate the insightfulness of others. That tradition is far less extensive in the case of Mark, however, than in the case of Matthew, Luke, and John. Mark was largely neglected by Christian interpreters through the centuries. Matthew's Gospel was the favorite of the church, John's Gospel the preference for the "spiritual." Mark, said Augustine, was simply Matthew's "epitomizer," and that was apparently sufficient to relegate the earliest Gospel to an obscure shelf in church libraries.

Interest in Mark blossomed in the 19th century. The Enlightenment institutionalized suspicion in the name of scientific method. People discovered that historical documents were not always reliable. Scholars began to wonder if the accounts of Jesus' ministry were "true"—particularly when there were disagreements among the Gospels and since the stories told of events, like miracles, that seemed singularly "unmodern." Scientific method legitimized suspicion and proposed ways of testing the historical veracity of the accounts. It was in this context that Mark came to be of interest to interpreters.

The features of Mark that most attracted attention were the lack of sophistication (e.g., the absence of a clear train of thought within the narrative, the ordinariness of the Greek) and the colorful detail. The detail in particular seemed to bolster confidence that the narrator knew "the facts." Of the Gerasene demoniac, Mark tells us that he was bound with both chains and fetters—and that he destroyed both fetters and chains, so uncontrollable had he proved to be (5:4). We learn of a young boy who fled the scene of Jesus' arrest naked, his linen garment in the hand of a soldier (14:51-52). We are told that the man who carried Jesus' cross—Simon of Cyrene—had two sons, whose names were Alexander and Rufus. The narrative seems "realistic," by which 19th-century interpreters meant a reliable reproduction of events.

Albert Schweitzer is perhaps typical of the era in his insistence that Mark was both completely accurate and totally naive. The author, he insisted, told things "as they really were," yet had not the slightest idea what held the story together. In fact, Schweitzer insisted, without additional information readers must find Mark's narrative "inherently unintelligible"—while at the same time an accurate reproduction of individual details. While Mark had finally attracted the attention of Bible readers, the Gospel served as little more than fodder for the guns of those who, like Schweitzer, were intent on blasting away at the strongholds of ecclesiastical dogma.

While there are still many interested in the Gospels as sources of historical information, scholars have proposed other goals for interpreters that offer promise. Born in an era when students of folklore had "discovered" the genius of preliterate societies, form criticism developed as a way of conversing with those anonymous believers who handed on stories about Jesus before they were written down. The Gospels, they insisted, can be studied as sources of information about that movement. Mark's lack of literary sophistication allows us to glimpse the contours of his oral sources prior to their incorporation into his work. Form critics pointed to telltale signs of oral transmission—easily remembered story patterns that reflect a typical setting within the life of a community. For them, the distinguishing stamp of the tradition that Mark included in his work was patterning rather than "history-likeness." Like the historians, however, they were interested in Mark principally as a source of information about something else—the "Geist," the spirit and character, of the early believers who remembered Jesus' sayings and told stories about him. A typical example of such a study is Rudolf Bultmann's *The History of the Synoptic Tradition,* or Martin Dibelius's *From Tradition to Gospel,* in which each episode is analyzed formally and studied for information about the Christians who told it and cast it in its present form.

The last 20 years have witnessed the rise of another version of this essentially romantic hermeneutic, one that suggests that the goal of interpretation is contact with other human beings—with "minds" or "geniuses." German scholars, trained as form critics, began to use their skills to get at the creative personality, not of the anonymous Christian community that handed on stories about Jesus, but of the creative genius of the editor who fashioned a whole tapestry from the strands of tradition.

"Redaction critics," as they have come to be called, profess interest in the story as a whole as testimony to a unified conception born in the mind of a creative personality. For them, meaning exists in larger forms than individual episodes, and "truth" lies in the intentions of an author. The task of the exegete is to distinguish between the traditional source material and the work of the editor so that a profile of this personality can emerge. Typical studies are Willi Marxsen's *Mark the Evangelist* and John Donahue's *Are You the Christ?*

The most recent developments in an increasingly complex hermeneutical world that includes deconstruction, structuralism, and rhetorical criticism—to name only a few—represent a further shift from "history." The term "literary" is probably a useful heading under which to group these various proposals. The Gospels are read as narratives, as communication events between a writer and an audience. The most important thing about these narratives, scholars propose, is not that they serve as sources of historical information about Jesus, or that they mediate an encounter with the creative personality of the early church or "Mark." As narratives, they generate a world into which we are invited as readers—a world, we may add, in which God is the primary actor and salvation the goal.

If the Gospels are first of all communication events, a host of questions arise about the nature of that communication—questions that may serve not to explain the material but to enhance its effectiveness. Such questions may include study of the audience—the nature of human imagination, the character of our expectations and their impact on what we hear and see. Or we may ask about literary or rhetorical "devices," the means by which an argument is made or an impression created. Those devoted listeners to radio dramas can appreciate, perhaps, that the world created by the various actors and technicians exists largely in the imagination of the audience. Students of literature speak of the world on "this side of the text"—the result of the communication that should occur between narrator and listener. The effectiveness of the story depends upon the involvement of the reader. Though a distance exists between the world in which Mark lived and our own, interpretation must finally achieve some merging of those worlds, some encounter with the "reality" Mark seeks to create with his story.

From such a vantage point, the "truth" of the narrative cannot be reduced to propositions or historical "facts"; nor can it be reduced to an encounter with the faith of the Christian community or of a discrete author; it cannot be exhausted by an explanation of how it came to be. The story creates a world that makes a claim on the reader; it is that world that must be the focus of interpretive effort and about which truth questions must be asked.

That is not to say other "truths" are thereby dismissed. The New Testament claims that the good news about God involves a historical figure, Jesus of Nazareth. The Gospels require that we pose historical questions. Their claim could in principle be falsified if it could be proved that Jesus never existed. The shape of the narrative may in turn require some comment about sources and the history of composition. One might well ask about continuities that exist or do not exist between Jesus and the church.

Historical studies are important in another sense. The strangeness of the Gospel should be protected from premature modernizing. There are things we need to know about first-century Greek, and expectations shared by author and audience to which we are not privy. We need to know the Old Testament Scriptures on which the New Testament authors could draw—and how those passages had been understood among Jews between the Testaments. We need to know the possible range of meaning of terms like "Son of God," "Christ," and "the Son of man."

Such study cannot substitute for our primary task, however, which is to enter the world created by the narrator. The "truth" involves the words and sentences of the Gospel, but it is larger than the individual parts. It must include questions about how the story affects us as well as what it "means." As with other stories, the place of various scenes in the unfolding of the plot and in the thematic development of Jesus' ministry is as important as what each scene means in itself. Though the commentary format, given such an agenda, is limiting, we may hope that it is sufficiently flexible to permit us to achieve our goals.

2. The Testimony of Papias

The first known comment about the Gospel according to Mark is recorded by the church historian Eusebius. It is attributed to Bishop Papias of Hierapolis, a city in Asia Minor. Papias lived in the early decades of the second century. The "testimony of Papias" reads as follows:

> Mark, who was the interpreter of Peter, wrote down accurately, though without structure, everything he remembered of the Lord's sayings and doings. For he had not heard the Lord or been one of his followers, but later, as I said, was one of Peter's [followers]. Peter used to adapt his teaching as needs required, without making a systematic arrangement of the Lord's sayings, so that Mark erred in no respect in recording some things as he remembered them. For his sole intent was to omit nothing he had heard and to make no misstatement about anything.

We may observe several things about Papias's comment. First, there is some interest in establishing the authorship of the work we know as the Gospel according to Mark. It would appear that concern with authors arose in the second century when alternative works were competing for acceptance and the church was pressed to provide justification for reading some books and not others. Given the large list of works reputed to have been written by Jesus' followers (e.g., the Gospel of Thomas, the Gospel of Peter, the Gospel of Philip), Mark's Gospel was a problem. None of Jesus' followers was named Mark. Where the name came from we cannot know; it was not customary to affix names to the beginning of a document, and "Mark" never reveals himself in the course of the story (the episode about the young man who flees naked at Jesus' arrest has sometimes been viewed as the author's "signature," but that is only one possible interpretation, and it seems unlikely; see the commentary on Mark 14:51-52).

Papias at least knows our Gospel as having been written by someone named "Mark." He seems concerned to identify this "Mark" as the companion of Peter. It may be that given the name "Mark," there are enough data in the New Testament to hazard an educated guess about his identity. Whether the guess is accurate is another question, one that will be discussed in some detail below.

Of greater concern to Papias is Mark's lack of structure. A German scholar, Josef Kürzinger, suggested that the Greek word *taxis* should be understood as a rhetorical term. Papias's statement, Kürzinger insisted, means that Mark's Gospel has no form, no structure—no "order" in the sense that an essay has a structure. Contrary to common opinion among scholars, Papias was not interested in chronology. Most of Papias's comment intends to explain this lack of rhetorical sophistication. His explanation: Mark never set out to write a real book. His only intention was to record what Peter said—and Peter did nothing more than recount anecdotes.

The testimony of Papias seems to reflect a troubling observation about Mark very similar to what we have noted in modern scholarship: the work is anecdotal. It lacks connection. Like modern scholars, Papias sought to account for this feature of Mark's Gospel—perhaps for the sake of learned neighbors scandalized by such a barbarous work—by appeal to his sources. While modern scholars propose that Mark made use of stories taken from the church's oral tradition, Papias argued for Peter as the oral source. The first recorded comment about Mark reflects some embarrassment about its lack of recognizable form.

Another possibility, of course, is that "Mark" did not respect aesthetic conventions because they did not permit him to do with his story what he intended. That is the point of Eric Auerbach in his epic work *Mimesis*. That Mark did not respect the rules of good literature does not mean the author was devoid of skill. It does not mean his Gospel should not be studied as literature. It does mean that it may represent literature of a different sort. We will assume, with Auerbach and others, that there is some logic to Mark's story, that the work is not devoid of artistry. Such hypotheses, of course, need to be tested. Comments about "artistry" must surely be qualified by observations about the episodic character of the narrative and the obvious lack of aesthetic polish—observations which date from the earliest interpretations of Mark. This commentary is an argument, however, that Mark is an important work deserving of close reading as literature—as a communication event.

3. Authorship, Date, and Location

According to tradition—a tradition that probably can be traced to Bishop Papias—Mark was composed by an associate of Peter (1 Peter 5:13). The figure is often identified with the John Mark who was a Jerusalem Christian, mentioned in Acts, in whose house the church met (Acts 12:12). This may even be the same John [Mark] who was related to Barnabas and who traveled at least for a time with Paul (Acts 13:5, 13; 15:36-41).

One major difficulty with this ascription is the language of the Gospel. Though Mark is not written in sophisticated Greek, the language is not translation Greek. The author spoke Greek, not Aramaic. It seems fair to assume that a Jerusalem Christian with a home in the city would have spoken Aramaic. Further, if arguments by form critics about the sources of Mark (individual stories and sayings, cycles of stories and sayings) are valid, there seems little reason to insist that the Gospel reflects the testimony of an eyewitness. The colorful details give evidence of an interest in the drama of narrative. They need imply nothing about eyewitness testimony.

It seems best not to presume on the evidence. Without more data, it is safest to regard the author of Mark as an anonymous Christian who fashioned from the tradition of the church a story of Jesus—perhaps for the first time. The most striking observation about the author of the Gospel is his anonymity. He scrupulously avoided providing any clues to his identity, and it seems only proper to respect that anonymity. Attempts to identify the author with an associate of Peter, even in the most recent commentaries, represent little more than imaginative fiction. There is nothing wrong with speculation about authorship, but basing interpretation on such fanciful reconstructions is unwise. Basing the authority of the Gospel on such speculations is unbiblical and comes dangerously close to unbelief.

The dating of the Gospel is only slightly less tentative. The host of proposals, with new suggestions constantly appearing, only indicates the scarcity of hard data. If there were indisputable facts, one study would suffice. The plethora of proposals suggests the evidence can be read in a variety of ways. The following considerations are relevant to the question of dating:

(*a*) Arguments for the priority of Mark still appear stronger than arguments for a contrary view. In terms of relative dating, therefore, Mark should be dated prior to Matthew and Luke.

(*b*) Evidence for the dating of the Gospel drawn from alleged Latinisms and evidence of Petrine influence provide an insubstantial foundation. Most of the Latin phrases have to do with military terminology or Roman currency that would have been consistent throughout the empire. And it is difficult to know what would constitute a "Petrine" influence.

(*c*) The greatest promise lies in references to the temple. Scholars have argued for decades about the reason for New Testament silence regarding the destruction of the temple in Jerusalem. We should note, to begin with, that none of the New Testament works sets out to tell the story of events that would include the war against Rome and the sacking of Jerusalem. The four Gospels seek to tell the story of Jesus, who died decades before Jerusalem was destroyed. Direct reference to the temple's demise can hardly be expected if the narrators confine themselves to the time of their story. The most we could expect are allusions.

There has been rather general agreement that Matthew and Luke provide clear hints that the temple had been destroyed by the time they wrote. The same may well be true of Mark. From the moment Jesus arrives in Jerusalem, the story is preoccupied with the temple—and its impending demise. Jesus quotes from Isaiah 56 and Jeremiah 7 as he indicts the temple leadership for corrupting God's house (Mark 11:15-18). He praises a lawyer who points out that obeying the *Shema* ("Hear, O Israel . . ." from Deut. 6:4) "is much more than all whole burnt offerings and sacrifices" (12:32-33). In chapter 13, Jesus predicts that there will not be left one stone on another in Jerusalem. At his trial, an alleged threat against the temple provides one of the charges against him—and at the moment of his death, the tearing of the temple curtain provides veiled testimony that the threat will be carried out.

The interest in the temple—both in its impending demise and in the question of its replacement—fits best in a period immediately after the destruction of Jerusalem. The date is not required by the data, but it seems their most reasonable explanation. Many other factors figure into the dating—factors that depend upon a reconstruction of early Christian history. It must suffice to note here that the hostility toward Pharisees and "the Jews," typical of Matthew, Luke, and John, is absent from Mark. That intensified hostility seems to reflect a later stage in the relations between Jesus' followers and the unbelieving Jewish community, typical of the last decades of the first century. Mark is thus best located prior to the deteriorating relations within the Jewish family which began perhaps a decade after the temple was destroyed.

About the circumstances under which the work was written we will have more to say later. All of the evidence is indirect. The various proposals about locating Mark in Rome or in Syria depend upon flimsy data and are no less fanciful than proposals about authorship. If we can say little about the place of composition, however, we may be able to say something about the nature of the group for whom Mark wrote. We can sketch a profile of the "implied readers" of Mark, the audience the Gospel presumes. We can make note of what that audience can be expected to know and to what concerns the narrative is directed. Such reconstruction remains hypothetical, but less so since the primary data are found within the Gospel.

Since profiling an audience presumes interpretation of the Gospel, the former must await the results of exegesis. Perhaps a few hints are in order—hints that must be developed and defended in the commentary. Mark wrote, it would appear, for "Christians" (though there is no evidence his audience used such a label)—for people who believed Jesus to be "the Christ, the Son of God," who knew something about his career and believed it to represent "good news." Mark's audience is expected to know about the Old Testament and about certain traditions that developed between the Testaments. The people for whom he wrote have some investment in the temple and need to understand its destruction. Contrary to much current opinion, that audience does not appear to be simply a beleaguered minority barely holding on. Mark writes for people who have tasted success. The portrait of the first generations of Christians as persecuted members of Greco-Roman society drawn principally from the lower classes does not square with the informaton Mark provides. Their "problems" may well include self-satisfaction, competition for positions of leadership, and taking the gospel for granted, rather than the often-advanced concern about the delay of the parousia or discouragement in the face of persecution.

It should be noted again that none of these external matters, like the identity of the author or the time and place of composition, can be used to guarantee the "truthfulness" of the narrative. The author of the Gospel provides no personal information on the basis of which we can evaluate his credentials. The story is written from "God's" perspective. The narrator knows how Scripture relates to events, what Jesus is thinking, what the disciples do or do not understand, and what the religious leaders suspect. He hears the voice from heaven addressed to Jesus alone; he knows about the conversation at Jesus' trial where none of the disciples is present. The narrator, in other words, knows more than any of the characters could know. This is at least partly what Christians have meant in categorizing his work as "inspired." The work claims an authority and a truthfulness beyond ordinary texts. Modern efforts to blunt the offense of this claim by identifying the author or accounting for his tradition cannot solve a problem that rests finally on belief or unbelief.

OUTLINE OF MARK

I. Outside Jerusalem (1:1—8:21)

   A. Opening (1:1-39)
       1. The Title (1:1)
       2. Preparer of the Way (1:2-8)
       3. Jesus' Baptism: The Rending of the Heavens (1:9-11)
       4. Testing (1:12-13)
       5. The Kingdom Is at Hand (1:14-15)
       6. The Call of the Disciples (1:16-20)
       7. The Battle Is Joined (1:21-28)
       8. Healings (1:29-39)

   B. Transgressor of the Boundaries (1:40—3:6)
       1. Cleansing a Leper (1:40-45)
       2. Healing a Paralytic (2:1-12)
       3. Summoning a Tax Collector (2:13-14)
       4. Eating with Sinners (2:15-17)
       5. New Skins for New Wine (2:18-22)
       6. Gleaning on the Sabbath (2:23-28)
       7. A Sabbath Healing (3:1-6)

   C. Insiders and Outsiders (3:7-35)
       1. The Crowds (3:7-12)
       2. The Commissioning of the Twelve (3:13-19)
       3. Family Troubles (3:20-21)
       4. A Question of Possession (3:22-30)
       5. True Family (3:31-35)

COMMENTARY

■ Outside Jerusalem (1:1—8:21)

Opening (1:1-39)

The Title (1:1)

The words "according to Mark," which stand as a title in present Bibles, were not original to the work. Titles, if they were used at all, appeared at the end of a book where the author might leave a signature of some sort. The wording reflects the standardizing efforts of the believers in the second century who preserved the New Testament writings. "The Gospel according to . . ." becomes the standard heading for the four untitled accounts of Jesus' ministry. The earliest manuscript evidence employs this convention, which indicates it is an early development. "Mark" is a name whose origin is unknown. "Mark's" book is anonymous. We will use the name "Mark" in light of Christian convention, while recognizing the importance of anonymity.

The beginning of the gospel of Jesus Christ, [the Son of God]. These few words provide the only title or heading to the book we know as the "Gospel according to Mark." The term **gospel** is not a literary term. It means literally "good news"; Paul uses it to refer to the message of salvation, which can be summarized in short formulas like that in 1 Cor. 15:3-7. Paul does not give the impression that "gospel" means a book. When Jesus says,

"Repent, and believe in the gospel" (Mark 1:15), he apparently is not referring to a book either. The opening sentence seemingly says something about the beginning of that message of salvation.

But a **beginning** in what sense? Unlike Luke, Matthew, and John, Mark provides little background information about his story. There are no introductory rubrics indicating the rules for interpretation. He gives no genealogy as a way of providing the pedigree of the main character. There are no birth stories, no accounts of promising moments in the life of the hero as a young man. The story opens in the middle of things. The "beginning" has something to do with scriptural promises and the career of John the Baptist. Does the author know more and assume that his readers do as well? Or does his silence about background indicate conscious choice not to include more? Or are his sources deficient? We can only guess at this point in our study.

At least the custom of beginning in the middle of things was not uncommon. In the ancient world such a beginning served to tantalize the reader. Questions about the background of the main character or the situation would be provided as the story progressed. Mark does provide at least some details about Jesus' background, including the name of his home town, the occupation of his father, and the names of some family members. Even so, background information is meager by any standards.

Even if the beginning raises many questions it does not answer, the little preface does provide a point of departure and a perspective. We are told from the outset that the story has to do with "the good news," and that it is about someone special. The name **Jesus** appears with at least one title, **Christ** (Messiah), and perhaps also with **Son of God,** depending upon assessment of the textual evidence. The oldest Egyptian witnesses are divided here, with one branch including "Son of God," the other omitting it. Textual experts are genuinely divided on whether to include or exclude the reading. The reading is included here, although it is far from certain. (In the next edition of the Nestle-Aland text, "Son of God" will be relegated to the footnotes as an alternative reading.)

The term **Christ** appears without a definite article. It is thus unclear at this point that **Christ** is actually a title (the Greek translation of the Hebrew "Anointed" or "Messiah"). Readers could regard it as Jesus' second name, except that later in the story it is employed as a genuine title (Mark 8:29; 14:61; 15:32). The term in Greek means something like "smeared"; without some background, Greek readers would find it only strange and confusing. The image of "anointing" makes sense, however, in light of the Old Testament practice of installation into office (anointing with oil) and in light of postbiblical tradition which came to speak of a savior figure as God's "anointed." Readers with knowledge of that tradition would immediately understand what it meant to speak of Jesus as **Christ**—an indication that Mark wrote for "insiders," for people who already had some knowledge of Jesus and of the background of his ministry in the traditions of Israel.

The expression **Son of God** is more clearly a title, though its meaning depends upon its religious setting. Is it a term whose setting is largely in the Greek world of savior figures and deliverers, or does it belong in the scriptural tradition of Israel as a term by which God may address the King (Ps. 2:7; 2 Sam. 7:14)? Recent scholarship has tended to become more aware of the term's place in Israel's eschatological tradition. In Mark, the royal connotations of the title and its association with "Messiah" are patent (1:11; 14:61). It would be unwise to decide for one setting or another, however, since even Israel's scriptural heritage had been developed in the Greek-speaking world. Titles are capable of more than one connotation.

Mark prefaces his story with an assessment: the story marks the beginning of the good news. It is about Jesus Christ, God's Son—one whose career must be understood against the background of Israel's hopes and dreams. Though other characters in the story will be uncertain about Jesus' identity, the reader is never in doubt. We are told from the very beginning who Jesus is and that he is the source of the "good news" (most likely, the genitive should be translated "*about* Jesus Christ," though Mark surely views Jesus' preaching as related to the "good news").

What it means to speak of Jesus as "Christ" and "God's Son," and in what sense he is the source of the gospel will be determined by the story that follows.

Preparer of the Way (1:2-8)

The narrative is introduced by a quotation ascribed to **Isaiah.** In fact, the quotation represents a conflation of Mal. 3:1 and Isa. 40:3, perhaps even with influence from Exod. 23:20 (a reference to a mysterious "angel" about whom God says, "for my name is in him" [Exod. 23:31]; the figure was the subject of considerable speculation in later times, speculation which subsequent rabbinic sages deemed dangerous, as Alan Segal has demonstrated in his work). Later copyists sought to correct the ascription by changing the text to "in the prophets." The presence of such a conflated quotation may indicate that a lively tradition of scriptural interpretation predates Mark's Gospel. It may even raise questions about the form in which the scriptural material came to Mark.

According to the narrator, there has been preparation for the story: it **is written.** In this instance, it is the career of John which has been anticipated. He is the messenger sent to prepare for someone else—the unidentified "you" in the scriptural passage (JB: I am going to send my messenger before you). The biblical **messenger** appears **in the wilderness** (that is the way Isaiah is read) to urge people to **prepare the way of the Lord.** The Baptist's audience would have understood the reference to the "Lord God." We might wonder whether Mark's audience was expected to know that John was preparing for the "Lord Jesus." We can only wonder in this instance, since the title "the Lord" is never used of Jesus in Mark (though see the commentary on 5:19-20 and 12:35-37).

John's preparation consisted of **preaching a baptism of repentance for the forgiveness of sins.** Ritual washing was an important component of Israel's worship. Priests in particular were expected to purify themselves before coming into the presence of God in the temple. Pharisees extended the notion of ritual purity to include the laity. The Essene community at Qumran, a group of dissident Jews who lived not far from where John preached, was preoccupied with ritual washing and purification. John says nothing about a regular practice of purification. He preaches repentance and washes penitents in preparation for the coming of the Lord. His baptism was to provide an important backdrop for later Christian baptismal practices.

John attracted considerable attention. Mark says with some exaggeration that **all the country of Judea, and all the people of Jerusalem** came out to John to be baptized by him. We know from contemporary records that John was one who developed a considerable reputation and following. In the annals of historians like Josephus, John, even more than Jesus, is viewed as someone worthy of note. When Mark (and the rest of the evangelists) portrays John as Jesus' forerunner, he is asserting something that was not obvious to everyone. We might even suspect, in view of the vigor with which the Baptizer denies every honor in the Fourth Gospel, that there were some who continued to view the Baptizer as the real luminary.

We should not fail to note the location of Mark's "beginning": the story opens in the desert and not in the holy city. Jerusalem is where the temple was located, the place of God's presence where every day priests offered sacrifices for sin. According to Mark, those who wished to obtain forgiveness left the city in droves to visit John in an unsettled desert place, where they could confess their sins and be washed. In Mark, Jerusalem is not a gracious place. It is where Jesus will die. Not surprisingly, at the end of the story the young man at the tomb directs Jesus' followers to Galilee: "there you will see him" (16:7).

Strange is the mention of John's diet and clothing. Considering how much information Mark does not provide about background, it is all the more striking that we learn about John's clothing. He wears a **camel's hair** shirt and a **leather** loincloth. The details suggest John is not "mainstream." He lives on the outskirts of civilization and does not abide by convention. His clothing apparently suits his life-style. The facts are also important for those who know the Old Testament; the prophet Elijah wore such garb as the mark of his prophetic office (2 Kings 1:8). The link with Elijah is likewise significant for those steeped in Israel's prophetic heritage. The last verses in the book of Malachi—the conclusion to the Christian Old Testament—promise Elijah's return:

> Behold, I will send you Elijah the prophet before the great and terrible day of the Lord. He will turn the hearts of the fathers to their children and the hearts of children to their fathers, lest I come and smite the land with a curse.
>
> (Mal. 4:5-6)

John's assignment and his clothing, even the location of his ministry, point to ancient promises now being fulfilled. John is Elijah who has come to prepare the way. It might be noted parenthetically that the verses from Malachi 3 about the "messenger" who is to "prepare the way," quoted in Mark 1:2, were customarily taken by Jewish interpreters as a reference to Elijah, whose return is promised in Malachi 4. This suggests the more strongly that Mark can rely on small details like the mention of John's clothing to conjure up familiar images from Israel's dreams of the future. It also suggests that Mark writes for people who know such dreams and traditions.

As great as John is, he is only a forerunner, a preparer of the way. Someone greater comes after him before whom he pales in significance. John does not mention Jesus' name; Mark expects the reader to make the connection when Jesus appears in the next scene. John concludes his preaching with a promise: **I have baptized you with water; but he will baptize you with the Holy Spirit.** Some manuscripts, imitating Matthew and Luke, add "with fire." Fire is a means of purification of a higher order than water. The same is true of the Spirit. The "baptism" has to do with cleansing. The one who comes after John will cleanse with the Spirit (cf. Acts 10, where the pouring out of the Spirit on Cornelius and his household is described as cleansing, fitting them to eat with Jews). There is no reason to see in this verse a contrast between water baptism and Spirit baptism. The contrast is between John's cleansing and the cleansing that will be provided by the one who comes after John.

The promise is left unfulfilled in the story—the first of many such throughout Mark. Those who know Acts may see the fulfillment of John's promise in the events of Pentecost, but Mark recounts no such event. His story breaks off before Jesus baptizes anyone. We ought not fill in such gaps too quickly. We will want to ask about all the unfulfilled promises when we come to the story's conclusion.

Jesus' Baptism: The Rending of the Heavens (1:9-11)

Mark takes little time with transitions. Verse 9 marks a typically abrupt shift. Jesus is introduced as coming **from Nazareth of Galilee** to the wilderness area where John is preaching, to be baptized by John. All sorts of questions are left unanswered. How did Jesus know about John? Did they have any previous relationship? At what point in his life did he seek John out? What preparation had been made? Did John recognize Jesus? What did he think?

Remarkably, the story does nothing to answer such questions. In fact, it poses them. Jesus comes to be **baptized by John.** The fact is an embarrassment for Matthew, who prefaces the story with a brief conversation in which John makes it clear that Jesus ought to be baptizing him. Although Jesus offers no real explanation for wishing to be baptized by John, he at least assures John—and the readers—that it is necessary "to fulfil all righteousness" (Matt. 3:14-15). In Mark, Jesus is simply baptized— identifying himself with the sinners who have come to confess their sins and be washed.

This simple event is the occasion for an extraordinary occurrence: as Jesus is baptized, **the heavens** are torn open, **the Spirit** descends **like a dove** into him, and God speaks **from heaven.** Sensitive translation is important here. The RSV reads, **the heavens opened.** That is the way Matthew and Luke tell the story. Mark, however, says that "the heavens were being torn apart." The image is quite different—dynamic, violent, final. What is opened may be closed; what is torn apart cannot easily return to its former state. Those familiar with Mark will immediately think

of the tearing apart of the temple curtain at the moment of Jesus'
death (15:38)—another uninterpreted comment about some mysterious event that teases the imagination. Christian interpreters—
like the author of the letter to the Hebrews—used the image of
the temple curtain to speak about the significance of Jesus' death.
The curtain separates the Holy of Holies from view; God's presence is threatening. With his death, Jesus has entered the Holy
of Holies once for all, and the curtain is no longer necessary (Heb.
9:6-14). The meaning may be that God's presence is no longer
threatening and that we have access to a gracious God. Or it may
be that God has now torn down the barriers and is among us—
on the loose. The sense that God's presence is frightening and
will spell disaster for some is the point of Isa. 64:1, a passage on
which the account in Mark may play. That sense of danger likewise
seems to fit Mark's story.

Perhaps such ideas lie behind the image in Mark 15, and perhaps they also inform his account of Jesus' baptism. With his
baptism, some cataclysmic change in the universe begins—a
change that is consummated only with Jesus' death. The curtain
that separates a threatening God from God's creatures is torn
away. More accurate than referring to our access to God would
be to speak of God's access to us. God comes whether we choose
or not. That presence may turn out to be genuinely dangerous.
Only the story will tell.

If this is behind the imagery in Mark, it is elicited by teasing
the readers' imaginations. It should also be apparent that insen-
sitive translation will short-circuit the imaginative process and
obscure possible connections within the story.

When the heavens are torn, there is a token of the change
which has occurred. **The Spirit** descends "into" (RSV: **upon**)
Jesus. The notion seems to be that Jesus now "possesses" the
Spirit—or rather is possessed by it. The image is like that of the
demon-possessed, except Jesus' Spirit is God's Spirit. Those who
attribute Jesus' power to demon-possession are guilty of blas-
pheming the Holy Spirit (3:28-29). Noting parallels to the conclusion of Jesus' ministry, we may observe that at the moment of

his death Jesus "breathes out the spirit." Like the tearing of the "curtains," the entrance and departure of the Spirit serve to frame the story of Jesus.

The image of the **dove** must derive from Jewish tradition, though there is little clear evidence of its use as a symbol for the Spirit. Probably the most likely source of the image is Gen. 1:2, where the Spirit "hovers" over the face of the deep.

The climax of the baptismal story is the **voice from heaven,** addressed to Jesus alone. The narrator is not interested in telling us whether or not anyone else heard or saw anything. We are given access to an event that takes place between Father and Son; what Jesus learns, we learn.

The heavenly words are familiar. They appear to come from the Old Testament. It seems only fitting that if God speaks, biblical words should be used. The passages from which the words are taken are important. The words **Thou art my [beloved] Son** come from Ps. 2:7, a royal psalm in which God speaks to his "anointed" (Messiah, Christ) as "Son." By the first century, Jews had come to regard this psalm as a prediction of the coming King from the line of David who would arise to save Israel. The few words from the familiar psalm identify Jesus with that traditional hope. God addresses Jesus as Son, and in so doing confirms the truth of the opening assertion that Jesus is "Christ, the Son of God."

The words "in you **I am well pleased**" seem to derive from Isa. 42:1: "Behold my servant, whom I uphold, my chosen, in whom my soul delights; I have put my Spirit upon him, he will bring forth justice to the nations." Jesus is thus identified with the mysterious "servant" on whom God pours out the Spirit, a figure whose task is to bring forth justice to the nations. The few words may even link Jesus' career as God's "servant" with other passages from Isaiah.

It is also possible that the reference to **my beloved Son** is intended to conjure up the image of another biblical "beloved son"—Isaac—whose destiny was that he would be offered as a sacrifice on a mountain of God's choosing (Gen. 22:3, 18). The story of Isaac's binding was central to Jewish identity; even today the story is read as the appointed text on Rosh Hashana, New Year's Day. Perhaps the reference suggests that Jesus is, like Isaac, another beloved Son destined to be offered up. There are hints that such an association was made in Christian circles (Rom. 8:32, and other places).

If such imaginative associations are not overly farfetched, it could be said that the words of the heavenly voice contain in summary form a preview of Jesus' career: he is the Christ, God's Son, the servant on whom God pours out the Spirit so that he may bring forth justice among the nations—God's beloved Son who is destined to be offered as a sacrifice. There are hints that the story of Jesus has "been written."

However, the most striking feature of the baptismal story emerges only from within the narrative setting. Jesus is introduced as the one greater than John who will baptize with the Holy Spirit—the Christ, Son of God. Yet when Jesus appears, it is not as the conquering warrior fitted with the appropriate trappings of a savior. The occasion for his confirmation by God and his anointing by the Spirit is his baptism by John—which is a washing for the forgiveness of sins. The tearing of the heavens, the descent of the Spirit, and the authoritative declaration of God all seem fitting testimony to the stature of the promised deliverer. The setting is all wrong, however. Jesus should be among the mighty, in the great city that served David as his citadel, not among sinners who have come to repent of their sins.

The story opens with a great shock. The promised deliverer has been confirmed and anointed for his appointed tasks. Yet he looks nothing like what was expected; he is in the wrong place, associating with the wrong people. Jesus' career begins with a tension between what is expected of God and what God actually provides. As the narrative progresses, the tension increases rather than decreases, ending with Jesus finally ironically hailed as King and Son of God by those who mock him—as he is tried, ridiculed, and executed on a cross.

Perhaps a parenthetical note is in order. Many modern interpreters see in the account of Jesus' baptism the features of some psychological drama: it is the "dawning of Jesus' messianic self-consciousness" or perhaps the resolution of some struggle with destiny. In the manner of a Descartes, such interpreters proceed from the assumption that what is "real" is internal. Yet in Mark—and one may add, in the whole New Testament—such a "self" seems hardly to exist. Mark makes no effort to portray any inner struggle. We learn virtually nothing about Jesus' self-reflection. The drama in the story has to do with social and political matters; it results from the impact of Jesus on the world to which he preaches, a world that is largely hostile to him. Collapsing the story into psychological categories represents a particular preoccupation—and one might say, disease—of our time that offers little promise as an approach to interpretation.

Testing (1:12-13)

The Spirit **drove . . . out** Jesus into the wilderness. The same language is used to speak of Jesus' "driving out" demons. Mark's view of the Holy Spirit is singularly undomesticated. It is the opinion of Jesus' detractors that Jesus is possessed (3:22), and they are right. It is not an unclean spirit, however, but the Spirit of God that serves as the driving force in his ministry.

The terse account of Jesus' stay in the **wilderness** raises more questions than it answers. What was the nature of the temptation? In Matthew and Luke, Jesus is "tempted" to sin by Satan. In the extended dialogues, Jesus makes crucial choices about the nature of his ministry and demonstrates his obedience to God. In Mark, there are no such dialogues. The forty-day period seems more like "testing" than temptation. The period of testing has precedent in the careers of at least two of Israel's greatest prophets, Moses and Elijah—and the symbolism surely recalls the experience of Israel in the wilderness. Perhaps the associations with the prophetic predecessors, who appear again at the transfiguration, are sufficient.

The reference to **the wild beasts** may suggest the dangerous nature of the desert, or it may suggest that we have here a recapitulation of the experience of Adam: Jesus is at peace with nature, recapturing God's will for the creation.

The ministration of **the angels** indicates that Jesus is no ordinary mortal. Like all the supernatural beings in Mark, the angels attest to Jesus' stature.

The precise nature of Jesus' wilderness sojourn is left to the readers' imaginations. Matthew and Luke give evidence of further reflection, depicting it as a temptation. For Mark, it is enough to know that Jesus was tested.

The Kingdom Is at Hand (1:14-15)

Jesus' ministry begins **after John was arrested.** We learn about the reason for John's arrest and his death only later (chap. 6). John is a forerunner in more ways than one. His preaching introduces a theme Jesus will develop: **repent,** for some great moment is at hand. John also anticipates in his career the fate of the stronger one for whom he prepares the way: John is **arrested** and executed by the established powers. In those ominous words about John's arrest the faint rumblings of a building storm can already be heard.

Unlike John, Jesus works in **Galilee,** in the north where he has made his home. There he proclaims **the gospel of God.** The use of the noun **gospel** is unusual in our "Gospels." The noun is never used in Luke or John. It is only the apostles who preach the "gospel" in Acts—where the term is used of the message that focuses on Jesus' death and resurrection. It is not this "gospel" Jesus preached. It is the gospel of God—summarized, perhaps, in the proclamation: **The kingdom of God is at hand.**

The expression **kingdom of God** has a long history in biblical scholarship. Jesus does not define what he means by **kingdom,** and interpreters have offered a wide range of explanations. There must, of course, be some way to test the various proposals, given the creativity of interpreters. Albert Schweitzer provided some ground rules: interpretation must take as its point of departure first-century Jewish views, since Jesus' lack of explanation can only mean he assumed his audience would understand the expression. While a number of interpretations are thus excluded, major interpretive possibilities still exist.

One major question has to do with the sense of the Greek word *basileia*. Is it first a spatial term, implying a sphere of influence, thus requiring the English "kingdom"? Or does it imply an activity, thus requiring the English "rule"? More recent scholarship has tended toward the latter.

A second major issue relates to the time when the kingdom is expected to dawn. Schweitzer—and most scholars in the 20th-century—have assumed that when Jesus said, **the kingdom of God is at hand,** he was convinced that the end of history was at hand. In this case, Paul's conviction that the "forms of this world are passing away" (1 Cor. 7:31) would be a fair interpretation. Those who regard "kingdom of God" as a future reality must then indicate how it is understood by the church—and by the audience for whom Mark writes.

An alternative was proposed by C. H. Dodd, who approached the question from the perspective of the Fourth Gospel and argued that the "kingdom" is already present.

It is premature to decide how the kingdom is to be viewed. It does seem unlikely that we should translate the opening words of Jesus' proclamataion as meaning "the kingdom is here." In any case, we can say that those opening words do not define the expression "the kingdom of God." Later in Mark, images will add some precision to the way "kingdom of God" is to be understood (chaps. 3, 4, 13). We may at least note that the language Jesus uses to speak of the future is eschatological language—imagery whose place is in talk about the end of things, about ultimate realities. The **gospel** about which Jesus speaks has to do with final matters. He is no ordinary preacher of revivals. Some great moment has arrived, a crisis: **The time is fulfilled.** In view of this great moment, the only appropriate response is to **repent, and believe.** While John and Jesus are agreed that a great crisis is at hand, Jesus urges people to "believe in the gospel"—a message in which he occupies a central role.

The Call of the Disciples (1:16-20)

With a terseness that is characteristic of the story, Mark immediately moves on to recount Jesus' summoning of the first of a special group of followers. Mark's Gospel is not only a story about Jesus but about his disciples, who have an important role to play in the story, as well.

The account of the call of **Peter** and **Andrew** and of **James** and **John** leaves much to the imagination. We view the event from the outside. Jesus calls, and they **follow.** The story provides no preparation of any sort. We have no idea what relationship Jesus might have had with the two sets of brothers earlier, no profile of the families that might explain the willingness to drop their work, leave their families, and follow Jesus on an unspecified mission. That the brothers are fishermen is important as foreshadowing: Jesus calls them to cast their **nets** for another catch. Even at this early point in the story, it is apparent that the two sets of brothers will have an important role to play in Jesus' mission.

Several things may be said. First, the initiative in summoning followers belongs exclusively to Jesus. There is no hint that the disciples sought Jesus out. Second, their summons requires that they abandon work and family. Though little is said, the call to leave family implies a radical break with society. We learn only a few verses later that Peter has a mother-in-law—in other words, he is married. With what justification do these four men abandon their means of employment and their families? One of the criticisms leveled at Christians in Roman society was that they were antisocial, that they broke down the bonds that held communities and families together. The terse account of the disciples' call does nothing to allay such fears; in fact, it may seem to raise warning flags. Who is it that can demand absolute obedience that seems to make no provision for all the realities that make up everyday life? The topic will emerge with some regularity throughout the Gospel.

The Battle Is Joined (1:21-28)

The opening scene in Jesus' public ministry is set in a **synagogue** on **the Sabbath**—a holy place on a holy day. The initial impression of the people is that Jesus teaches **as one who had authority and not as the scribes.** He does not appeal to precedent; he speaks without benefit of tradition. The danger of such unauthorized speaking is obvious from the outset.

Appropriately, the first scene in Jesus' ministry involves a confrontation. The one who heralds the kingdom of God and who teaches with authority is confronted by a man possessed by **an unclean spirit.** The unclean spirit is in a holy place on a holy day, where it ought not to be. As in all exorcisms, the diseased man does not ask for aid. He is helpless, completely under the influence of the spirit. The spirit, speaking for his kind, acknowledges Jesus as a threat: **What have you to do with us, Jesus of Nazareth? Have you come to destroy us? I know who you are, the Holy One of God.** The spirits, even if evil and unclean, know the truth about Jesus; they recognize him as "the Holy One of God," "Son of God," and "Son of the Most High God." Until the account of Jesus' trial, no human being calls Jesus "Son of God." Only God and supernatural beings know his identity. The demons also recognize that Jesus' coming means their time is up.

Jesus "rebukes the spirit" and casts him out. The story includes some graphic detail as a way of proving that something has happened. It also concludes in a way appropriate to such stories: people are amazed at Jesus' **teaching** and his **authority.**

Translating the response of the crowd involves some decision about punctuating the Greek (an editor's decision, since the original Greek had no punctuation). The response is either, "What is this? A new teaching with authority?" or **What is this? A new teaching! With authority he commands.** . . . In either case, the point is that Jesus strikes people with unprecedented authority, both in what he says and what he does. He does not depend upon majority opinion or precedent, as do the scribes. Even unclean spirits are subject to him. In many respects his actions are without precedent among religious authorities. His reputation spreads everywhere; people will have to take account of him.

This initial story in Jesus' public ministry provides a foretaste of what is to come. Though Mark regularly refers to Jesus as "teacher" and makes general reference to his "teaching," his main character is more a man of action than a philosopher or sage.

Healings (1:29-39)

And immediately he left the synagogue and entered the house of Simon and Andrew. The abrupt movement is typical of Mark. The connective **and immediately** seems at first to have an adverbial function, lending to the narrative a sense of rapid movement. By the end of the second chapter, it seems to lose that adverbial sense and functions as a simple transition.

The information that **Simon** has a **mother-in-law** suggests, as we learn later, that he (and perhaps the other disciples) has indeed left home and family to follow Jesus. We hear nothing about a wife and children. The healing of Simon's mother-in-law is described without detail. She is **sick**; Jesus touches her; immediately **the fever** is gone. Little is made of the faith of the disciples, nothing of the faith of the woman. The story is simply a summary that testifies to Jesus' power.

It is, we must presume, still the Sabbath when Jesus visits the house; only with v. 32 do we learn that the sun has set and that people from the town have come to the house. If there is any sense of narrative movement, we are to presume that Jesus healed the woman on the Sabbath. His extraordinary power will become even more problematic for religious authorities if he heals on the Sabbath—as we discover more definitely later (Mark 3:1-6, where this becomes a public issue).

That evening, at sundown. . . . Even if Jesus does not wait to heal, the people who need Jesus' help wait to come until after the Sabbath is past (sunset marks the end of the Jewish day). His success seems instantaneous: **the whole city was gathed together about the door.** (Mark is fond of hyperbole; earlier it was "all the people of Jerusalem" who came out to John.) The little summary introduces a familiar theme: Jesus heals those who are **sick** and casts out **demons, but he would not permit the demons to speak, because they knew him.** On the one hand, demons testify to the truth they are obliged to acknowledge. On the other, they are not permitted **to speak** because they know the truth. We are not told why Jesus wishes to conceal the truth about himself, only that some things are to remain secret. We shall have occasion to return to this theme again and again throughout the story. These "injunctions to silence" are termed features of the "messianic secret" in Mark. It is worth noting that Jesus' identity is not a secret hidden from demons any more than it is hidden from Mark's readers. For the other characters in the story, it is another matter.

That Jesus is not simply a healer concerned with localized suffering is made clear in the exchange with Peter. Jesus goes off by himself to pray. Peter finds him and calls him back to his work: **Everyone is searching for you.** Jesus is called to more than this one group, however. **Let us go,** he tells Peter. There are other places he must preach. His message must be heard at least **throughout all Galilee.** There is some urgency to his preaching about the nearness of the kingdom. Others need to hear the message and to be freed from the power of unclean spirits.

Transgressor of the Boundaries (1:40—3:6)

Cleansing a Leper (1:40-45)

Jesus' healing of the **leper** is the first of several stories that deal with Jesus' violation of ritual boundaries. Among Jews, these boundaries were established by the Torah. The law was not viewed primarily as a means of salvation but as the mark of Israel's election and a way of ordering life. Boundaries were for the protection of the community. In the controversy stories that follow, Jesus' conversation partners are the Pharisees. This group, mostly laity, was concerned about maintaining Israel's identity in an increasingly secular and hostile world. Their defense was the law, by which they sought to safeguard holiness. (For more on the Pharisees, see the comments on 2:15-17, below.)

Lepers were out of bounds, and for good reason. They posed a threat to society. There was no cure for chronic leprosy. Lepers could be sustained by the charity of others, but they were kept at a safe distance outside the city in order to protect the health of the community. Laws of ritual uncleanness thus served to protect the community from danger. Even the **leper** acknowledges such boundaries. He knows that he is "unclean" and requires purification.

Jesus refuses to recognize such boundaries. He reaches out and touches the leper. The story is about faith; the leper asks for help and receives it. It is also about Jesus' willingness to risk ritual defilement (not to mention contracting leprosy) for the sake of saving a life. As is regularly the case when Jesus transgresses these ritual boundaries, he is not contaminated by contact with the unclean. Here a leper is cleansed.

Verse 43 is difficult. Translators generally clean up language that in the Greek is strangely harsh. The Greek literally says, "And snorting at him in indignation, Jesus cast him out." The language sounds more typical of exorcisms. A few manuscripts in the Western tradition have attempted to make sense of the Greek by substituting "and having become angry" for **moved with pity** in v. 41, suggesting perhaps Jesus' anger at the disease. One commentator has attempted to explain the strange language by suggesting this is really an account of an exorcism: the man is plagued by a demon as well as leprosy. If that is not the case, we can only note the strange tone. Mark does not provide enough information to understand why Jesus might be angry.

The injunction to silence is already familiar and will be repeated with regularity. Jesus instructs the leper to **say nothing to any one**—except **to the priest,** to whom the leper is to offer the appropriate sacrifice as testimony to his cleansing. Jesus may violate sacred boundaries, but he apparently does not intend to tear down the whole cultic apparatus—at least not yet. The temple and its priesthood seem to have a role to play in the life of the religious community that at this point Jesus affirms. Later we will learn that the religious leaders have failed in the performance of their duty and that the temple will be destroyed.

The leper, commanded to tell no one, instead tells everyone what has happened. The exceptions are frequent enough to make any simple explanation of the "messianic secret" unlikely. Most often Jesus tells people to be silent after performing a miracle (e.g., 5:43; 8:26). Once he enjoins someone to testify to what "the Lord" has done, and the recipient of Jesus' healing does (5:19-20). On other occasions (here and in 7:36), those who are instructed to be silent cannot contain themselves. The play between silence and speaking will continue throughout the story to the very end. The great irony is that when followers are finally told to speak, they say nothing to anyone.

The testimony of the cleansed leper becomes a basis for further action. Jesus' reputation spreads. People come from everywhere to seek his help. And the religious authorities begin to be interested.

Healing a Paralytic (2:1-12)

The account of Jesus' healing of **a paralytic** is set in **Capernaum,** apparently a center of activity in Jesus' ministry. The synagogue is where Jesus began his public ministry with a dramatic exorcism. The present scene is set in a **home.** We are not told to whom the house belongs, only that it has become a public place. Jesus' popularity has spread to the point that people are so crammed in to hear his teaching there is **no longer room for them, not even about the door.** The story that follows is, on the one hand, about the remarkable persistence of a group of people who believe Jesus can heal a paralytic, and, on the other, about religious people who are troubled by the implications of the healing.

Finding no room at the door, the **four** who have brought the paralytic to Jesus "dig through" **the roof** to get the paralytic into the room. (In Luke, they "remove the tiles"; Luke's account reflects the experience of city people; Mark's presumes knowledge about rural housing.) In response to **their faith,** Jesus heals the paralytic. This is one of several stories in Mark that offer extravagant promises to those who have **faith** in Jesus.

The story is not only a testimonial to the power of faith, however. Jesus' response to the paralytic claims far more: "Child, **your sins are forgiven.**" Jesus' words presuppose a link between sin and disease. It would be sheer anachronism to speculate about psychosomatic illness, seeking to apply modern psychological theory to an ancient text. We may note only that in the view of our narrator and his audience, physical disease is not attributable to neutral forces. There is something mysteriously evil about illness that links it to the power of sin. The coming of the kingdom spells the end of both.

With Jesus' declaration of forgiveness, another group of characters emerges: **the scribes.** We have heard of them earlier. The crowds impressed with Jesus' authority offer a comparison: "for he taught them as one who had authority, and not as the scribes" (1:22). "Scribe" refers first of all to professionals trained in the interpretation of the law. In the centuries before the Christian era they had come to replace the priests as guardians of the tradition and teachers of law (see Schürer, 2:322–37).

The references to scribes in the Gospels presume that they are the primary interpreters of the law—and that their authority resided in the tradition in which they were trained. In contrast, Jesus relies on no such external authority. He speaks in his own name; the typical form of his interpretations is "pronouncements." Scribes appear frequently in the stories as critics of Jesus, particularly impressed by his lack of credentials (11:27-33). Scribes are sometimes identified with Pharisees ("The scribes of the Pharisees" [2:16], by which the author presumably means scribes who belonged to the Pharisaic school); sometimes they are included among the officials who ran the Jewish government in Jerusalem ("scribes, chief priests, and elders" [8:31, etc.]).

The response of these religious experts is ominous: **It is blasphemy! Who can forgive sins but God alone?** In the material that follows, controversies explore the function of the law as a boundary. As we have noted, Pharisees saw the law not as a means of salvation but as a way of ordering life in response to God's electing grace. The law, and its application in the "tradition of the elders," defined the world in terms of clean and unclean, permitted and prohibited. The purpose of the law was to define a zone within which life could be lived as God intended. It was the task of religious experts to determine precisely where the boundaries lay. Jesus' behavior threatens the boundaries and thus elicits discussion among the pious who are concerned about the law. Interestingly, Mark chooses to begin the series of controversies with the most serious: **blasphemy.**

The most important boundary the law provided was the one between God and creation. The basic sin of the human race, as defined in Genesis, is the refusal to let God be God. Adam and Eve succumbed to the temptation to become "like God." The first of the commandments has to do with honoring God as God. Blasphemy is thus the most serious of all sins. Compromising the oneness of God, claiming what belongs to God alone, is a sin so serious, so damaging to society, as to merit death. If the charge of the scribes is true, if Jesus is guilty of blasphemy, he must die.

Interpreters have raised the question whether Jesus' statement constitutes blasphemy. The passive of the verb "forgive" (**Your sins are forgiven**) should be taken as a circumlocution for God. Jews avoided speaking not only the special name of God but even the word "God," if possible. The passive means the statement ought to be read as "God forgives your sins."

According to this reading, Jesus says nothing essentially different from the scribes. It is God who forgives sins.

Our question should be how the scene is to be understood in Mark, not how the statement appears in light of precise rabbinic law from the second century. Most significant in that regard is Jesus' comment in v. 10: **But that you may know that the Son of man has authority on earth to forgive sins. . . .** Here, Jesus at least claims the right to speak for God. While this may not qualify as blasphemy by any known legal code, the religious leaders certainly understand Jesus' willingness to make declarations on God's behalf as the kind of infringement that constitutes a violation of the sacred boundary. Jesus blasphemes!

In that accusation, we have not simply an introduction to a series of controversies but a foreshadowing of what is to come in the rest of Jesus' ministry and an indication of how high the stakes are. When Jesus finally arrives in Jerusalem and appears before the court, he will be tried on precisely this charge—blasphemy—and condemned to death (14:63-64). While there may be precedent for many of Jesus' specific interpretations of the law, he will prove too dangerous in the view of the religious and political leaders. Forced to choose between Jesus and the tradition, they will choose the tradition.

Jesus makes no attempt to explain himself or to defend his right to pronounce forgiveness. He merely provides a graphic demonstration of his power and authority. **Which is easier,** he asks, "to forgive sins or to heal a paralytic?" He commands the paralytic to take up his bed and go home as a demonstration that **the Son of man has authority on earth to forgive sins** (on the meaning of "the Son of man," see excursus, below). The paralytic does as he is commanded. People are appropriately astonished, and they **glorify God.** For the religious authorities, however, a problem is posed that will have to be dealt with. Jesus has power and cannot be ignored. Does he really speak for God? Is God's reign somehow tied to his ministry? Or is he simply presumptuous and, worse, a blasphemer? As guardians of the tradition, it is their responsibility to answer.

Excursus: The Son of Man

A few comments are in order regarding the use of the strange expression "the Son of man" in Mark, an enigmatic term that continues to generate articles and volumes that promise an explanation.

The first comment is that the expression does not qualify as a "title" in the same way as "the Christ" and "the Son of God." "The Son of man" never appears as a predicate nominative; no one ever says, "You are the Son of man." The observation is important. The strange expression, uncommon in Greek, appears in Mark only on Jesus' lips. It should be examined, therefore, as a self-designation; it is a way Jesus refers to himself. If we begin by examining the usage in Mark and not with a theory about the expression, there is no justification for hearing a single occurrence of the expression as a reference to anyone besides Jesus.

In present scholarship there are two basic lines of investigation. The first approaches "the Son of man" as a title, investigating the traditional background of the title as a way of understanding what the self-designation means in the Gospels. The second approaches "the Son of man" not as a title at all but as a self-designation whose awkwardness in Greek is likely the result of an attempted translation of an Aramaic idiom. Scholars like Geza Vermes and Barnabas Lindars explore the Aramaic possibilities behind the Greek. In their view, the New Testament usage must be derived from Jesus' use of an Aramaic form of self-reference that translates poorly into Greek (similar, perhaps, to the use of "man" in German or "a person" in English).

The matter need not be decided, except to observe how heavily scholarship has been weighted toward a titular approach—and how little evidence exists for such a view. As noted in the commentary, in Matthew's recasting of the confession of Peter in Mark 8:27-33, the interchange of "I" and "the Son of man" indicates that Matthew does not regard the expression as a title at all.

For the purposes of interpretation, it is perhaps best to view "the Son of man" as an enigmatic expression by which Jesus refers to himself. How to nuance each translation of the expression must await further discussion; "Man from heaven," however—the translation chosen in the new *Lectionary for the Christian People*—is the least likely and least appropriate of all possibilities. Where allusions to the "human" who comes with the clouds are present, they are clearly marked by the explicit use of imagery from Daniel 7 (Mark 13:26 and 14:62). (See bibliography on Juel, Lindars, and Vermes.)

Summoning a Tax Collector (2:13-14)

The call of **Levi** is reported in a single sentence. The only significant piece of information is that he was **sitting at the tax office.** Levi was a tax collector, a member of a despised class. Working in Galilee, he would have been in the employ of Herod Antipas. While not as contemptible as those Jews in Judea who collected taxes for the Roman administrators, Levi would have been regarded as an outcast. The Babylonian Talmud includes tax collectors among the most notorious of sinners, unfit for participation in the life of the synagogue. One reason the whole system was so detested was that collection was franchised. Tax farmers were assigned a region and a fixed sum. Anything collected beyond the assessment was profit. The burden of taxation was extraordinary. The collectors have always been resented; excessive profits would only heighten the resentment.

Jesus' summoning of Levi implies another transgression of boundaries. Jesus not only touches lepers and claims the right to forgive sins; he also accepts into his inner circle one who is an outcast in Jewish society.

Excursus: The Controversies

The call of Levi, a tax collector, introduces the first in a series of controversies. The controversies have several regular features. A question is asked, implying a criticism of Jesus' actions in view of the tradition. Jesus settles the issue by making a pronouncement of some sort. The stories are given general settings and are only superficially woven into the narrative. It is the series of such stories in the opening chapters that gives Mark's Gospel its episodic character.

Students of oral tradition have argued that the stories bear the earmarks of preliterary tradition and offer clues to the culture within which stories about Jesus circulated prior to their incorporation into the Gospels. The topics they address—dietary laws and Sabbath observance—were of obvious importance to the faithful who remembered the stories. Concerns about such questions, at least in these instances, were settled by recalling a statement of Jesus. With the quotation of the statement, the little episodes conclude, with no interest in the impression made on Jesus' opponents or other matters.

Jesus' interrogators in these stories are often called "adversaries" by commentators. Perhaps the term is a bit strong. Jesus is asked to defend his behavior by observant Jews who regard him as someone sharing common values. If Jesus were perceived by the pious as a common sinner, they would not have dignified him with questions.

Debate about interpretation of a law was not unusual within Jewish tradition. In fact, one might say that difference of opinion was a prominent feature of the tradition, something to be treasured. In the legal rulings of the sages written down more than a century and a half later in the Mishnah, legal opinions regularly include minority views. In still later tradition, it became customary to state legal opinions in terms of opposing perspectives ("the house of Shammai says . . . but the house of Hillel says"). That Jesus' behavior should become an occasion to debate his interpretation of the law and his attitude toward the "tradition of the elders" does not suggest that his critics are enemies.

The typical conversation partners are identified as **Pharisees.** The term designates a party or sect within Judaism rather than an office. Pharisees represented one perspective on Jewish identity. In Mark, they appear regularly as defenders of Sabbath observance and ritual purity—a major concern of Jewish tradition later recorded in the Mishnah. The preoccupation of such Jews was not salvation as much as sanctification. In a confusing world, often openly hostile to Jewish tradition, Pharisees sought to provide a safeguard for their way of life. Their Torah was understood as a constitution, regulating and ordering life. It provided the desired stability and regularity in terms of holiness. Pharisees applied to everyday life patterns of purity developed for priests. God had called Israel to be "a kingdom of priests and a holy nation" (Exod. 19:6—words which introduce the giving of the law). Pharisees sought to work out that vocation for laity as well as for priests.

We know little about the historical Pharisees from Jewish sources, but what little we know accords well with the portrait sketched by Mark. They were concerned with dietary laws and Sabbath observance—not as a mark of particular pride but as a way of making life holy. They regarded mealtime as sacred. They ate the food prescribed in the law and abstained from what was forbidden. They sought to reinforce their resolve to swim against the cultural stream by eating together. Mealtime provided a means of public testimony to their faith in the God who gave the law.

We do the Pharisees an injustice when we regard them as petty hypocrites. Mark does not portray them as petty. They have a definite view of Jewish identity that differs at points from Jesus', and they ask questions. We ought not trivialize these differences of opinion by caricaturing the opposition. We might also note that Jesus would have looked more like a Pharisee than a member of any other of the various groups in the story. The reason for the Pharisees' concerns is that Jesus seems sympathetic to their religious cause while doing things that seem to undermine its foundations. If he were not a religious Jew, they would have had no interest in him.

Eating with Sinners (2:15-17)

The first of the controversies has to do with Jesus' associates at meals. Jesus calls Levi, a tax collector, to follow him. Then he eats with him, as well as with other **sinners and tax collectors.** The place of the meal is **in his house.** Luke takes the reference to "his house" as meaning the home of Levi (5:29). Perhaps that is the proper way to read Mark. Jesus accepts an invitation to eat with the notorious sinner he has just called. His behavior scandalizes pious Jews (**the scribes of the Pharisees**); it suggests indifference to dietary laws. It may imply that Jesus condones the actions of **sinners and tax collectors.**

Jesus' response suggests a wholly different preoccupation: **Those who are well have no need of a physician, but those who are sick; I came not to call the righteous, but sinners.** Jesus' preoccupation is not so much with the creation and preservation of a stable order as much as it is with bringing strays back into the family. Jesus ventures outside boundaries in order to bring back the lost, heal the sick, cleanse the sinful. Implied, perhaps, is a critique of piety so intent upon securing its own purity that it is powerless to redeem the lost. The question, of course, is whether such a preoccupation as Jesus' can be tolerated in an uncertain world where stability is so rare—and so essential to survival.

New Skins for New Wine (2:18-22)

The next story addresses the question of **fasting.** Fasting had been a sign of reverence for God since ancient times, and an entire section of the Mishnah (*Taanith*) is devoted to days of fasting. The festival of the day of atonement, for example, was "celebrated" by fasting and repentance. Since Jesus preached that people should repent in the face of the impending kingdom of God, fasting would seem an appropriate accompaniment. It apparently was seen as such by **John's disciples.** But, as John's disciples and **the** (disciples of the?) **Pharisees** observe, Jesus' **disciples** do not fast.

Jesus' "pronouncement" is more lengthy in this case. He first addresses the question by comparing himself to a **bridegroom** and his followers to the marriage party. When the wedding party is in progress and the bridegroom present, can fasting be appropriate? Certainly not. That is a time for feasting and celebrating. The time will come soon enough when the bridegroom must leave.

What is the point of the imagery of a wedding party? Elsewhere in the New Testament the imagery appears in contexts where its eschatological overtones are obvious. In the visions of John the seer, Jesus is the bridegroom to whose marriage feast the elect are invited (Rev. 19:6-10). Jesus compares the Kingdom of God to a marriage feast the king gives for his son (where God is clearly the King) (Matt. 22:1-14). The imagery is eschatological, describing features of the last days. Jesus' use of the analogy claims that his presence signals the inauguration of that messianic feast when fasting will be quite inappropriate. The reminder that the bridegroom will be **taken away** suggests that the presence of Jesus cannot be regarded as the consummation but as an anticipation of what is to come. The kingdom is at hand, not yet fully present. While the groom remains, however, there can be no fasting. The imagery is reminiscent of the opening miracle ("sign") in John's Gospel, when Jesus turns water into wine at a wedding at Cana.

Jesus' second group of images (**cloth** and **patches, wine** and **skins**) deals with the relationship between the new and the old. The imagery implies a radical sense of discontinuity guaranteed to awaken in his religious audience considerable disquiet. Implied is an incompatibility between new and old. Compromises will not work. They will succeed only in spoiling both the old and the new. New wine is for new skins. Jesus is indeed something unprecedented, and the tradition will not be able to accommodate him. Something is bound to be destroyed. That is, of course, precisely what his questioners fear.

Gleaning on the Sabbath (2:23-28)

The third in the series of controversies focuses on **Sabbath** observance. Again, disagreement about what constitutes proper respect for the Sabbath has precedent. An entire tractate in the Mishnah discusses in minute detail what is and is not permissible on the Sabbath. That discussion of the scriptural injunctions against work on the Sabbath was necessary in view of the rather general character of the biblical material. The Pharisees were aware that respecting the Sabbath did not need to be unreasonable. Certain acts were necessary—like a farmer's care for animals and some of the ordinary business of daily life. In specifying precisely what was not allowed they wished to offer a more accurate sense of how respect for the Sabbath could be lived out—one of the aspects of Jewish life that distinguished Jews from their Gentile neighbors.

According to the story, the **disciples** plucked **grain** while walking through a field. Such a practice is explicitly permitted in Deuteronomy as a general sign of neighborliness:

> When you go into your neighbor's standing grain, you may pluck the ears with your hand, but you shall not put a sickle to your neighbor's standing grain.
>
> (Deut. 23:25)

One could argue that "plucking the ears with your hand" is not really "work," like reaping, and thus does not constitute a violation of the Sabbath rest. Sages were concerned, however, to protect against any possible violation of the law (this is the meaning of "putting a hedge around the Torah"). Sages discussed such matters as precisely how much grain could be picked before it was considered work—and thus a transgression. **The Pharisees** here regard plucking even a few ears of grain as work. Their question invites Jesus' opinion.

Striking here is Jesus' approach to settling the dispute. Like the sages, he cites precedent—but not the precedent of prior legal opinion. He compares his situation to that of King David, who ate the **bread of the Presence** when he was hungry. (In fact, the event, recorded in 2 Sam. 15:35, occurred when Ahimelech, not **Abiathar,** was **high priest**.) In what sense can Jesus claim David as precedent-setter—unless he is understood to be the offspring who will sit on David's throne?

The debate is concluded with a double pronouncement. The first, that **the sabbath was made for** humans, **not** humans **for the sabbath,** enunciates a view that accords well with what can be found in Jewish tradition, particularly with the opinions later associated with the disciples of Hillel. It represents the kind of reasoning common in the wisdom tradition.

The second pronouncement seems a more appropriate statement of personal authority: **so the Son of man is lord even of the sabbath.** While there are questions about how to understand the strange title **the Son of man,** here as throughout Mark it must be understood as a self-reference: Jesus is lord of the Sabbath. As did King David, Jesus approaches tradition, even Sabbath observance, with a special claim to authority.

Precisely what tone is added by "the Son of man"—whether it conjures up visions of Daniel 7 and hints at a messianic claim—cannot be determined from this passage.

A Sabbath Healing (3:1-6)

The last in the series of controversies continues the theme of Jesus' transgression of **Sabbath** observance, providing a climax for this little portion of Mark. The brief tale contains features typical of both controversies and healings. In the story, however, the man with the malady never asks for help and Jesus' adversaries never say a word. Jesus' action dominates from start to finish. What is distinctive here is the open concern of the religious Jews to trap Jesus. Though episodic, the narrative gives the impression of increasing hostility. Jesus' detractors (**the Pharisees** and **the Herodians,** 3:6) are no longer interested in Jesus' reasons for what he does. They hope simply to **accuse him.**

Disputes about healing on the Sabbath were not unique to Jesus and the New Testament. The question he addresses to his would-be critics has precedent in the discussions of Jewish sages. It is not impossible that other Jewish teachers would have applauded Jesus' opinion that "doing **good**" on the Sabbath is to be commended. The normal principle, however, is to refrain from doing on the Sabbath what is not absolutely necessary to life. If there is a genuine risk of life, Sabbath rules may be transgressed. The Mishnah, while written down a century and a half later, offers a sense of the issue:

> If a man has a pain in his throat they may drop medicine into his mouth on the Sabbath, since there is doubt whether life is in danger,

and whenever there is doubt whether life is in danger this overrides the Sabbath.

(Mishnah, Yoma 8:6)

The point of Jesus' critics is that the healing was not absolutely essential, since there appeared to be no risk of life. Jesus regards this distinction, however, as a sign of **hardness of heart.** According to Jesus, they do not recognize the intent of the law. He heals the man, thus issuing a direct challenge to his audience. In this case, the healing serves as a pronouncement. And as in the previous episode, Jesus relies not on precedent but on his personal authority.

For his adversaries, **the Pharisees** and **the Herodians,** Jesus seems intent upon making an issue of Sabbath transgression. The man did not have to be healed; Jesus could have waited at least until sundown. The Pharisaic enterprise involved building and maintaining a legal structure within which life could be lived. Jesus threatened that structure. The power he demonstrated made him all the more dangerous. There was a good possibility that he would pull the whole structure down, making civilized life impossible, removing the last barrier to the wave of Hellenism that threatened to sweep Jewish tradition into oblivion. Jesus' Sabbath transgressions, however trivial they may appear to us, were genuinely dangerous.

The Pharisees and the Herodians consult about **how to destroy** Jesus. The Greek could be translated simply "ruin," suggesting some frustration at having been unable to accuse Jesus (3:2). In the context, however, it points forward to the climax of the story when Jesus' opponents destroy him by putting him to death.

The Herodians are introduced here without comment. They play little role in the story, appearing again only in the controversies in chapter 12 where, again in conjunction with the Pharisees, they ask Jesus about payment of tribute to Caesar. They were apparently partisans of the family of Herod. Herod the Great, known prior to his death as "the King of the Jews," was a half-Jew (an Idumean) who owed his position to close relations with the Romans. With his death, his kingdom was divided among his three sons. When Archelaus, ruler of Judea, proved incompetent, Judea became a Roman province, while Galilee remained under the jurisdiction of Herod Antipas—the ruler who beheaded John the Baptizer.

Like the Pharisees, the Herodians perceive Jesus to be a threat. Because he is enormously popular with the common people, Jesus will become an increasing threat to those in power. Herod (Antipas) will eventually become concerned (Mark 6:14). By the end of the story, officials in both the religious and political realm will decide he is too dangerous to live.

Insiders and Outsiders (3:7-35)

The Crowds (3:7-12)

Karl Ludwig Schmidt, in his famous work on the "framework" for the story of Jesus, suggested that the sense of movement and coherence in Mark's Gospel arises from a handful of summaries, of which this is one of the more important. The controversies are episodes, grouped together with little effort at weaving them into a single cloth. The summary, Schmidt argued, represents the author's attempt to pull the strands of the story together and to suggest some movement. While he underappreciated the artistry within the narrative, Schmidt was certainly correct in highlighting the significance of the summaries as ways of focusing the story.

As is customary in these early chapters, Jesus goes to the seaside as a favored location for healing and teaching. It proves to be a convenient location, since the crowds have now grown enormously. Jesus must do his teaching from **a boat** lest he be crushed by the mob. **The crowd** is large, we are told, because his reputation has spread—not only through **Galilee** but also into **Judea** and **Idumea,** the Transjordan, **Tyre** and **Sidon.** People flock to him from everywhere; his popularity may even rival that of John, who attracted "all the country of Judea and all the people of Jerusalem." The mention of the Transjordan and Tyre and Sidon suggests that Jesus has attracted the attention even of non-Jews, since these were Gentile territories. Little is made of the issue at this point. His encounter with Gentiles will be emphasized later.

The summary seeks to establish Jesus' enormous popularity with the sick and the poor. Those who were sick came in hopes of having Jesus **touch** them. He did, and they were healed. The summary also reminds the reader of Jesus' encounter with the demons, a typical feature of his ministry since the outset. What is stressed, however, is not simply that Jesus was able to cast out **unclean spirits.** The summary underlines that the demons, as always, know who Jesus is: the "Holy One of God," **the Son of God,** and the "Son of the Most High God" are all titles employed only by demons—at least prior to Jesus' trial. Knowledge that Jesus is "Son" is apparently reserved for supernatural beings.

Here, as elsewhere, Jesus "rebukes them greatly"—not because what they say is false but because they know who he is. His rebuke intends that they **not make him known.** We are told no more than earlier about the reasons for the secrecy—except that it is intended by Jesus. Speculation about Jesus' reasons is still unwarranted because there are no data provided by the narrator on the basis of which to formulate a theory. We will have to rely on Mark to provide more information.

The summaries are obviously intended for the reader and reinforce the distance that separates reader and characters in the story. Though the demons **cried out,** we are offered no indication that any in the audience understand what they say. Until the very end of the story, no human being uses the titles employed by the demons. Jesus' followers do not suggest he is the Son of God. Only God and the demons call Jesus **Son**—until the concluding chapter, when the chief priest and a centurion use the phrase. How the various "confessions" are related will be addressed later. Apparently knowledge that Jesus is **the Son of God** is of supernatural origin—and is privileged information. As readers, we are the privileged.

Excursus: The Son of God

The expression "the Son of God" qualifies as a title in Mark. It appears as a predicate nominative, designating an office of some sort. The title is not used with frequency, and the patterns of usage merit attention. In the opening chapters, only demons address Jesus as "the Son of God" (3:11 and 5:7). In the concluding chapter, the chief priest and a Roman soldier use the expression (for the grammatical difficulties in the Roman's "confession," see the commentary on 15:39). No follower of Jesus and no other humans employ the title.

Related to these occurrences is the use of "my Son" by God at Jesus' baptism (1:11) and at the transfiguration (9:7).

Completely uncertain is the reading in 1:1. Nestle's 26th edition of the Greek New Testament includes "Son of God," while the 25th edition relegated it to the margin. Nestle's 27th will again place the reading in the margin, so that the most recent English translations of Mark should exclude "Son of God" from the opening verse.

While much has been written about the title "the Son of God," it is still the case that outside Christian literature the term is remarkably rare. The only attestation of the title in Jewish writings is a fragment from the Qumran Scrolls in which a royal figure is identified as "Son of God" and "Son of the Most High God." While the fragmentary nature of the occurrences makes any inferences difficult, we at least know that the expression (in Hebrew) was not unknown. In the Greco-Roman world, "the Son of God" is rarely attested.

The following observations may be made regarding the expression and its place in Mark's Gospel:

1. Until the account of Jesus' trial and death, the term is reserved for supernatural beings: demons, who are enjoined to be silent, and God, who calls Jesus "Son."

2. In 1:11 and 9:7, the wording of the heavenly voice is reminiscent of Ps. 2:7, in which God addresses the king as "son." There is evidence from the Qumran Scrolls that Psalm 2 and 2 Sam. 7:14 were interpreted as messianic oracles, pointing to the coming King. "Son" and "Son of God" are thus titles appropriate to the coming king, as the question of the high priest likewise presumes ("Are you the Christ, the Son of the Blessed?"). While the royal tradition may not provide the exclusive traditional background for the title in Mark, it certainly predominates. "Son of God" thus should not be heard as an alternative to "the Messiah."

3. Jesus' absolute use of "the Son" (13:32) and his reference to God as "Abba" (father) is another factor in the way "the Son of God" is heard. This usage cannot be derived from royal tradition and has appropriately been investigated as arising from Jesus' own usage. Those who have

studied Jesus' unique "God consciousness" and have made it an essential element in a New Testament Christology must base a great deal on speculation. In the exegesis of Mark, such study may be of interest but is not foundational for interpretation of the Gospel and its use of "the Son of God." (See the bibliography, Hengel and Juel.)

The Commissioning of the Twelve (3:13-19)

While the episodes that follow are only loosely connected, there is a definite strategy observable in the narrative. Thus far we have witnessed differing reactions to Jesus among several groups: disciples Jesus has called, the crowds who come for healing, and religious Jews. Here, boundaries are now more clearly drawn. Jesus appoints a circle of **twelve** who are given special responsibilities. Immediately after the formation of this inner circle, we witness the reaction to Jesus of Jesus' family and of **scribes who came down from Jerusalem** (v. 22). Both groups, in differing ways, view Jesus as out of his senses. The imagery in the chapter's concluding scene provides structures within which the story is played out: some are inside, others outside. The roles of "insiders" and "outsiders" are central to the reality Mark's Gospel creates.

Since the opening verses in the Gospel Jesus has been summoning various individuals to follow. Now he begins to weld them into a group. The site of this gathering is specified only as **the mountain.** While the term may imply simply the hill country, its use elsewhere in Mark may suggest some symbolic significance. Particularly suggestive is the "mountain" where Jesus appears with Moses and Elijah and is transfigured (9:2-10). Association with Mount Sinai and with theophanies is apparent in this account. The "mountain" also appears in 6:46 as a place of retreat, where Jesus can go to pray by himself. Perhaps the image suggests both the sense of isolation and "elevation" appropriate to the authority of the one who will now make fateful decisions.

From these heights, Jesus appoints a circle of **twelve.** Some weighty manuscripts add that they are called "apostles," but the reading seems too clearly an explanatory addition (we are told they are **to be sent out**). The absence of a title like "disciples" or "apostles" is perhaps worth noting. There is no effort to identify "the apostles" with the circle of the Twelve, reflecting perhaps the same perspective as 1 Cor. 15:3-7, where "all the apostles" are distinguished from "the twelve." Furthermore, we learn in Mark that the "insiders" include more than the Twelve ("those who were about him with the twelve" [4:10]). The group, whose names are provided, represents a special circle of insiders. We will learn that there is yet a more intimate group of insiders— Peter, James, and John—with a special role to play.

The **Twelve** are assigned specific responsibilities: they are **to be with him, and to be sent out to preach and have authority to cast out demons.** This commissioning specifies a role for Jesus' intimates that will carry beyond the confines of the story. They are called to share Jesus' ministry, to do what he does. We can already understand that if Jesus is to make any lasting impact it will be through the efforts of the **Twelve.** From this point on, the group is at the center of the story. Mark's Gospel is about the **Twelve** almost as much as it is about Jesus.

The reason for appointing twelve is not explained by Mark (as it is in Matthew and Luke, where Jesus tells his followers explicitly that they will sit on thrones "judging the twelve tribes of Israel" [Luke 22:30; cf. Matt. 19:28]), but it is undoubtedly presupposed. In view of the impending dawning of God's kingdom, Jesus' followers are given some special responsibility for Israel, the people of twelve tribes. Their call does not suggest that Jesus is appointing representatives of a new Israel but that his emissaries are sent to Israel—the only one there is—to carry through his own mission. Like Jesus, they are to preach about the kingdom of God and to heal.

Mark includes mention of two symbolic names. **Simon** is **surnamed Peter,** from "rock." The symbolism suits Peter's role as a fundamental figure in the story. **James** and **John** are called **sons of thunder.** Matthew offers some explanation of Peter's name ("You are Peter, and on this rock I will build my church"), though not of the name **sons of thunder.** In popular Christian tradition, the name is explained by the alleged "temper" of the two young people (they are ready to call down fire from heaven on inhospitable Samaritans according to Luke 9:54). The explanation is unwarranted. More plausible is some derivation that relates to the imminence of the end—the great storm about to burst on the present. Whether Mark or his readers know the derivation of the nickname is impossible to say, based on the little evidence we possess.

The reference to **Judas** as the one **who betrayed him** indicates the degree to which the narrator is not bound by time—he can refer to events that happen much later as an explanation of features in the narrative—and that Mark's readers must certainly have known the story of Jesus at least in rough outline. The little hint of what is to come—betrayal—is only one in a long list of pointers that direct us to the great crisis that will occur at the story's end.

Family Troubles (3:20-21)

An evaluation of Jesus' ministry follows immediately his selection of a group of intimates. The occasion is a massing of people so great that there is no opportunity even to **eat. The crowd,** of course, believes Jesus can help them. The enormous popularity apparently provokes a crisis. Jesus can no longer be ignored.

The first to offer an appraisal are his relatives (*hoi par' autou*), who come **to seize him.** The word *krateō* should be translated as **seize**; it is used in the sense of "get one's hands on someone" in Mark 6:17; 12:12; 14:1, 44, 46, 49, 51.

There is some ambiguity in the explanatory comment. One possible translation might be, **For they [people] were saying, "He is beside himself."** The more natural translation would take "his relatives" as the subject of the verb **were saying.** In other words, according to Mark, Jesus' relatives come to lay hold of him because they fear he is insane.

A Question of Possession (3:22-30)

The evaluation that Jesus is **beside himself** is shared with the religious authorities who have come **from Jerusalem** (the first hint of what is to come in the great city). No one can deny that

Jesus is extraordinary, that his power and authority are not derived from internal resources. **The scribes** attribute his power, however, to demons. Jesus is **possessed**!

Jesus chooses to respond indirectly, with illustrations (**in parables**), but there is nothing cryptic about his response: their evaluation is absurd. Attributing his power to cast out demons to demonic possession violates common sense. The scribes fail to appreciate the way **kingdoms** or households work. For a ruler to take up arms against himself would be the prelude to disaster. Divided households cannot survive. In fact, if Satan's host is at war with itself, people ought to rejoice—for he has come **to an end.**

Jesus offers the only reasonable interpretation of what is occurring: someone has invaded the domain of the **strong man** (**Satan**)—and that someone is the "stronger one" of whom John the Baptist spoke. Satan is being deposed and his domain plundered.

The imagery provides a glimpse of how healings and exorcisms are related to Jesus' announcement that the "kingdom of God" has drawn near. Jesus is the agent as well as the herald of God's rule. Exorcisms, the typical features of his ministry, constitute an invasion of alien territory—the dispossessing of Satan and his host. The parallel drawn between **kingdom** and **house** may suggest that the Greek *basileia* is not to be understood simply as denoting an activity ("The rule of God," as some would translate the expression). The world is portrayed as a household in which Satan is master. Jesus is wresting control from him.

That such imagery has significance for Mark's view of the kingdom is apparent also in 13:34-35, where Jesus pictures the days preceding the end of the ages by speaking of a "house" whose owner ("the master of the house") leaves his slaves in charge, commanding them to watch for his return. It would be reductionist and anachronistic to speak of this "household" as the "church." There is nevertheless a sense in which spatial imagery is implied in the expression "kingdom of God." Jesus not only seeks to "plunder Satan's fold" but to establish a new "household" (see the commentary on chap. 10). (For the idea that the devil is in control of the world, see the temptation stories in Matthew and Luke, where Satan presumes that political authority belongs to him.)

The imagery Jesus employs in speaking of his work is "uncivilized." He is one who has come to bind and to plunder. It is precisely that socially destructive possibility that Jesus' opponents fear. When he is arrested, Jesus asks, "Have you come out as against a bandit?" (14:48). He will be executed between two bandits, hung on a cross as a threat to the state. In view of that charge, there is a certain abandon in Jesus' choice of imagery. He is God's Son, the agent through whom the kingdom of God will be established. There is little attempt, however, to mask the offense his ministry will cause among those in authority. He will be perceived as a law-breaker and a threat to society. Jesus does little to allay such fears.

In their assessment that Jesus is possessed, **the scribes** are correct. Jesus is not his own; the driving force in his ministry is the **Spirit** within him. But it is the Spirit of God, not an unclean spirit, that inspires his work. The attribution of that inspiration to **the prince of demons** thus constitutes blasphemy **against the Holy Spirit.** Ironically, the religious authorities do not know what the demons themselves must acknowledge: Jesus is the "Son of God." While the initial reaction of religious people to Jesus is that he commits blasphemy (2:7), it is in fact Jesus' detractors who are culpable. Just as the earlier charge of blasphemy anticipates Jesus' trial before the Sanhedrin (14:53-64), so too Jesus' words about blasphemy **against the Holy Spirit** indict those who condemn Jesus to death.

True Family (3:31-35)

With those chilling words still echoing, the story returns to Jesus' family. **His mother and his brothers** come, we are told, and stand **outside.** They do not venture "inside" but send someone to summon Jesus. This is the first mention in the story of Jesus' close family, and in this context they are introduced as outsiders.

The earlier comment that Jesus' relatives believe he is beside himself casts the summons of his family circle in shadows: their "call" is hardly neutral. While perhaps not included among those guilty of blasphemy against the Holy Spirit, his mother and brothers are nevertheless definitely on the outside. The repeated references to the circle about Jesus (**crowd sitting around him; looking around on those who sat about him** in a circle) drive home the point. Jesus' own flesh and blood, those who should be closest to him, are not intimates at all. His true family—his **brother, and sister, and mother**—are those who do **the will of God,** presumably as Jesus is interpreting it.

The statement is explosive. Jesus threatens the most fundamental of all structures, the family. Blood relations guarantee nothing. What will alone unite, he seems to say, is fidelity to the truth.

Those who are troubled by Jesus have good reason to be. He appears as the opponent of structured life—of civilization. His language is reminiscent of cults that seek to break ordinary social ties and forge new ones. Real "family," cults suggest, is found among those united by the same faith or ideology. Ties with parents and siblings may be obstacles to real community. Jesus seems to say the same thing. "New skins for new wine." But at what cost? Who will be able to pay?

The section concludes with a divided world. Those clustered around Jesus, including his disciples and others "around them," as well as the crowds, are insiders. The rest, including the respectable elements of society like family and religious leaders, are outsiders. As the story develops, the categories of "insider" and "outsider" become central to the narrative.

Promising Instruction (4:1-34)

This little collection of parables represents the first account of any sustained teaching by Jesus. There are earlier references to Jesus' teaching in the synagogue (1:21-27) and a reference to instructing crowds (2:13), but Mark has recorded only declarations about controversial matters within debates with scribes and Pharisees. The debates contribute to the plot, with Pharisees and Herodians plotting how to get rid of Jesus after the confrontation. The parables play no such role in the plot. They are addressed to crowds who have come to listen. In Mark, the parables serve as ways to understand the whole narrative. In particular, they relate the ministry of Jesus to the "kingdom of God" that is the theme of his preaching.

Jesus' parables have been the subject of intense scrutiny in the last century. An important turning point was Adolf Jülicher's study that marked a break with the church's tradition of allegorical interpretation. Students of the parables have sought to find a more stable basis for interpretation than the imagination of preachers. Joachim Jeremias, perhaps the most influential of these scholars, insisted that we can know what the parables mean only if we know the intention of Jesus in telling them and the situation in which they were uttered. For those persuaded by his approach, the form of the parables encountered in the New Testament is regarded as a source of information about something else, a starting point for reconstructing a history of interpretation that will lead to the "authentic words of Jesus."

In a commentary on Mark, such a historical reconstruction cannot be a priority. The focus of interpretation will be the parables as they are encountered in their scriptural setting. How closely the parables in Mark correspond to those actually spoken by Jesus is a question worth pursuing, but interpretation does not depend upon the results of such historical reconstruction. The results of such historical reconstruction will always remain speculative, providing an even more insubstantial basis for interpreters. The historical approach leaves interpretation in the hands of a few experts. And in any case, locating truth and meaning only in the intention of the historical Jesus betrays the strange conviction that the "word of God" must be identical to the "words of Jesus"—a view that no Christian tradition has ever espoused.

The matter is worth noting because so few commentators seem willing to regard the New Testament books as the primary context for interpreting parables. In most current studies, the prior history of the parables turns out to be decisive for interpreting Mark.

Jesus teaches **the crowds** in **parables.** The word **parable** has a wide range of meanings. The term identifies a type of figurative speech. In his controversy with the scribes, Jesus discusses the way of kingdoms and households; the illustrations he uses during that discussion are termed "parables" (3:23). The **parables** in this chapter, three in number, are typically introduced with some variation of the formula, **The kingdom of God is like. . . .** The term **like** identifies the parables as extended similes. The function of the illustrations drawn from rural life is to shed light on something else—in this case, the kingdom of God. Since the disciples require explanations, however, and in view of Jesus' statement in v. 11, the term must also imply "veiled speech"—perhaps even "riddle" (see especially 4:11).

Speaking the language of the countryside, Jesus uses agricultural imagery to speak about the kingdom of God. The parables presume that the audience knows something about the kingdom of God—the glorious time when God will rule after defeating all enemies. They speak of a reality whose coming God's people anticipate (14:25; 15:43).

While the kingdom of God may be a commonplace, its relationship to Jesus' preaching and teaching is not. It is that questionable relationship that elicits the parables. In Luke, Jesus tells three stories in response to the grumbling of the scribes and Pharisees that he "receives sinners and eats with them" (Luke 15:1). Though Mark provides no such introduction to the parables in this chapter, we can determine from the larger context implied questions and criticisms to which Jesus' stories are a response. People, in particular religious Jews, are not persuaded that Jesus' ministry has anything to do with the kingdom.

Jesus begins his ministry by announcing that the kingdom of God is at hand. He preaches, heals the sick, and drives out demons—summoning a group of twelve to share in that ministry. In response to scribes who believe him to be possessed, he speaks of kingdoms and households, of binding the strong man to plunder his house—implying that his ministry is related to the establishment of God's kingdom. One question looms large in the minds of supporters and detractors alike: Is there reason to believe Jesus' ministry has anything to do with the glorious kingdom of God? Religious Jews and Jesus' relatives certainly have serious doubts, and the list of the suspicious will grow as the story unfolds. The parables address those doubts.

The Sower and the Soils (4:1-20)

The movement from the house (3:20) to **the sea** is abrupt. The new scene, set at the seaside, is familiar from the previous chapter. Jesus is teaching the **very large crowd** that has flocked to him. As in 3:9, he chooses to speak from **a boat** just offshore so as to address the crowd.

Of the **many . . . parables,** the narrator records only three.

The parable of the sower is exceptional in several respects. It is not introduced with a formula, as are the parables of the seed growing of itself and the mustard seed. We must infer that this parable, like the subsequent two, is about the kingdom of God. That is, after all, the theme of Jesus' preaching, according to 1:15.

This story is likewise the only one to be interpreted. In vv. 13-20, Jesus explains the parable to his followers, treating it as an allegory. Most current interpretations of the parable choose to distinguish between the actual parable (vv. 3-8) and the explanation, attributing the explanation to Christian exposition. There is, they argue, a difference between parable and allegory. Jesus told parables.

The allegorical reading in this case, however, is within the New Testament. While the parable of the sower may be capable of various interpretations, the narrative limits possible readings by offering an interpretation and by placing the parable in a particular context. The meaning of the parable of the sower, then, can be determined only in light of vv. 13-20 and within the narrative context Mark has provided—if we are to interpret Mark.

The actions of the farmer in Jesus' first story seem somewhat outrageous. There is a carelessness about his scattering of **seed,** a lavishness that does not bode well in view of all the potential hazards to the harvest. Perhaps because plowing was done after sowing, the farmer's actions would not seem as strange to an ancient audience as to moderns. For any audience, however, there is a sense of waste and risk: **birds** take their toll; weeds will prove troublesome; hidden rocks and paltry soil will impose additional limits on the farm's productivity. One might wonder why the farmer is not more cautious about his seed, more prudent. Surveying all the threats to the harvest, from birds to weeds to poor soil conditions, people may well wonder if the efforts of the farmer will bear any fruit.

It turns out the farmer knows his business. Despite the obstacles, the harvest comes. To the doubters, the yield will be a glorious surprise. The exaggerated yields, **thirtyfold and sixtyfold and a hundredfold** (a return of ten times the seed sown was considered excellent), serve as dramatic vindication of the planter.

The parable is an analogy. It speaks about the kingdom of God. The bountiful harvest is employed in Jewish tradition as an image for the coming days. The focus is not the kingdom in general, but its relationship to Jesus' preaching and teaching. Expectant Jews did not doubt the kingdom would come; there were many reasons to doubt, however, that Jesus' efforts would result in the bountiful harvest signaling the arrival of the promised days. He invested his efforts in singularly unpromising circles. Troubles lay ahead that might well frustrate his efforts. In the face of such doubts, Jesus promises that his work will bear fruit, however careless he may appear and however many obstacles stand in the way. His efforts will result in nothing short of the coming of God's kingdom in all its splendor and glory.

Note that the parable says nothing about taking precautions to minimize the risk. The sower does not distribute his seed in more calculated fashion in view of all the hazards; nor are there provisions for weeding or driving off pests. The only effort expended is in sowing seed. The abundant harvest comes—in spite of all the obstacles.

The parable ends, as it began, with an encouragement to listen. Those who have **ears to hear** should give heed. The following verses indicate, however, that ears are not necessarily open to instruction, just as eyes may prove to be blind.

The next three verses mark a break between parable and explanation. They presume a change of scenes: **And when he was alone.** The narrator is, of course, not bound by time and space. He is free to move back and forth as he chooses.

The scene pictures Jesus alone with an inner circle. Note that **the Twelve** are not exclusively members of this inner circle. There are others with them. Central to the passage is the distinction between this group and those outside, picking up the theme from the preceding chapter. The former are insiders—Jesus' real family—who "do the will of God." And there are those "outside" who do not. Because Jesus has chosen the insiders, it is difficult to understand the distinctions in terms of some moral category. There is a distinction first of all because Jesus chooses to treat the groups differently.

Significantly, insiders need explanations. Their question deals not simply with the story Jesus has just told but with **the parables**—perhaps the "many things" to which Mark refers in v. 2. The parable of the sower is only an example within a series. Jesus' response intends to make a statement about the form of teaching in general. The general nature of the statement has led many commentators to speak of the verses as a "parable theory," which most attribute to Mark and not to Jesus. For many, such attribution means that the verses do not need to be taken seriously since they were probably not spoken by the "historical Jesus" in this setting—a strange notion for which there is little foundation in interpretive theory of any sort.

To this group of insiders, Jesus insists, has been given the mystery (RSV: **secret**) **of the kingdom of God.** The enigmatic phrase appears only in this context in the Gospels and is not explained. The term "mystery" or **secret** refers to some heavenly reality that requires disclosure (1 Cor. 14:2; 15:21; Rom. 16:25; Eph. 3:3, 9; Rev. 1:20; 17:7). "Giving" the mystery implies revelation: to the disciples has been disclosed some heavenly secret about the kingdom of God. That is presumably what distinguishes the "insiders" from the "outsiders." We are not told precisely what the "mystery" entails or when it was entrusted to this group. Such a disclosure will apparently prove decisive; it is perhaps to such a possession Jesus refers a bit later when he says, "To those who have it will be given; those who have not, even what they have will be taken from them" (4:25).

While insiders receive mysteries and explanations, outsiders get only "riddles." Jesus' words only veil the truth for those who do not already perceive the heart of the matter. And that is what he intends. In words reminiscent of Isaiah's call, Jesus declares that by means of riddles he veils the truth so that people will not see or hear **lest they should turn again, and be forgiven.**

It is hardly surprising that interpreters have sought every means to escape the implications of these words, from attributing the "in order that" (Greek, *hina*) to a mistranslation of the Aramaic to dismissing the whole section as "Mark's parable theory"—as though that meant that this portion of Scripture need not be taken seriously. Noting that Jesus' words come from Isaiah does not make them easier. They come from Isaiah's call, where the prophet is told to preach, knowing in advance that his words will succeed only in hardening hearts until God has carried out punishment (Isaiah 6). God alone can open eyes and ears, and will not. The present, Isaiah is told, is a time of veiling and punishment.

There seems no escape from the implication: God has the sovereign right to determine who will and who will not see and hear—and repent. Jesus claims the right as his own. He intends—at least at this stage in his ministry—to keep outsiders in the dark.

It may seem easier to understand these verses in retrospect as a reflection on how Jesus' preaching turned out. Seeing and hearing require something more than sounds and sights. There must be some openness to the truth, some will to understand. That will was apparently lacking among Jesus' audience. His preaching did not serve to open eyes and ears but to harden hearts and finally to secure his own death warrant. The one who told parables was hung on a cross. That does not remove the offense, however, but only deepens the mystery. The evangelist does not shy away from seeing the will of God at work in unbelief as well as belief.

Jesus intends that people should not understand, and it is for that reason he speaks in "riddles." The statement is of a piece with Jesus' silencing of the demons and his injunctions to people he has healed not to make him known. We are not given an explanation of his reasons. We are only directed to the Scriptures, providing a reminder that secrecy is in accordance with the will of God. There is no embarrassment here about the idea of election, no attempt to evade the implication that it is by God's grace alone that there can be insight that leads to repentance.

The passage, however, does not allow the construction of some theory about double predestination. We learn only a few verses later that Jesus' ultimate intention is not veiling and concealment. The goal of his mission is disclosure. Nothing is hid except to be made manifest (4:22). The story is headed somewhere. Jesus' sowing will lead ultimately to the harvest; Jesus has already suggested that the kingdom has "come near." When it fully comes, perhaps, the time of secrecy will end. Until then, Jesus reserves the **secret of the kingdom of God** for a few.

Those who possess the secret of the kingdom still require explanations. Everything is apparently not clear to the insiders (indeed, we may ask later whether anything at all is clear to them). While his intimates have asked about "the parables," Jesus responds to a question about **this parable** and treats it as symptomatic: If you do not understand **this parable**, how will you understand the others? Indeed!

In the explanation given the disciples, the parable of the sower, interpreted as an allegory, becomes the parable of the four soils. Each feature of the story is explained. The seed equals **the word.**

The birds equal **Satan.** Thorns equal **cares of the world.** The explanation does not work equally well throughout, and is possible only by wrestling with the grammar. While the parable focuses on four batches of seed, the explanation treats the four groups as receptors—in other words, as types of soil. In the explanation, application is made explicit. The story is about the variety of "hearings" the word will receive. Some will receive the word and produce fruit; others will not.

The reasons for fruitless hearing are many: **Satan** works against the harvest by snatching the seed; **persecution** will prove too much for others; **riches** will choke out the good intentions of still others. While the parable does not provide an outline for the story, the themes it introduces run through the Gospel. Mark offers numerous examples of people whose lives attest the devastating effect of Satan. Jesus warns his followers about the danger of wealth and the realities of persecution (10:23-27; 13:9-13); at least one rich man is unable to escape the lures of possessions (10:17-22), and when faced with the prospect of arrest, Peter and the disciples collapse.

The power to resist the threats does not lie with the **soil,** however. "Soil" is a passive image. Like the "original," the interpreted parable speaks of promises and not demands. No injunction is offered to "Be good soil." The parable, even as interpreted, includes no exhortation. **Satan** will endeavor to destroy the harvest; temptations and **persecutions** will come. Yet **the good soil** will produce more abundantly than anyone can conceive—however unlikely it may seem. The soil will produce—not because it can make some Herculean effort but because it is good soil and the farmer knows his business.

The parable, with the other seed parables in the chapter, reinforces the sense of direction and momentum in the narrative. Jesus' efforts are part of a larger enterprise—the establishment of the kingdom of God—and are headed somewhere. There is purpose in what Jesus does, and however many obstacles block his achievement of those purposes, the planting will succeed in producing a rich harvest.

The parable, with the others in the chapter, will have an important bearing on how the ending of the Gospel is read. The similes provide assurance that Jesus' goals will be accomplished. Mark ends with one final disappointment and a host of promises awaiting fulfillment. Interpretation of this Gospel will require understanding the relationship between hopeful anticipation and disappointment.

While the parable of the sower (or the soils) makes promises, it leaves readers with disquieting questions. To whom are the promises about productivity directed? Who are those who represent **the good soil**—particularly if soil is passive and cannot be expected to change itself? Are the fruitless receptors forever destined to be unproductive? What about the disciples, the obvious candidates in the narrative for "good soil"? Will they produce? Even an elementary knowledge of Mark makes that question urgent.

The parable makes promises, but there is good reason to ask for whom the promises are intended. A general promise is of little comfort to anyone in particular. Will the Gospel provide a warrant for declaring God's promises to any particular person? Does Jesus address even his disciples? Taken by itself, the parable provides confidence that Jesus' ministry will bear fruit. That confidence is crucial for interpreting what is to come. It is not enough by itself, however, to provide comfort and consolation to any particular audience. Fruitfulness belongs to God. But what can be expected from God? There must be more to the story.

The Purpose of Secrecy (4:21-25)

Verses 21-25 represent collected sayings that shed light on the message of the parables. Jesus has just told his followers that he intends to keep outsiders in the dark. Here he speaks of giving light and revealing secrets. The purpose of **a lamp** is to illumine; it is thus not to be covered but placed **on a stand.** Likewise the purpose of secrecy and concealment, according to Jesus, is eventual disclosure. What is secret for now will eventually come to light. As seedtime drives toward harvest, so secrecy strains toward disclosure. Expectation of disclosure is one of the themes that carries the narrative forward.

The next two sayings are introduced by a warning: **Take heed what you hear.** The well-known saying about "measure for measure" is here appended to the warning about listening. It may seem strange that Jesus offers warnings about the consequences of not listening when he has just spoken in riddles so that outsiders will not hear. The point of this saying and the next is not so much exhortation as a statement of fact: everything will depend upon hearing, just as everything will depend upon "having." Those who do not have the truth, who have not listened, will remain outsiders. They will lose even what they have. The warning is cruel if the deaf and the have-nots are never given access to the truth. If Jesus has indeed come for "those who are sick" and for "sinners," outsiders may yet be given an opportunity.

The Patient Farmer (4:26-29)

Jesus' second seed parable is explicitly introduced as speaking about **the kingdom of God.** This parable also deals with the contrast between seedtime and harvest. Drawing another lesson from the world of agriculture, Jesus emphasizes the importance of patience. While the farmer may cultivate his field after the seed has been planted, he has only limited control of the natural process. In our own modern society as well, fertilizing, cultivating, even irrigating cannot hasten or force growth. It must come in its own time. But it will come; the signs will be unmistakable. And when the harvest arrives, it will again be time for activity.

It may seem that Jesus' ministry is not bearing fruit. Jesus' followers may be tempted to force the growth. Be patient, says the parable. The kingdom will come as surely as harvest follows planting. Until it does, you can only wait. Growth cannot be coerced.

The Mustard Seed (4:30-32)

The last of these seed parables compares **the kingdom of God** to a tiny **mustard seed** that, when planted, produces the largest of all garden **shrubs**—large enough to provide protection for **the birds**. Here the contrast between the humble beginning and the magnificent conclusion is stressed. Mark notes correctly that the mustard seed produces a **shrub**; in Matthew and Luke, it produces a "tree"—incorrect botanically, but correct traditionally as a symbol of the kingdom of God.

In context, the little simile comments on the relationship between Jesus' mission and the coming kingdom of God. Once again the question the parable addresses is not whether the kingdom will come. The question is whether Jesus' efforts have anything to do with the kingdom. His movement seems so small and insignificant! Just wait, Jesus promises. The mustard seed is tiny, but once it is planted it will produce a glorious shrub. An organic connection exists between Jesus' ministry and the kingdom, just as between seed and shrub. What is required of the faithful is patience that arises from hope.

Secret Instruction (4:33-34)

The summary that concludes Jesus' teaching stresses again the contrast between insiders and outsiders. Outsiders are given only **parables,** as they are able to listen. The disciples receive explanations, since they are the privileged, the ones to whom the mystery of the kingdom of God has been given. The narrator is emphatic: to them Jesus **explained everything.**

The narrative now takes a surprising turn. The contrast with Matthew is instructive. The collection of parables in Matthew 13 concludes with Jesus' characterization of his disciples as "scribes trained for the kingdom of heaven" (13:52). The story moves immediately to Jesus' preaching in his home town, where his former neighbors are scandalized. The boundaries between insiders and outsiders are solidified. In Mark, the first of several scenes set in a boat on the Sea of Galilee provides unsettling evidence about this little group of insiders that becomes a counter-theme in the ensuing chapters. Jesus' ministry moves toward disclosure. Harvest will follow seedtime. The disciples, as those entrusted with the mystery of the kingdom of God and the recipients of explanations, should know that and perform accordingly. What we learn about them, however, is not encouraging.

Spectacles (4:35—5:43)

Without doubt, the most spectacular miracles in the Gospel are recorded here at the end of chapter 4 and throughout chapter 5. Mark's relish for drama is apparent. The vocabulary is rich, the description lavish (Matthew and Luke have abridged the stories in chap. 5 considerably). The sketches of Jesus in the accounts of the Gerasene demoniac, Jairus's daughter, and the woman with a hemorrhage make little effort to distinguish him from typical healers or wonder-workers in Greco-Roman society. Traits appear that may even seem "magical" (power flows out of Jesus' clothing without his consent). Stories such as these are to awaken a sense of awe and amazement. The narrator is by no means naive about human reactions to power, however. Not everyone will welcome one who can perform such remarkable signs. Even miracles of healing contribute to the growing sense of unease among those who must finally decide on behalf of the common people what to make of Jesus.

Calming the Storm (4:35-41)

The boat which has served as Jesus' pulpit now serves to convey him and his followers to the other shore. Precisely where he and his disciples have been is unclear. Their destination is simply **the other side.** In transit **the boat** is struck by a **storm.** Pounded by **the waves,** the boat seems about to sink, and the disciples are terrified. Jesus' sleep seems to the disciples a sign of his indifference to them—a poignant contrast to the disciples' sleep in the garden later in the story.

When he is roused, Jesus **rebukes the wind** and **the sea,** addressing them as he does demons (the vocabulary is consistent). They obey, just as do unclean spirits.

God's power over nature is familiar from the Old Testament. The image of water as symbolizing chaos has roots far back in Near Eastern mythology and in the Psalms. Two passages reminiscent of this account are Job 38:1-11 and Ps. 74:13-14. God's deliverance of those at sea by calming storms is described in Ps. 107:23-29. The event of the Exodus is sometimes described with similar imagery ("He rebuked the Red Sea, and it became dry" [Ps. 106:9; see also Ps. 114:3-4]). The stilling of the storm, in other words, draws on traditional imagery used to speak of God's power over nature. Jesus operates with the authority of God.

Jesus' question assumes the form of a mild rebuke. Translation is crucial here. "Do you not yet have faith?" he asks (according to the best-attested text; RSV: **Have you no faith?**). The question of the disciples, **Who then is this . . .?** suggests that faith is not yet fully formed. Or, to shift images, what has been planted in them has not yet germinated. They do not yet know what they can expect from Jesus.

This miracle story makes promises: Jesus exercises God's control over nature. It must be subdued, like the demonic powers, and Jesus has the power to do so. Later Christian art has taken **the boat** to be symbolic of the church whose safety Jesus' presence guarantees.

The story in its present setting also raises questions. To what degree can Jesus' promises be trusted? The disciples are the inner circle, those who have been entrusted with the mystery of the kingdom of God; they have been given explanations of Jesus' "riddles." If there is any good soil, it is surely here. Yet the disciples perform poorly on their first test. They do not yet trust Jesus; they are afraid (note the prominence of the image throughout the Gospel). When will they learn? When will they begin to produce?

The Gerasene Demoniac (5:1-20)

Though the description is a bit general, **the other side of the sea** apparently means that Jesus and his disciples cross into Gentile territory. It does not seem possible that **country of the Gerasenes** can be geographically correct. The actual city is at least

20 miles from the lake. Matthew's attempted correction and the numerous textual variants testify to the geographical uncertainty.

More important than precise location is the description of the territory: it is unclean, out of bounds. A **herd of swine** is there, suggesting impurity; pigs were forbidden food for Jews. A cemetery is nearby, also unclean. The man who comes to Jesus has **an unclean spirit.** The whole land is taboo for Jews, but as has become customary, Jesus ventures precisely into such forbidden territory.

The one who meets him from **among the tombs** is possessed. The signs are graphically depicted: he exhibits superhuman strength. He cannot be subdued even when bound by **chains.** The detail is lavish: the man possessed was bound **with fetters and chains, but the chains he wrenched apart, and the fetters he broke in pieces.** The poor soul cannot be civilized. He apparently poses no danger to anyone else; he is a threat only to himself. He **bruises himself,** moaning **night and day,** living **among the tombs,** alone.

This is obviously not a story about faith. The man is possessed, so far gone that he cannot help himself. It is a story about an invasion of alien territory, reminiscent of Jesus' parable about plundering the house of a strong man after binding him (3:27), with the twist that Jesus binds the strong man by liberating one in his clutches.

As soon as Jesus sets foot on land, the possessed man races to meet him. The translation **worshiped him** is not quite right. The idea is that the demoniac prostrates himself before Jesus as a sign of submission ("they fell down before him" [3:11]). The demons fear Jesus; as supernatural beings, they know who he is—the **Son of the Most High God,** one who has power to drive them out. There is something almost comic in the demon's attempt to invoke God's protection (**I adjure you by God, do not torment me**), since the demon is dealing with the Son of God. The somewhat clumsy explanation of the demon's request (**For he had said to him . . .**) may reveal signs that the story has been edited.

Jesus asks the demon his **name.** According to ancient lore, there was power in knowing the name of an evil spirit. It gave the exorcist control over the demon. The interchange between Jesus and the demon exhibits some humor. The demon responds: **My name is Legion; for we are many.** The statement is a boast. No wonder the hapless man was impossible to subdue! The boast, however, is a foolish disclosure, since now Jesus has power over the demons and can cast them out. There is yet more significance in the boast. The name **Legion** conjures up imagery of particular significance to a subject people. "Legion" is a Latin word, not Greek, and it can only be intended to offer some comment about the link between Roman soldiers and demons. It is all the more interesting, then, that the standards of the legion stationed in Palestine bore the image of the wild boar—a link with the pigs in the scene who will serve as the demons' hosts.

The popular character of the story is evident in the continued exchange between Jesus and the demons. We know from earlier in the story that Jesus can cast out demons with a word. Here, there is some play. The demons beg for a concession: they do not wish to be sent **out of the country.** It is, after all, unclean territory, a hospitable abode—with pigs and tombs nearby. But they need a new host. They suggest the **herd of swine**—an appropriate place for an army of demons, from the perspective of a Jewish audience. Jesus' concession is only an apparent victory for the legion, however. Now bearers of the demons, the pigs race down the embankment and fall into the water—which then cleanses **the unclean spirits.** Both pigs and demons meet an appropriate fate in the cleansing waters of the lake.

Concern about private property is absent from the story. For the original audience, pigs were unclean animals unfit for consumption, and their destruction would have been regarded as fitting. There is even humor, since the unclean pigs provide the means by which unclean spirits are cleansed. The destruction of the army of demons and the salvation of a human life are considered worth a herd of swine—at least by the author and his readers.

The swineherds and townspeople are not as approving. When they come to see what has occurred, they find the demoniac **clothed and in his right mind.** The marks of civilization are obvious: he is wearing clothing again and is obviously in possession of himself. He has obviously been cured. Their response, however, is not to celebrate the redemption of a life and to worship Jesus as savior. They ask him **to leave** the region. Their request seems motivated less by their dismay over the loss of pigs than by their encounter with a man of unimagined power. Their initial reaction is to the sight of the former demoniac—a reaction familiar throughout the Gospel: **And they were afraid.** Like the religious authorities in Jewish territory, they find Jesus threatening. Their world is tolerable. Even demons can be endured as long as the possessed can be relegated to a place outside civilized territory— among the tombs on the outskirts of town. What is frightening about Jesus is that he refuses to leave the world as it is. He transgresses the boundaries and rescues those beyond help. He has the power. Such a person cannot be controlled, only followed. The people in the land of the Gerasenes are unwilling, so they ask Jesus to leave. The cure of the demoniac is too expensive— not just in terms of the swine but in terms of social stability.

As Jesus departs, the cleansed demoniac begs to follow. The request is unusual—as is Jesus' response. He tells the man to return home and offer testimony to what **the Lord has done for you.** Jesus' regular response is to enjoin those healed to say nothing. Here, the man is urged to tell. Why the exception? Perhaps, as some have suggested, the reason is that Jesus is on Gentile soil. The story is possibly a foreshadowing of preaching to all the nations. While that may be true, any proposal is difficult to sustain because the information is so sparse. In any case, the cure results in a mission in **the Decapolis,** cities populated principally by Gentiles. Jesus' reputation spreads into Gentile territory, so that when he visits such places as Tyre and Sidon crowds still flock to him (7:24). The former demoniac is likewise an example, perhaps, of preachers and healers other than the Twelve who work in Jesus' name (see Mark 9:38).

There is an intriguing shift in the concluding verse. Jesus tells the man to tell **how much the Lord has done for you.** He in fact reports **how much Jesus had done for him.** The term "Lord," customarily reserved for God, is not employed elsewhere in Mark as a title for Jesus. The shift here suggests Mark knows that "Jesus is Lord."

The Healing of Two Women (5:21-43)

The two stories, the healing of Jairus's daughter and the healing of the woman with a hemorrhage, separated in the lectionary, belong together. The dramatic connections and contrasts are signs of artistry. The stories provide an example of a simple and effective narrative technique: one story brackets another, so that the two become mutually illuminating. (Other examples of such bracketing in Mark include the cursing of the fig tree and the cleansing of the temple [11:12-26], and Peter's denial and Jesus' trial [14:53-72].)

Jesus' return to **the other side** is marked by instant recognition and the gathering of crowds. That Jesus is back on Jewish soil is obvious, since the first to make a request is **the ruler** of a **synagogue.** The term, familiar from Acts (one of Paul's converts, Crispus, is identified as the "ruler of the synagogue" [Acts 18:8]), refers to the one in charge of physical arrangements for worship. The mention of a name and an office is unusual in miracle stories, where we usually are told only the particulars of the ailment. The identification of **Jairus** as a religious official is important to the story, however, and not an incidental detail. It is significant because, for the first time, a respectable religious person shows interest in Jesus. It is important, second, that in his attention to a woman regarded as unclean by the religious community, Jesus appears to miss the chance to impress a religious official.

The desperation of Jairus is poignant: he prostrates himself before Jesus. His **daughter is at the point of death.** Jesus must come immediately, or there will be no chance for her recovery. We are not told how Jairus has learned about Jesus, but only that he has confidence Jesus can heal his daughter if only he arrives in time.

On the way to the leader's house, Jesus is interrupted by a nameless **woman.** She is sick and obviously as desperate as Jairus. Following the logic of miracle stories, Mark describes her problem in graphic detail with a long string of participles. The more graphic the depiction of her plight, the more striking will be the cure. We learn that the woman has been hemorrhaging **for twelve years,** that she spent everything she had on **physicians** and for all that has not been cured but in fact has gotten **worse.** The comments set up the extraordinary healing power of Jesus—and they betray the social orientation of the narrative: it is told from the perspective of the underclasses, for whom professionals like doctors exist only to prey on the helpless. The omission of these details by Matthew and Luke may offer an indication of the different social stratum for whom the other two evangelists wrote.

The strange behavior of the woman—creeping up to Jesus from behind, without wishing to draw attention to herself—indicates that her "hemorrhage" is associated with ritual uncleanness. That is true whether the hemorrhage is related to menstruation or to any other "issue of blood" (compare Leviticus 15; Mishnah, *Zabim* and *Niddah*, where the elaborate casuistry reveals the seriousness of ritual impurity and the lengths to which the pious were willing to go to avoid contamination). Her problem is not simply that she is sick, but that her illness has rendered her unclean. **For twelve years** she would have been regarded as an untouchable, unwelcome at the synagogue. Anyone touching her would be rendered unclean, unfit for participation in worship. Her illness is in every respect a social disease. She cannot expect help from anyone, therefore, and must not call attention to herself.

Like Jairus, the woman has confidence that Jesus can heal her. She has heard about Jesus, and that hearing has generated faith. So convinced is she of Jesus' power that she wants only to **touch his garments.** The idea that the clothing of a healer can have healing properties is present in Acts as well, where we learn that anything that has touched Paul's body can drive off demons or heal the sick (Acts 19:11-12); in a similar vein we are told that the sick in Jerusalem line the streets in hopes that Peter's shadow will fall on them (Acts 5:15). Such notions are characteristic of a widespread popular piety; amulets supposed to possess magical powers were common even among Jews. Official disapproval of such beliefs by religious leaders did little to discourage them among the populace. However much it may seem like superstition, in this case the woman's confidence is not misplaced, for when she touches Jesus' robe, she is **healed.**

The statement about Jesus' recognition that **power had gone forth from him** is unusual in the New Testament, where Jesus is always in control. Matthew, by modifying the story, has taken precautions to guard against the impression that Jesus' powers are "magical." In Matthew, the woman is healed only after Jesus sees her and speaks the healing word (Matt. 9:22). Both Mark and Luke reveal no embarrassment about the idea that power can flow from Jesus unintentionally.

Jesus' question, **Who touched my garments?** and the disciples' response, **You see the crowd pressing in around you, and yet you say, "Who touched me?"** are rather standard dialogue features. The disciples play the role of straight men, speaking for common sense (similar to the role they play in the accounts of the feeding of the 5000 and 4000): How can you ask such a question when everyone is touching you? As readers, of course, we know what Jesus knows: someone has touched him with special expectations and with remarkable results. By bringing it to the attention of the crowds and calling the woman forward, Jesus has an opportunity to praise the woman's faith, which is the real point of the story. Ask, and it will be given.

Jesus' statement probably ought to be translated, "Your faith has saved you." The RSV **has made you well** fails to capture the sense in which the physical cure results in a more comprehensive restoration: the woman is no longer unclean and can participate fully in the religious activities of the community. She is no longer an outcast.

While he was still speaking marks the transition to the story of Jairus. The interruption, it turns out, has been life-saving to the unclean woman but fatal to Jairus's child. **Your daughter is**

dead. Jesus' healing of a social outcast, and a woman at that, has apparently deprived a young child of a chance at life and perhaps spoiled the opportunity to win the favor of a religious official. The ebb and flow of expectation contribute to the drama of the story.

The death of the young child provides a new opportunity for surprise: **Do not fear, only believe,** Jesus tells the leader of the synagogue. There are possibilities even where hope appears to be lost.

The circle of observers begins to narrow. If the Twelve represent an inner circle of insiders, **Peter, James, and John** represent the innermost circle. They alone among the disciples will witness the miracle, just as they alone will witness the transfiguration and, with Andrew, will be privy to Jesus' warnings about the future (Mark 13); Jesus brings the three along to share his last hours of agony in Gethsemane (14:32-42). The reader is expected to remember the larger crowds, of course, who will eventually want to know what has happened.

When the little group reaches the **house** of the synagogue leader, there is a crowd and **a tumult.** It was customary to begin mourning almost immediately, with particular individuals designated as "professionals" whose task it was to stir up mourning and lamentation. In many cultures, mourning at death is a public ritual in which the community is invited to participate.

Jesus' insistence that the little girl **is not dead but sleeping** elicits laughter. People know death when they see it, and in any case the "professionals" have witnessed enough dying to know when the end has come. The laughter, of course, has an important function in the story: it sets up the remarkable character of the miracle which we know will take place. The mourners represent common sense. Jesus' statement is nonsensical.

Jesus' declaration that the young girl is only sleeping might suggest that the ensuing miracle is not really so miraculous. Perhaps the narrator in our story is a realist, one who views Jesus more as a sage than a wonder-worker. That Mark views the young girl's restoration as a genuine return from death is apparent in view of a story told about one of Jesus' contemporaries, Apollonius of Tyana, by his biographer, Flavius Philostratus.

> Here too is a miracle which Apollonius worked. A girl had died just in the hour of her marriage, and the bridegroom was following her bier lamenting as was natural his marriage left unfulfilled, and the whole of Rome was mourning with him, for the maiden belonged to a consular family. Apollonius then witnessing their grief, said, "Put down the bier, for I will stay the tears that you are shedding for the maiden." And withal he asked what was her name. The crowd accordingly thought that he was about to deliver such an oration as is commonly delivered as much to grace the funeral as to stir up lamentation; but he did nothing of the kind, but merely touching her and whispering in secret some spell over her, at once woke up the maiden from her seeming death; and the girl spoke out loud, and returned to her father's house. . . . Now whether he detected some spark of life in her, which those who were nursing her had not noticed—for it is said that although it was raining at the time, a vapour went up from her face—or whether life was really extinct, and he restored it by the warmth of his touch, is a mysterious problem which neither I myself nor those who were present could decide.
>
> *(Life* 4.45)

Philostratus's brief commentary clearly reveals his own skepticism. For him, Apollonius is more a sage than a wonder-worker. Genuine resurrections of dead people are most unlikely, in the view of this sophisticate. Mark exhibits no such skepticism, as should be clear from the rest of the Gospel. We are not to doubt the girl is dead. Jesus' statement about "sleep" should be understood as in 1 Cor. 15:51: it is "sleep" in view of a resurrection to come. It is also similar to the statement in John 11:11: "Our friend Lazarus has fallen asleep, but I go to awake him out of sleep." John appends the explanatory comment, "Now Jesus had spoken of his death, but they thought that he meant taking rest in sleep" (John 11:13). As in John's Gospel, the surprise is that Jesus has the power to interrupt that "sleep" and to bring the dead back to life. Jesus' audience, of course, does not understand what he means.

Once again Jesus narrows the group. Mark says literally that he "threw out" the mourners. Bringing his few disciples and the parents into the room, Jesus takes the girl by the hand and says, in Aramaic, **Little girl, I say to you, arise.** The use of Aramaic by Mark represents an appreciation of the aesthetic dimensions of narration. Mark's audience does not know the foreign words; they require translation. On three other occasions Mark recalls Jesus' words in his native Aramaic: once in another miracle story (7:34), once in recounting Jesus' prayer in the garden (14:36), and finally in repeating Jesus' sole word from the cross (15:34). The Aramaic gives the story a taste of authenticity and a mysterious feel.

At his command, the little girl arises, alive. Jesus indeed has the ability to transform death into sleep and to awaken those who sleep. The note that the girl **walked** around should be taken as a typical feature of miracles: there is dramatic proof of her cure. The explanatory comment that **she was twelve years of age** is less clear. It may explain that she is indeed old enough to walk. It may also be related to the mention of "twelve years" in the story of the woman with a hemorrhage. The occurrence of the temporal designation may indicate how stories could be linked in oral tradition, in catchword fashion, or there may be some deeper significance in the association of the two women. If so, however, it has eluded interpreters and must remain a topic of speculation.

The reference to the amazement of the onlookers is again typical of miracle stories. Such references are to awaken a sense of awe and amazement in the reader as well. Likewise the instructions to give the girl **something to eat** may be understood as a proof that she has really been returned to life. Spirits do not eat (see Luke 24:39-43).

One feature of the ending, however, is anything but typical of miracle stories. Jesus' command that **no one** make this known fits neither the situation nor the formal ingredients of the story. As in most miracle stories, there is a certain logic in the narrative that drives toward eventual disclosure: the gradual exclusion of everyone but an inner circle, the laughter of the mourners—all set up the eventual spectacle at which Jesus' detractors will be silenced. Given the logic of the story, the skeptical mourners must learn of the miracle and be silenced. Matthew's version, even in its abridged form, ends appropriately: "And his fame spread throughout that whole region" (Matt. 9:26).

Speculation by commentators about Jesus' reasons for silencing the spectators short-circuits the interpretive process. When there are gaps in the story, of course, the temptation is to fill them in. It seems natural to move immediately to an analysis of Jesus' thinking to provide a reason for this strange injunction. There is little justification for resorting to a psychological analysis of characters in the story, however, unless the author has provided us with sufficient data. Mark has not. We are given little access to Jesus' thinking. Though insiders, we glimpse only the externals of the events.

The problem is that the "externals" of this story—as of others in Mark—do not provide a perfectly coherent picture. Viewed from the perspective of the narrative, there is a certain artlessness about the injunction to silence. The story offers us no possibility of imagining a situation in which the parents could keep the matter a secret. The mourners, after all, are just outside, waiting to see Jesus proved the fool. And the rest of the disciples, with the crowds that had flocked to Jesus, still remain in the picture. Interpreting the injunction as referring to the manner of the girl's resurrection ("Don't tell anyone the details of what went on in here!") or to some other feature of the event is an expedient to which some commentators resort without justification. The fact is the story does not end as we were led to expect.

Interpreters must respect the logic of the narrative. There is no way around the sense that there is some awkwardness here. However, this is not the only instance in the story when Jesus commands people not to make known what he has done. If we are to do all we can to appreciate the Gospel, our only resort is to ask if these injunctions fall into any discernible pattern. In numerous instances Jesus tells people not to speak about what has happened to them; he regularly tells demons not to make him known. His disciples are instructed not to speak about certain matters—at least not until after he is raised from the dead (9:9). We are not given reasons for the silence, only an indication that it is part of a plan. The time for disclosure has not yet come. Understood in this way, the instructions to the little group make "sense."

We may legitimately ask to what degree the conclusion of this story represents Mark's sense of endings. The episode ends without resolution. Tension remains. Readers are forced to wonder if the command was obeyed and how the spectators could have kept quiet. The lack of resolution is familiar from elsewhere in the Gospel, in particular from the conclusion in 16:8. There, too, it seems inconceivable that the women could have avoided telling what they had seen and heard. Perhaps the best we can do is to pay attention to this refusal to resolve stories and to ask if the tension introduced is important for understanding the narrative.

These four miracle stories—spectacles, as we might term them—demonstrate that Jesus has extraordinary power. He is the one who has come to bind the strong man and despoil his house. He has control over nature. He restores to health and wholeness those who have no reason to hope to be cured. He even raises the dead. Traditional boundaries between clean and unclean, designed to protect the faithful, are regularly transgressed for the sake of a greater good. Jesus ventures into the realm of the unclean, even the dead, and brings back into God's family those who, for a host of reasons, have been excluded. Jesus will not leave the world as it is. His ministry offers promise for those who are on the outside—and a challenge for those in the story who feel at home in the world as it is. Such people have reason to fear Jesus. As someone with such extraordinary power, he is obviously a man to be reckoned with.

Varied Responses (6:1-29)

Rejection at Nazareth (6:1-6)

The transition to the account of Jesus' visit to his home town is abrupt. Little effort is devoted to explaining the logic of Jesus' movements. The contrast to the preceding miracles is appropriately striking. What is important is the reception he receives among his home town people. We have been prepared for the reception in chapter 3, where Jesus' relatives and family are cast in the role of outsiders.

Jesus' visit to **the synagogue** results in astonishment, as is customary in the stories about Jesus' ministry. His teaching strikes his audience, particularly people from his home town, as extraordinary. They are interested in the source of his wisdom and knowledge: **Where did this man get all this?** The astonishment does not lead to appreciation, however, but to scandal, much as in the land of the Gerasenes. The problem his former neighbors have is Jesus' origin. The people from his home town know where he is from, and that derivation precludes what they perceive to be extraordinary claims to authority. Their world is understood in simple terms: a person is defined by family and community. They know where Jesus is from—his mother, his brothers and **sisters.** The unspectacular nature of his origin does not allow for the spectacular events. And so they are offended.

In chapter 3 we learned that Jesus had brothers and sisters. Here we learn more about his origin. He has a "fatherland." The name of the village, Nazareth, is not used here, though it is in 1:9, and the term "the Nazarene" is used in 1:24, 10:47, 14:67, and 16:6.

More interesting is the identification of Jesus as **the son of Mary.** While arguments can be adduced for the variant ("son of the carpenter"), this remains the best-attested reading. The failure to mention his father's name is striking. Not surprisingly, several manuscripts modify the phrase to read, "Is this not the son of the carpenter, the son of Mary . . . ?" The variant is most likely an attempt to harmonize Mark with Matthew. The copyists (and Matthew) recognized the implied insult in speaking of Jesus as Mary's son: it is an intimation that he was illegitimate (a claim presumed in later Jewish legends and in the Fourth Gospel [John 9:29]). Mark offers no explanations. Whether or not he presumes the reader knows traditions about Jesus' birth is a matter of guess-work.

In addition to commenting on his origins, the people note that Jesus is a **carpenter** (perhaps, more generally, a builder). In the opinion of his neighbors, this fact presumably disqualifies him from being a learned man.

The questions likewise presume that Jesus has brothers and sisters, some of whose names are mentioned. Of particular note is the mention of a brother named **James,** a figure who will become prominent in the early church, though he plays no role whatsoever in Jesus' ministry. According to Paul's confessional summary in 1 Corinthians, James was the recipient of an appearance by the risen Christ (1 Cor. 15:7). Since we are offered no additional information about James and his history as a member of Jesus' family, we are left to guess the circumstances of his life and the events that brought him to a position of prominence in the movement founded by his brother.

Jesus' aphoristic statement about a prophet's **honor** is the first use of a recognized category by which to evaluate his career. His activities, including miracles and teaching, are reminiscent of the careers of prophets like Elijah and Elisha. There may, of course, be other "types" to which Jesus bears some resemblance, though salvation-figures were probably not as stereotyped as many scholars have suggested and are not easily identified by an epithet like "prophet." "**Prophet**" is at least a category known from Israel's tradition and from the Scriptures. Apparently others agree with Jesus that this label is appropriate: a bit later, people hazard the guess that Jesus is John the Baptist raised from the dead—or Elijah, or another of the prophets.

The refusal—or inability—of Jesus' neighbors to accept his status confirms what the story has suggested thus far: the world's standards of judgment appear to run headlong into God's ways. Jesus does not measure up. The circumstances of his origin allow no way of accounting for the stories about him. His common beginnings do not fit the assessment that he is a prophet. The result is scandal and fear. The reaction of the people from his home town also suggests that real insiders are not necessarily those who by birth or circumstance are closest to Jesus. In fact, those who ought to know best turn out to be the most incapable of insight.

Jesus **could do no mighty work there.** Matthew tones down the sentence to indicate simply that Jesus did not perform miracles there. Mark's sentence suggests that faith is a necessary ingredient, though the Gospel includes a host of stories in which faith has no place at all (e.g., the exorcisms). A woman has faith and is healed. The leader of a synagogue has faith, and his daughter is restored to life. The people of Jesus' home town do not believe, and he can do no mighty work. The trick, it would seem, is to have faith. How one gets faith—how one comes to understand matters that are contrary to ordinary sense and that Jesus seems intent upon keeping hidden—are questions the narrative has yet to answer.

Jesus "marvels at their unbelief." Does that mean it is a genuine surprise for him? Is it a matter he can do something about? We are not told at present. We know only that Jesus' neighbors remain imprisoned by their unbelief, and as a result, Jesus does no mighty works in their midst—except, the narrator adds, for a few healings.

The Sending of the Twelve (6:7-13)

In contrast to Jesus' family and his neighbors, the disciples are insiders. They have been chosen to be with Jesus and to carry out his mission (3:13-19). An initial phase in their preparation is now apparently concluded, for they are sent out to do what Jesus has done: cast out demons, heal the sick, and preach repentance—since, as Jesus indicates at the beginning of his ministry, the kingdom of God is at hand.

There is something elusive about this preaching tour. Precisely what did Jesus have in mind? Albert Schweitzer's reconstruction of Jesus' ministry makes a good deal of this preaching mission, which he interprets via Matthew as a prelude to the coming of the kingdom: Jesus believed, Schweitzer argues, that before the disciples finished their preaching tour the kingdom would have arrived ("For truly, I say to you, you will not have gone through all the towns of Israel, before the Son of man comes" [Matt. 10:23]). When it did not, Jesus had to make a change in plans—and decided to go to Jerusalem to force God's hand.

Mark provides no basis for such a view. The problem is there are few clues on the basis of which we might understand how this mission fits into Jesus' long-term plans. The sending out seems purposeful, but we are offered little sense of where it will end. Perhaps that is one reason Schweitzer felt justified in filling in what he perceived to be a gap in the story.

The sending out of those chosen by Jesus has been prepared for. In chapter 3, their commission is stated and they are "sent out" (according to a variant reading, they are actually called "apostles," or "sent ones"). The disciples have been selected to carry on Jesus' work, and here for the first time they are given an opportunity.

Jesus' emissaries are sent out with no means of support. They are to rely solely on those to whom they are sent. There is no way for such preachers to amass wealth from their work, since they are not paid a wage and in any case have no way to take acquired possessions with them. Preaching is not for profit. Yet these apostles must eat and have a place to stay. Such necessities the beneficiaries of their ministry can be expected to provide. It is clear from Paul's correspondence with the Corinthians that this support was to be expected. By Paul's time apostles apparently traveled with their families (1 Cor. 9:3-5). Paul's refusal to accept support from his churches is viewed as unusual, even objectionable (2 Cor. 11:7-11), since it may suggest preachers are unwilling to entrust themselves to their congregations.

According to Mark, the apostles are to remain with a family for the whole period spent within a particular village. In the later church, the pattern was to share the burden of support among various households. Wandering preachers, sometimes called "prophets," continued to be an important social feature in early Palestinian Christianity for some decades. The *Didache* makes it clear, however, that it was not uncommon for traveling preachers to take advantage of hospitality.

> And concerning the Apostles and Prophets, act thus according to the ordinances of the Gospel. Let every Apostle who comes to you be received as the Lord, but let him not stay more than one day, or if need be a second as well; but if he stay three days, he is a false prophet.
>
> (*Didache* 11:3-5)

In his instructions, Jesus prepares the disciples for rejection as well as success. Some villages **will not receive you.** That is only to be expected. These emissaries represent Jesus, and we know that he has encountered opposition among his own people, among the religious, and even among Gentiles. The gesture of **shaking off the dust** from the apostles' **feet** dramatizes their break with a community: not a trace will be carried with them. The gesture likewise anticipates judgment with ultimate consequences: "For whoever is ashamed of me and of my words in this adulterous and sinful generation, of him will the Son of man also be ashamed, when he comes in the glory of his Father with the holy angels" (Mark 8:38).

The disciples have apparently been sufficiently prepared for this venture. Though we are given no details, we learn that their preaching tour is a success. They **cast out many demons** and **healed** the **sick.**

The Death of John the Baptizer (6:14-29)

The sending out of the disciples is of sufficient consequence to attract the notice of King Herod, who is troubled by the reports. The activity sounds too familiar, and Herod fears that John the Baptist **has been raised from the dead.**

The connection between Jesus and John is a bit puzzling. The story has not prepared readers to view John as a healer and exorcist. There is apparently enough similarity between these two preachers, however, to regard both as "prophetic"—and even to confuse one with the other. It should be noted that the prophetic figures with whom Jesus is identified are eschatological prophets whose arrival would signal some decisive crisis: **Elijah,** whose return was prophesied by Malachi (Mal. 4:5-6), or perhaps the "prophet like Moses" mentioned in Deut. 18:16-20 (cf. Acts 3:22-23). The evaluation of the crowds, to be repeated just prior to Peter's confession (Mark 8:28), suggests people viewed Jesus as a figure whose career was reminiscent of scriptural redeemer-figures.

The mention of John provides an occasion to complete the unfinished story of the Baptizer. The flashback fills in details about events that occurred after John's arrest—the last time John was mentioned in the story. Jesus' ministry begins with John's arrest. The return to John at a time when Jesus seems to be enjoying success and popularity introduces a sobering note into the story again. It serves as a reminder of what happens to preachers who threaten established authorities. The confusion between Jesus and John insinuates that a similar fate awaits Jesus.

The death of John at the hands of **Herod** Antipas is attested in other sources. The Jewish historian Josephus confirms Mark's information about Herod's marriage to **his brother's wife** (though, according to Josephus, Antipas's half-brother and the husband of Herodias cannot be the "Philip" identified in Luke as the tetrarch of Ituraea and Trachonitis), as well as the fact that from **Herodias** he had a daughter, Salome. Josephus offers his own account of John's demise: John was arrested because he was popular with the wrong sorts of people and because Herod perceived him to be a political threat (*Antiquities* 18.116-19). According to Mark, John was arrested for his denunciation of Herod's marriage to his brother's wife. The accounts view the same issue from different perspectives: since Herod Antipas's first wife was the daughter of Aretas IV, King of Nabataea, a kingdom bordering on Herod's territory, John's attack on Herod's divorce of his wife would have been politically potent. In fact, it was. Aretas used the divorce as an occasion for attacking Herod, in which battle he routed Herod's army (*Antiquities* 18.113-15). According to Josephus, some Jews believed the defeat was divine judgment on Herod for his execution of John (*Antiquities* 18.116).

The wealth of detail about John and Herod is striking, suggesting perhaps some deeper significance, as in the description of John the Baptist's clothing and diet. Some scholars have detected overtones of the story of Elijah's quarrels with Queen Jezebel. As we have noted, Mark intimates a relationship between John and Elijah on at least two occasions (1:5-6; 9:11-13). The manipulation of a man by a clever woman is hardly a unique motif, of course, and the account of Herodias's intrigues is not convincing evidence of a dependence on scriptural precedent. What the story tells us is that John's fate, like that of Jesus, rests in the hands of a ruler who can be manipulated by others. Herod, like Pilate, reluctantly agrees to an execution he would not have chosen himself.

The concluding words of the story report simply that John's **disciples** came and buried their teacher. Jesus' story will provide a dramatic contrast. When he dies, none of his followers will come to bury him. They will all have fled. The burial must be left to a stranger.

The Provider (6:30—8:21)

The Feeding of 5000 (6:30-44)

With the flashback complete, the narrative returns to the disciples who have now returned from their successful mission. They are termed **apostles** here because they were sent out (Greek, *apostellō*). There is no indication that the term designates an office. Jesus suggests they withdraw for **rest**—as Jesus has withdrawn on at least one occasion (1:35-38). The *erēmos topos* (a **lonely place**) is not specified, except to note that Jesus and his followers must go there by **boat**.

The strange comment that the crowd is able to beat the disciples there by land is apparently intended to demonstrate Jesus' immense popularity. The crowd is relentless; Jesus cannot avoid them even by his retreat. The crowds seem to know Jesus will not ignore their needs. Jesus sees them as **sheep without a shepherd.** The imagery has a familiar place in Israel's tradition—used both to speak of God as shepherd (Psalm 23; Ezekiel 34) and of the king who, like David, guarded the flock from danger.

The deserted setting turns out to be a problem. The hour is late, the disciples tell Jesus, and there is nothing for the people to eat. They reasonably advise sending the crowds to the surrounding villages while there is still time to travel so that they can find food. Jesus' response—You give them something—elicits only a commonsense reply: we couldn't possibly provide for them. The disciples speak for reasonable people; they obviously do not expect anything of Jesus. There are matters they do not yet understand.

In response to Jesus' question about what food is available, the disciples report they can find only five small loaves and two fish. That, it turns out, is enough. Jesus miraculously extends the food, so that there is enough for everyone with a great deal left over.

Several things must be said about the simple story. First, it plays on a theme familiar from the Old Testament. On several occasions, God miraculously provides food for people or for an individual. The best-known story, of course, is the provision of manna for the Hebrew slaves escaped from Egypt. The account of the feeding in John 6 plays on the story of Moses and the Israelites in the wilderness, the two stories being linked under the theme "bread from heaven." The parallels may not be as explicitly stated in Mark, but readers may well have been expected to appreciate parallels with the famous stories of Israel's sojourn in the wilderness. The strange interest in the division of the five thousand into groups of hundreds and fifties may recall Moses' division of Israel into administrative groups, though the reason for such an association would be difficult to specify. If Mark suggests some parallel between Jesus and Moses, it is interesting that the question posed by the disciples (Shall we go and buy two hundred denarii worth of bread, and give it to them to eat?) is asked by Moses in Numbers: "Shall flocks and herds be slaughtered for them, to suffice them? Or shall all the fish of the sea be gathered together for them, to suffice them?" (Num. 11:22).

Another story about the miraculous provision of food has to do with Elijah (with whom Jesus has been confused by the crowds [6:15]), who provides for the widow at Zarephath.

The most remarkable parallel, however, is a story told about Elisha in 2 Kings 4:42-44:

> A man came from Baal-shal-ishah, bringing the man of God bread of the first fruits, twenty loaves of barley, and fresh ears of grain in his sack. And Elisha said, "Give to the men, that they may eat." But his servant said, "How am I to set this before a hundred men?" So he repeated, "Give them to the men, that they may eat, for thus says the LORD, 'They shall eat and have some left.' " So he set it before them. And they ate, and had some left, according to the word of the LORD.

The story not only offers a parallel to the substance of the Gospel account; it also features a similar structure and a similar punch line. It is difficult for those who know the story not to see a relationship between Jesus and the prophet Elisha. It is not surprising that people believe Jesus to be a prophet. He speaks with authority, he performs signs and wonders—he acts like Moses or Elijah or Elisha.

A second point that should be made about the story is its link with the Last Supper. Like a pious Jew, Jesus blesses the bread before he gives it to the disciples to distribute to the crowds. It is difficult, however, not to recognize a sequence of actions that will be echoed in Jesus' last meal with his followers. The string of verbs ("took bread, . . . blessed, broke, and gave") is identical to that in the account of the last meal (14:24). In the account of the feeding of the 4000 that follows in Mark 8:1-9, the sequence of verbs is the same, with the exception of the second, which is "give thanks" (*eucharisteō*) instead of "bless"—the former being a term that has a special place in Christian eucharistic practice. That is all the more important in view of the account Paul gives in 1 Corinthians about what he had "received from the Lord." The wording of the Last Supper in the Gospels, as in Paul's letters, had been shaped by decades of liturgical usage. We are to see, in other words, a relationship between the miraculous provision of bread and the last meal Jesus has with his followers—a meal that will be commemorated by Christians for all time. We will have more to say about what is implied by this relationship in discussing the Lord's Supper.

A third point to make about the story has to do with the interesting conclusion of the account. The usual miracle-story references to the astonishment of the crowds are absent. The ending is somewhat anticlimactic, focusing on numbers: **twelve baskets full** of fragments, **five thousand men.** The account of the feeding of the 4000 in Mark likewise emphasizes numbers: seven baskets full of fragments are gathered after the meal (8:8). And in Jesus' question addressed to his disciples in the last of three boat scenes (8:19-20), the numbers are recalled. It may be that the numbers are intended simply to add color to the story. It is also possible that they have some symbolic significance—though the various attempts to decipher the code have been singularly unsuccessful.

Disciples at Sea (6:45-52)

The miraculous provision of food is followed by the second of three **boat** scenes in Mark. It is noteworthy that the only two miracle stories John shares with the synoptic Gospels are the feeding of the 5000 and Jesus' walking on the water—in precisely the same order. The stories must have circulated together in pre-Markan tradition. In this strange account, Jesus sends his followers ahead **to Bethsaida** (they arrive only in 8:22). Jesus remains behind by himself, **to pray** in the hills. How he plans to follow his disciples we are not told. As in the first account of their trip across the lake, the disciples encounter difficulty from the weather. Once again they are delivered by Jesus.

The circumstances of their deliverance this time are rather different. Jesus sets out **walking** on the water. The author offers no explanation for the extraordinary behavior. Further, Jesus intends to pass his disciples. In view of their distress, however, he does not.

When they see him, the disciples believe he is a "phantasm" (RSV, **a ghost**). Mark again employs a rich vocabulary to describe terror and distress. Jesus silences their fears with his majestic, **It is I.** Whether the expression is employed, as in John, with a sense of its history in Old Testament tradition as a divine self-reference (particularly in Second Isaiah) is unclear, though the scene does bear some of the marks of a theophany. Jesus' presence, as in the first of the boat scenes, brings calm to nature. The disciples are not calm, however. They are beside themselves.

The author adds an interesting explanatory note: **they did not understand about the loaves.** Apparently the miraculous provision of bread should have disclosed a truth that the disciples have failed to grasp. What truth? That Jesus is able to provide for all needs? That Jesus, like Moses, Elijah, and Elisha, not only provides food but has power to command nature itself? No detailed explanation is given, apart from the little comment that casts a pall over the whole scene: for **their hearts were hardened.**

The little comment about hardened hearts is sobering. It is again familiar from Old Testament tradition, where God hardens the heart of characters like Pharaoh. If the disciples' failure to understand is due to a "hardening" (and the verb is passive—it is not something they do to themselves), their plight is more serious. How will they reverse this hardening? How will they see? If the problem were one of will, encouragement could perhaps suffice. If the problem is a hardened heart, something more than exhortation will be required. If the seed planted in them is to bear fruit, it will not be because they have made extraordinary efforts. **Their hearts were hardened.** Deliverance can come only from outside.

Popular Support (6:53-56)

The disciples arrive not in Bethsaida but in **Gennesaret.** They will not arrive in Bethsaida until 8:22—until after their third "voyage." The somewhat confused geographical references in between confirm the suspicions of many that Mark fashioned a story from fragments (or cycles)—and that he was probably not intimately familiar with the geography of Palestine.

With Jesus' arrival in Gennesaret, the reaction of people is typical: when they **recognize** Jesus, they flock to him—and he heals the **sick** when they come. Jesus is still immensely popular with those who need help. **The fringe of his garment** is no less potent than it was in the case of the woman with a hemorrhage. Whatever the impediments to his exercise of power in Nazareth, there are none in the land of Gennesaret.

Pharisees: Clean and Unclean (7:1-23)

The lengthy discussion of ritual purity that follows is the first dispute about legal matters outside the opening chapters. The contrast between **the Pharisees** and Jerusalem **scribes,** on the one hand, and the woman who begs for crumbs in the following story is striking. While Jesus feeds crowds with an endless supply of bread, religious Jews seem concerned only with washing before eating. By juxtaposing stories as he has, the narrator seeks to explore some of the dramatic ironies in responses to Jesus.

The linking of **Pharisees** with **scribes who had come from Jerusalem** marks this interrogation as more than a friendly disagreement about ritual. The scribes from Jerusalem have already suggested that Jesus is possessed (3:22), and it is in Jerusalem that those fearful of Jesus' influence will take action against him.

The issue of **defiled hands** is not trivial. Concern for purity arose out of concern for the law as the measure of holiness. The washing of hands, commanded regularly for those engaged in temple service (see Exod. 30:19 for rules regarding entry into the Tabernacle, where washing hands and feet before entering the sacred place was necessary "lest they die"), became a mark of testimony to the sanctity of all of life—or, better, a means of sanctifying all of life. Priestly rules were extended to the laity as well on the assumption that holiness was expected of all Israel ("You shall be holy to me; for I the LORD am holy, and have separated you from the peoples, that you should be mine" [Lev. 20:26]).

The explanation of washing practices is offered to Mark's readers who are unfamiliar with such matters. That does not mean Mark's readership is exclusively Gentile or that his audience understands itself as distinct from Israel. The matter of labels and self-identification is more complex than many have acknowledged (see below on Mark 12).

The explanation corresponds almost exactly with the language that became part of official Jewish tradition in the Mishnah and Talmud. The issue is cleansing **hands** before eating bread. The relevant tractate in the Mishnah (*Yadim*, "Hands") discusses valid and invalid ways of cleansing the hands, including how much water is necessary and how the hands are to be washed (Mishnah, *Yadim* 1:1-2). The matter was obviously regarded as important. Such technical discussions may help to explain a particularly puzzling reference to the "fist" in Mark 7:3, which the RSV does not attempt to translate. Rabbinic discussions specify that a handful of water is sufficient to cleanse the hands (M. Hengel, "Mc 7,3 *pugmē*: Die Geschichte einer exegetischen Aporie und der Versuch ihrer Losung," ZNW 60 [1969], 182–98). Apparently the term in Mark relates both to the required amount of water and to the proper manner of washing. The hand was cupped, fist-like, to make the most efficient use of available water. The practice is not derived directly from the Torah but from the "oral law"— the **tradition of the elders,** which Pharisees regarded as having equal authority with the written law. This tradition, eventually recorded in the Mishnah and developed in the two Talmuds, sought to spell out as clearly as possible what obedience to the commandments entailed.

Those who dismiss such questions as trivial betray a fundamental misunderstanding of the whole Pharisaic enterprise, which is to sanctify all of life. The **tradition of the elders** was not an attempt to bury the commands of God in trivia but to apply the Torah to every facet of life. The question the Pharisees and scribes put to Jesus, a variation on earlier controversies, betrays a genuine concern. Jesus is asked why his followers are not concerned with ritual purity. The suspicion, here as earlier, is that Jesus' behavior conveys—at least to others—disrespect for the law, threatening the whole Pharisaic construction and (in their view) the Jewish way of life. Religious Jews fear that Jesus will frustrate their attempt to sanctify all of life. Washing of hands is a mark of respect for every aspect of God's created order; it signals the desire to bring mealtime under the sacred canopy of the Torah. Jesus' followers display a basic disrespect for the tradition of the elders.

Jesus' initial response is to attack the whole Pharisaic enterprise: the tradition of the elders, he insists, is nothing more than "human tradition" that seeks to evade **the commandment of God.** The characterization is taken from Isa. 29:13 (in its LXX form), where the prophet seeks to expose the emptiness of religious forms in his time. Traditions themselves are not the problem; people cannot live without form and structures. Such traditions, however, cannot guarantee fidelity to God. They can become a refuge within which even the most devoted evade God's will. Pharisaic opposition to Jesus is the sure sign this is the case.

Using the Scriptures against the tradition that claims to be its legitimate extension, Jesus attacks the oral law for its opposition to God's will as expressed in the commandments. The failure to acknowledge the priority of the written commands of God, Jesus insists, marks the Pharisees and scribes as **hypocrites.** They, not he, are the offenders.

The case Jesus argues is intricate and reveals something of Jewish casuistry. The specific example Jesus chooses has to do with the dedication of property to some special use by means of an oath (*corban,* meaning "dedicated"; Josephus translates this word as "gift" for his Greek readers [*Antiquities* 2.4.4]; the vow is discussed in Mishnah, *Nedarim* ["Vows"] 1:2-4). Once something had been dedicated by means of the oath to some special holy purpose, it could not be used in any other way. In the example Jesus cites, a child dedicates the profit his parents may receive from him to special (religious) causes, thus excluding his parents from receiving the profit. The practice, Jesus insists, violates the commandment about honoring one's parents (Exod. 20:12; Deut. 5:16), a serious offense. The extreme case of dishonoring one's parents, as Jesus reminds his detractors, is punishable by death

103

(Exod. 21:17). In this instance, according to Jesus, **the tradition of the elders**—intended to serve as a "fence around the Torah"—justifies disobedience to the commandment. The traditions about dedicated property **make void the word of God.** It is but one instance among many.

We have devoted time to understanding the perspective of the Pharisees (and of later rabbinic Judaism) both in order to correct a history of misunderstandings among Christians and to grasp the precise nature of the disagreement. **Making void** the written law was certainly not the intention of the Pharisaic sages. They saw no contradiction between the oral law and the Scriptures. According to the Pharisees and their successors, the rabbinic sages, both "Torahs" were equally valid. In the mythology underlying the oral law, both the oral and written law had been given to Moses. While one form was committed to writing, the oral Torah was reputed to have been handed on from generation to generation by pairs of sages until the time of Judah the Prince, the head of the rabbinic academy who edited the Mishnah toward the end of the second century. The pairs of sages who handed on the tradition are listed in a tractate of the Mishnah known as *Aboth*, "Fathers."

Not all Jews accepted the validity of this oral law. Discussions about the legitimacy of **the tradition of the elders** were not unique to Jesus or to the early church. Sadducees disputed the legitimacy of the oral law, holding exclusively to the written commandments. Such scriptural conservatism also explains their refusal to accept concepts such as resurrection that were not grounded in the Old Testament (see Mark 12:18-27). Jesus' attack, however, seems more sweeping in light of the discussion that follows. The issue, according to Mark, is not simply the interpretation of a particular law, or even the validity of the oral law. Jesus calls into question the whole matter of ritual purity and food laws.

Such matters were of considerable import among the early circles of believers in Jesus. We know from elsewhere in the New Testament that battles were fought over the rules governing table fellowship between Jewish and non-Jewish followers of Jesus. It appears that Jewish and Gentile believers began worshiping together soon after the church spread to areas outside Palestine. Justification for such table fellowship came later, and no single argument prevailed for some time.

One perspective is represented by Luke-Acts. The story of Peter's visit to the home of the Roman Cornelius and the repercussions of that visit occupy several chapters in Acts (10; 11; 15). The issue in Acts is not whether or not Gentiles will be saved but under what circumstances they will be allowed to eat with Jewish believers. When Peter returns to Jerusalem after his fateful visit, he is asked by the "circumcision party," "Why did you go to uncircumcised men and eat with them?" (Acts 11:2). As Peter's initial vision suggests, the issue is ritual purity (Acts 10:9-16). The eventual "agreement" worked out in Jerusalem, according to Acts, permits table fellowship between observant Jewish believers and uncircumcised Gentiles as long as Gentiles observe a minimum of dietary laws (Acts 15:22-29). While Luke includes accounts of Jesus' attack on Pharisaic piety, he fails to report the story about Jesus' declaration of **all foods** as **clean** (Mark 7:19). The view is too radical.

Paul seems to have had his own view about such matters. When he discusses the matter of eating food dedicated to idols in 1 Corinthians 8–10, there is no suggestion that the Jewish law is in any way relevant to the discussion. His principle is that while believers should be free to eat meat of any sort, they must take account of those with weaker consciences within the community of the faithful. Paul's dispute with Peter and the church at Antioch, reported in Galatians 2, seems to have been over the same issue. Paul believed that his visit to Jerusalem for the so-called Apostolic Conference had confirmed his position that dietary laws could not serve as barriers to table fellowship among those who believed in Jesus. In other words, Gentile Christians were not obliged to observe dietary laws.

The extended discussion in Mark sketches a view closer to Paul's than to Luke's.

Jesus' statement addressed to **the people** marks a return to the initial criticism posed by the Pharisees and scribes: Why do your disciples eat with defiled hands? Jesus' response is short and enigmatic: Only what **comes out** of a person can defile. As in chapter 4, the disciples are in a privileged position. They ask about the strange statement and receive an explanation: purity is a matter of the **heart** rather than the digestive system. According to the narrator (**Thus he declared all foods clean**), the statement marks the end of food laws. Food cannot defile. Nor, apparently, can unwashed hands. The suspicions of the Pharisees seem to be correct. Jesus' terse explanation undermines the whole enterprise of constructing a system by which the world is structured in terms of pure and impure, clean and unclean. Jesus shapes the categories "pure" and "impure" into typical moral categories. Thus sin is a matter of the **heart**, the will, rather than a matter of violating laws of purity. Sin involves principally acts harmful to the neighbor. These actions, arising from a corrupt will, are what defile.

The list of **evil things** itself is similar to others in the New Testament (Gal. 5:19-21; Rom. 1:29-31; 1 Peter 4:3); the specific "vices" appear throughout the New Testament, particularly in Paul's letters. Such catalogues were common among Greco-Roman moralists and within Hellenistic Judaism.

It is important to understand what Jesus' critique of Pharisaic piety means. The common notion that Jesus rejects a decadent religion of externals in favor of a religion of internals is grossly oversimplified. Judaism cannot be viewed as a decadent religion; it has remained vital throughout the centuries. Nor is it exclusively focused on externals rather than internals. There is a difference, however, between "Christianity" and Judaism, at least as viewed from the perspective of this controversy. What distinguishes the two groups is the view of the law and its function. For Judaism (certainly later rabbinic Judaism, and also the perspective of the Pharisees in Mark), the relationship with God and the world is mediated by the Torah, understood as a structure that orders all of life in terms of holiness. For Jesus' followers, the relationship with God and the world is mediated by Jesus, whose desire to heal and to save acknowledges no boundaries. Dietary laws, like Sabbath observance, are viewed as barriers to extending the family of God and bringing back the strays. New wine requires new skins, to use an image familiar from the Gospel.

One might well ask what it is that will shape the new community of faith and how it will define itself over against the world. The moral transgressions Jesus outlines suggest that his followers will structure their lives in terms of principles enunciated in the commandments (no **theft, murder,** false witness, etc.). Other boundaries are not yet obvious, however. Perhaps Mark could assume that the world, by its opposition to the new community of faith, would itself provide boundaries by its resistance and even persecution (see chap. 13).

What should be said is that religious Jews found Jesus a threat to their religion. Mark, more radically than Matthew or Luke, senses the threat—and the reverse, namely, the new social possibilities for those who followed the Christ.

A Gentile Woman: Crumbs from the Table (7:24-30)

As if to emphasize the radical crossing of boundaries, Mark tells next of Jesus' visit to the region of **Tyre** and **Sidon**—Gentile territory—and of his encounter with a Greek woman. We learn that Jesus' fame has spread even among Gentiles in this region, and that Jesus cannot escape attention here any more than in more familiar surroundings.

Once again we are told of an encounter with **a woman,** by itself exceptional. That she is a **Greek (Syrophoenician)** is even more remarkable. Social mores discouraged such contact between men and women; Jewish attitudes toward Gentile women provided additional boundaries.

Like other desperate people who came to Jesus, the woman throws herself **at his feet** and requests that he heal her **daughter.** In this story, little detail is provided about the nature of the illness. There is a miracle; the little girl is healed. The narrator is more interested in the interchange between Jesus and the woman, however, than in the details of the cure. The miraculous cure is, of course, a demonstration of Jesus' extraordinary power: he is able to heal at a distance as well as by touch. The cure is simply reported, rather than described. It is not the main element in the story.

While Jesus appears as one who constantly transgresses boundaries, he does not simply do away with them. In response to the Gentile woman's initial plea, Jesus responds that **it is not right to take the children's bread and throw it to the dogs.** The offense of the language is palpable. Numerous commentators have tried to minimize the insult by insisting that the Greek should be translated "little dogs"—household pets. Even if that were to be the case, the insult remains. Bread is **thrown** to dogs, even if household pets. Jesus' response reflects a widespread Jewish conviction that Gentiles are unworthy, even **dogs.** A comment in the Babylonian Talmud makes the comparison:

> As the sacred food was intended for men, but not for the dogs, the Torah was intended to the given to the Chosen People, but not to the Gentiles.
>
> (bHagigah 13a)

Such sentiments arise from an awareness that Israel is God's elect. While Jesus' ministry may mean a radically new way of understanding that heritage and election, he does not abandon God's choice. If Gentiles are to be included, it will not be because Jews have been rejected and not given an opportunity to hear the promises of God. Even Paul, whose career was built on the equality of Gentiles within the church, insists that the word of God is "to the Jew first and also to the Greek." Jesus expresses such sentiments without attempting to conceal their offensiveness.

The Gentile woman has no pretensions. She makes no effort to justify her request; she accepts her status as a non-Jew. She comes as a suppliant, without any claim on Jesus—or on God. She is satisfied to be regarded as a dog—so long as she can have **the children's crumbs** that fall from the table. Jesus provides bread for thousands. Religious Jews worry only about washing hands. And a Greek woman is satisfied with crumbs!

Her faith is rewarded. **For this saying,** her petition is granted. Such faith, we learn later, can move mountains. Here, it succeeds in winning the life of a daughter.

The Deaf Hear, the Dumb Speak (7:31-37)

The geographical comment forming the transition to the next episode seems somewhat confused. It seems as if to get from **Tyre** to **the Sea of Galilee** and to **the Decapolis** one must go **through Sidon.** In fact, Sidon is north of Tyre. The Sea of Galilee is far south of Tyre, and the western regions of the Decapolis still further to the south. The comment does not suggest Mark was familiar with the geography of the area.

The healing of a man unable to hear or speak, narrated immediately after the reference to the Decapolis, relates a second encounter with Gentiles. The unspecified group that brings the man to Jesus to be healed is presumably composed of inhabitants of the region. Like the Syrophoenician woman, they have heard reports about Jesus and believe he has power to heal.

The healing is the second of three in which an unidentified group brings someone to Jesus to be cured (2:1-12 and 8:22-26). The stories demonstrate the results of faith, though it is not the faith of the sick that is the focus of attention.

The relationship between this story and the healing of the blind man in 8:22-26 is particularly close. The wording is almost identical: **They brought** someone to Jesus and **besought him to lay his hand upon him.** In both cases, Jesus takes the sick man away from the crowd and performs the cure; in both cases spittle and touch serve as means by which Jesus heals; and in both stories, Jesus exhorts the one healed not to speak to anyone (though the results are apparently different in the first episode, since the healed man speaks). The patterns may indicate something about the origin of the stories in oral tradition; they may also serve to underscore the theme of "hearing" and "seeing," introduced in

4:12 and picked up in 8:18. Jesus opens ears that cannot hear, just as he gives sight to unseeing eyes.

Mark gives color to the story by employing the Aramaic of **Be opened.** That Jesus is speaking to someone from the Decapolis who presumably speaks Greek is unimportant. Aramaic is the language of Jesus, and it adds a sense of mystery to the story. Mark translates into Greek, perhaps to avoid the impression that Jesus is using some magical words.

The results of Jesus' actions are instantaneous: the man's **ears were opened** and "the tongue's bond was loosed." The language indicates how close are notions of illness and possession. Sickness is not a neutral state but the result of forces hostile to God that will be destroyed when the kingdom of God comes.

Jesus gives strict orders that **they** say nothing to anyone. The command presumes Jesus is speaking to more than the deaf and dumb man. Once again the injunction seems unreasonable. Such a cure cannot be hidden. There is no suggestion that Jesus is speaking about only the manner of the cure or the identity of the healer, as some commentators have suggested. The result of his command is interesting: **the more he charged them, the more zealously they proclaimed it.** Some interpreters, resorting to psychology, have argued that this was Jesus' strategy all along: people who are told not to do something are bound to disobey. If you want something spread, tell people not to speak! Whatever we make of Jesus' commands, this surely cannot be the way they are to be understood.

More likely, we are to sense that this "good news" is too extraordinary to keep secret. Jesus enjoins secrecy, for the time of proclamation has not yet come. But the good news cannot be hidden. This is perhaps a glimpse of what is to come—a mission carried out by those whose ears have been opened and whose tongues have been released, and who therefore simply cannot be silent. What can the recipient of such a miracle do but preach? Nothing is hidden except to be made known. The whole story, like this healing, presses toward disclosure.

The results of this preaching are utter astonishment among listeners. Jesus **has done all things well.** There has never been anything like this. And in the review of the amazed crowds we may even hear overtones of Isa. 35:5—"Then the eyes of the blind shall be opened, and the ears of the deaf unstopped." The great day is dawning.

Bread for the Gentiles: Feeding 4000 (8:1-10)

The transition, **in those days,** is artificial, but it does link the feeding of the 4000 with Jesus' healing of the deaf and dumb man in the region of the Decapolis. We are thus to think of the story that follows as occurring in Gentile territory.

The situation described is familiar: there is a large **crowd,** and it does not have food. Little effort is expended in explaining how the crowd got into this situation. Presumably, readers can be expected to remember the earlier miraculous feeding and the circumstances that led to that crisis.

In the previously narrated feeding of the 5000, the disciples took the first step, asking Jesus what to do. Here Jesus takes the initiative. The crowd, Jesus reminds his followers, has been with him **three days** without anything **to eat.** They cannot be dismissed, lest people faint on the journey home.

The response of **the disciples** is disturbingly familiar: although they have witnessed a miraculous provision of food for a large crowd in the wilderness not long before, they seem completely at a loss what to do. They ask the same question as before: **How can one feed these** people **with bread here in the desert?** Jesus' response is as before: **How many loaves have you?**

Students of the Gospel have often taken the parallels as a sign that Mark is reproducing a doublet of one tradition. There was one story about a miraculous feeding in the desert, so the interpretation goes, but the details were different in circles where the story was told. Mark, being unsophisticated and concerned to omit nothing, simply reproduced the two versions without realizing they recounted the same story.

The inadequacy of such exegesis should be obvious. The repetition is intentional; the details of the two stories are recalled with precision, and in the summary of the two accounts in 8:19-21, the small differences in wording are reproduced exactly (see below on 8:19-21). The effect of the repetition on readers is perhaps more to the point. Those who have listened to the whole Gospel read at one sitting generally laugh at this point. It is almost comical. It has all happened before—and the disciples do not yet understand about the loaves. They still do not expect a miracle.

The story is the same, the numbers slightly different. Rather than blessing the bread, Jesus **gives thanks** (*eucharisteō*). The same variation in terminology between "blessing" and "giving thanks" occurs in accounts of Jesus' Last Supper. In Mark 14:22 and in Matt. 26:26, Jesus "blesses" the bread; in Luke 22:19 and in 1 Cor. 11:24, Jesus "gives thanks." As noted above, it seems likely that the feeding of the crowds anticipates Jesus' last meal while at the same time it reflects the church's special "breaking of bread" that had become a regular feature of corporate life long before Mark's Gospel.

Both bread and fish are distributed, and, as before, the people eat and are **satisfied.** This time **seven baskets full** of fragments are gathered. The word used for **basket** is different from that used in the earlier version. Perhaps the only significance is that the distinct vocabulary is preserved in the summary in 8:19-21. The number of those fed is **4000** (it is not specified here that there were 4000 "men," as was the case with the 5000). As in the earlier account, little is made of the reaction of the crowds. Jesus simply dismisses them, and we are told no more about them. What is emphasized is that once again Jesus is able to provide food for a large crowd and have some left over. Whether the numbers are included as features of a "realistic" story or as symbolic of some deeper meaning is unclear at this point (see below on 8:19-21).

Demand for a Sign (8:11-13)

Immediately after providing for the crowds, Jesus and his disciples leave by boat for the regions of Dalmanutha. The place is

unknown. Matthew's "Magadan" (15:39) appears in some manuscripts of Mark, probably as an intended correction. It is at least
clear that Jesus lands in Jewish territory. **Pharisees** appear, ready
to argue, and they demand **a sign from heaven.** Their question
is quite without any preparation in context, though it nicely suits
the varied reactions to Jesus Mark presents in vignettes. Chapter
7 was introduced by a dispute with Pharisees about washing hands
before eating bread; a Gentile woman demonstrated her willingness to feed on crumbs from the master's table. Listeners are
utterly amazed by reports of Jesus' healing. He feeds another
large crowd miraculously. And the conclusion is that **the Pharisees**
are still unimpressed: they demand from Jesus a **sign.**

The term is an important one. **Signs** are what prophets provide
as pointers to their call by God. "Signs and wonders" are viewed
as supporting evidence. The term calls to mind the miracle-
working prophets, like Moses, Elijah, and Elisha. As in the Gospel
of John, there is considerable irony in the request for a sign
immediately after Jesus' feeding of the crowd. As Moses provided
sustenance for the Israelites, so Jesus provided for his audience.
The point is lost on the Pharisees—though not on the people,
who believe Jesus to be "Elijah" or "one of the prophets" (see
below).

Jesus refuses the request of **a sign from heaven.** What, after
all, would be convincing? **This generation** has eyes, but it cannot
see what is being enacted before its face. The decision about Jesus
will have to be made on evidence from his ministry. There is no
escape from the decision that must be made. The tension between
Jesus and the tradition will have to be resolved, and Jesus will
not do the resolving.

The Disciples: Unseeing Eyes (8:14-21)

The scene now shifts to the disciples for whom numerous foils
have been provided. The religious are not impressed with Jesus.
They have not understood his ministry as an inauguration of God's
kingdom. They have rather seen him as a threat to piety and to

113

their tradition. His family does not understand about him. People from his home town are scandalized. The crowds at least understand that he can heal and can provide for their needs. The disciples, however, have witnessed everything; they have been entrusted with the mystery of the kingdom of God; they have been given explanations. Twice they have witnessed a miraculous multiplication of loaves and have presumably eaten their fill. They at least will understand! Yet the ensuing scene, the third in the series set in a **boat** on the water, serves as a chilling conclusion to one phase of Jesus' ministry. The disciples—those selected by Jesus to carry on his ministry—appear to understand little more than when their education began.

The scene is ostensibly about **bread** and the disciples' inability to understand that Jesus can provide for their needs. They are concerned about having brought along no provisions—or rather only **one loaf**—after witnessing two spectacular demonstrations of Jesus' ability to supply food. They still expect nothing of Jesus.

There seems to be another level, however, at which these events are to be understood. Jesus warns his disciples about **the leaven of the Pharisees and the leaven of Herod.** The image of leaven is related to bread, but it moves the discussion into a different realm. The Pharisees have consistently expressed concern about Jesus' disregard for the tradition of the elders. They fear that his behavior will undermine the structure that gives meaning to their lives, and they are unwilling and unable to trust his sovereign authority. That concern is corrupting, like leaven. Perhaps that is the matter to which Jesus' warning is directed. All we know of **Herod** (Antipas) is his execution of John the Baptizer and his fear of Jesus' popularity (perhaps the political consequences?). In both cases, such concerns undermine faith in Jesus and in the coming of the kingdom.

The disciples appreciate none of the subtlety. In fact, they seem completely bewildered. They know only that they have no bread (except one loaf). They do not understand about the loaves—about Jesus' ability to provide for their needs in all respects. The disciples understand nothing, and their confusion elicits a strong statement from Jesus. He applies to them terms earlier reserved for "outsiders" who would receive only riddles: **Having eyes do you not see and having ears, do you not hear?** The words are reminiscent not only of the earlier narrative but also of Isaiah's sobering call.

Jesus carefully recounts the details of the two feeding stories: **five loaves, five thousand, twelve baskets; seven loaves, four thousand, seven baskets.** The use of the precise imagery, including two different terms for **baskets,** makes it impossible to understand the recounting of both stories as somehow unthinking. The narrator is interested in both stories, attending even to small details. The repetition only underscores the disciples' inability to understand.

The impulse to see in the numbers some symbolic significance is great. The **twelve baskets** would seem clearly an allusion to traditions about the twelve tribes: Jesus provides for all Israel. The **seven baskets** is more difficult. The feeding of the 4000 is set in Gentile territory, and it would be tempting to link the imagery to the Gentile mission: Jesus will provide not only for Israel, but also for non-Jews. Thus far, however, commentators have been unsuccessful in offering a compelling derivation of the symbolism. If the imagery has a symbolic dimension, it will probably remain inaccessible to those who lack the code.

We can grasp that the disciples should now understand about Jesus. The poignant **Do you not yet understand?** brings their lack of insight to something of a climax. The words aptly speak for readers who have observed the disciples from the beginning and can only wonder how they can possibly fail to comprehend what is going on around them.

Jesus' words do more than simply raise the problem; they offer an assessment of the disciples' problem. Their lack of insight is like blindness and deafness; it is like having hardened hearts! Their problem is not simply attributable to sloth or a lack of effort. They are unable to see and hear, blocked from understanding by a malady that requires a cure from outside. If the seed planted in the disciples is to bear fruit, it will not be because they have successfully made of themselves good soil. They require deliverance no less than the helpless demoniacs Jesus has healed, no less than the blind and the deaf who were brought to Jesus for release.

It is with the words of Jesus still ringing that the story of the healing of the blind man is recounted. The strange tale provides a crucial transition, introducing the account of Peter's confession, which, as most commentators have noted, represents an important turning point in the narrative. Not to appreciate the function of the healing story as an interpretation of Peter's confession is to miss a crucial element in the story.

■ Toward Jerusalem: The Way of the Cross (8:22-10:52)

Gradual Enlightenment (8:22-26)

This healing story is unusual by any estimate. Though Bultmann classifies it as a typical miracle story, he lists several exceptions, most notably Jesus' failure to heal the blind man completely on the first attempt. People did not tell miracle stories to highlight the inabilities of their hero. Other stories, as those in chapter 5, contrast Jesus' power with that of other healers, demonstrating his overwhelming superiority. The failure of Matthew and Luke to include the story is evidence of its problematic character.

There are, of course, recognizable features. As in the earlier story of the healing of the deaf mute, **some** bring to Jesus **a blind man** to be healed. Again, no name is mentioned, only the malady. This is the first time blindness has been identified as a problem requiring Jesus' attention. Jesus takes the blind man aside to heal him in private, as in the story of the deaf mute. Again, spittle is employed as a healing agent.

Strangely, the blind man is not immediately healed. Jesus must ask if he can see. The response, "I see people, **but they look like trees walking,**" is most unusual. The comment suggests the man has some standards by which to evaluate what he now sees. He cannot have been born blind, it would seem (cf. the comment in John by the blind man: "Never since the world began has it been heard that any one opened the eyes of a man born blind" [9:42]).

The fact remains that he cannot yet see clearly. There must be a second stage in the process. Only after Jesus' second touch is he completely healed and able to see **everything clearly.**

Jesus' enigmatic response, **Do not even enter the village**, should be understood in light of other injunctions to silence. The man is instructed to go **home** without saying anything. The narrator does not bother to mention the reaction of the blind man or his friends, unlike the earlier account of the deaf mute's restoration.

The symbolic function of the story is apparent. Jesus has just spoken of the disciples as having ears and eyes but being unable to hear and see. Mark has already told of Jesus' healing of a deaf mute who cannot be prevented from sharing the good news. Here is the story of a blind man who is healed. The story will be followed by the first breakthrough, when Peter confesses that Jesus is "the Christ." But as we learn, Peter's "insight" is no more functional than the blind man's glimpse of walking trees. The words, we learn, are correct—but Peter and the disciples are nevertheless still in the dark. The two stages necessary for complete healing of the blind man—for total clarity of vision—may well foreshadow what must occur with the disciples as well.

The disciples' problem is that they are in the grasp of a power from which they must be delivered. Their plight is like blindness that must be cured. Peter's confession offers the first evidence that light has penetrated the darkness; he has a glimmer of insight. In view of the preceding healing, that insight is promising. However much Peter and the rest fail to grasp, there is an implied promise that Jesus will finish what he began. Nothing is hidden except to be revealed. What Jesus plants will bear fruit. But when? The promise of a harvest is restated in other terms, but without a clear indication of when it will come.

The Confession of Peter (8:27-30)

This little episode marks a critical transition in the story. Jesus' interrogation of his disciples is both retrospective and prospective. There is some taking stock of what has been and a glimpse of what will be. For the first time since the opening verse, the term "Christ" is used in the narrative. And for the first time Jesus explicitly predicts that he will **be killed.** Not surprisingly, this becomes an occasion for instructions on discipleship which occupy most of the next two chapters.

The location of the conversation between Jesus and his followers is Philip's **Caesarea,** the seat of Herod Philip. Some commentators have seen in the location some play on pagan associations or perhaps reference to the substantial Roman contingent located there. Such speculation remains highly hypothetical.

Jesus' question, **Who do people say that I am?** provides an occasion for a retrospective. "People" here obviously does not include Pharisees and relatives. We are aware of what they think. The reference is to the crowds who have flocked to Jesus.

The labels all presume that Jesus is a prophet. They have been employed earlier, in chapter 6. Some—Herod among them—are impressed by the parallels between Jesus and **John the Baptist.** Others believe Jesus to be **Elijah** come back to herald the new age. **One of the prophets** may make reference to the "prophet like Moses" of Deut. 18. At a time when prophecy as an institution had ceased and prophets were either past figures or future hopes, some believed Jesus to be such a figure. The crowds offer a high estimate, and in view of the evidence it is not surprising. The closest parallels to the stories told about Jesus are in the cycles (and legends) involving Elijah and Elisha.

It is too strong to term these evaluations "wrong." Mark did not recount stories about Jesus' miracles and his teachings only to deny absolutely the significant parallels to the careers of prophets and holy men. The appraisals do not get to the heart of the matter, however, and that is what the Gospel is about.

"But you," Jesus asks the disciples, **Who do you say that I am?** Peter's response represents a new departure: **You are the Christ.**

The title designates a royal figure from the line of David (see excursus, below, pp. 124–26). Peter identifies Jesus as a king— as the King.

Albert Schweitzer, in his famous book *The Quest of the Historical Jesus*, comments that nothing Jesus had yet done could have convinced Peter he was the promised Messiah. Interpreters have tried to supply connections where they do not exist, from seeing in Jesus' announcement of the kingdom of God an implied claim to be king, to redefining "Messiah" to include the prophetic office. The solutions do little to solve the problem. In view of tradition and Jesus' performance thus far, Peter's "confession" is unwarranted. To make the point, Matthew adds, "Flesh and blood have not revealed this to you but my Father who is in heaven" (Matt. 16:17).

We do best to understand Peter's confession as anticipatory. If Jesus has done nothing regal yet, perhaps he will. Speaking for the disciples, Peter gives voice to the hope that Jesus is the one born to be King and that he will come to power in the days ahead.

Jesus' response is enigmatic. The verb, translated **charged,** is used twice in the following verses, where it means **rebuked.** The same verb is regularly used of Jesus' rebuke of demons. In 4:39, Jesus "rebukes" the wind and the sea. The translation **charged,** while one possible choice, seems weak. The term is rarely used in Mark without a pejorative sense, and **charged** fails to connote that. On the other hand, "rebuke" would imply Jesus' disapproval of the confession, and that connotation would also seem misleading. **The Christ** is one of the principal titles of Jesus in Mark and elsewhere in the New Testament. It appears in the opening sentence of Mark's Gospel, and it occurs at the climax of the story. When asked by the chief priest, "Are you the Christ, the Son of the Blessed," Jesus replies with an unambiguous, "I am" (14:61-62).

The strange response is best understood in view of Jesus' rebukes of demons elsewhere in the narrative. Many commentators resort to psychological explanations of his silencing the disciples, but there is no data to support such speculation. Demons are silenced "because they knew him" (1:34). An almost identical phrase is employed in 3:12, where Jesus "strictly ordered them not to make him known." We are given no reason for silence—only that it is Jesus' desire that his identity be kept a secret, and that the time of secrecy will eventually give way to disclosure. Though Peter speaks the truth, the time for public testimony has not come.

Jesus' response may also suggest there is some ambiguity about what Peter has said. Perhaps he has said more than he knows. The narrative now develops that theme.

First Prediction: Rejection and Vindication (8:31-33)

Peter's glimpse into the future is followed by Jesus' own forecast. For the first time Jesus tells his followers **plainly** that he must die—and be raised. The prediction is the first in a series of three. The story has offered many hints of the storm that lies ahead. Now the foreshadowing becomes explicit prediction. Notable is the use of *dei*: it is necessary (RSV, **must**). Jesus' ministry stands under the constraint of God's will. What happens is not accidental. It is in accordance with the Scriptures: the Son of man goes as it is written of him.

Not too much should be made of the phrase **the Son of man.** The disciples understand that Jesus is here speaking of himself. Note that Matthew exchanges "I" and "Son of man" in his account. Jesus asks, "Who do people say the Son of man is?" and the disciples reply as they do in Mark, understanding the term as a self-reference. On the other hand, Matthew says that he began to teach them that he would have to suffer. Matthew understands "I" and "Son of man" to be equivalent, as do the disciples in Mark's narrative. There is thus no justification for viewing "the Son of man" as a title—and certainly not as a title intended to replace "the Christ." It is best to view the expression as Jesus' unusual and mysterious self-reference.

The formulation of the first of Jesus' three forecasts shows evidence of biblical interpretation: the term **be rejected** is from

Ps. 118:22, a passage quoted in full in 12:11, "The very stone which the builders rejected has become the head of the corner; this was the Lord's doing, and it is marvelous in our eyes." The verse from the psalm played a prominent role in Christian reflection on the meaning of Jesus' resurrection. Jesus' first prediction thus begins to interpret what is to come as well as to foreshadow. Jesus will be "rejected" by the religious leaders and "vindicated" by God, as foretold in the psalm. The Psalms in particular provided the means by which Jesus' followers made sense of his death. Traces of language from the Psalms need not give the impression that Mark planted clues for the careful reader. The biblical phrases probably indicate that by the time Mark wrote, Jesus' story—particularly the account of his passion and resurrection—could not even be narrated without using the language of the Scriptures.

The Jewish opponents of Jesus noted in this prediction of his rejection appear with regularity from this point on. **The elders and the chief priests and the scribes** are all official designations, specifying the groups who made up the Jerusalem government. **Scribes** were the professional religious interpreters; **the chief priests** were members of the aristocratic families who ran the temple; **the elders** were lay members of the high court. It is no longer Pharisees who serve as Jesus' critics; they largely disappear. The problems in Jerusalem will involve principally matters of political consequence. Those responsible for Jesus' "rejection" are the religious officials. Mark is the most careful of the evangelists in distinguishing various groups within the Jewish community. There is no basis for the claim that "Israel" rejects Jesus.

Though Jesus will be killed, no agent is specified. We learn later that "Gentiles" will put him to death. Of more importance, apparently, are the scriptural "builders" who reject Jesus. The role of the Jews is more theologically significant than that of Pilate, as we shall see—even though they are not the ones who will put him to death.

Jesus' prediction of his rejection and death includes a forecast of his resurrection. It is thus somewhat misleading to call this a "passion prediction," as has become customary. Labels have a way of obscuring as well as illumining. Jesus anticipates what is to come, and, while his rejection receives more attention, the future holds resurrection and vindication as well. That the disciples do not get the point is not at issue. This explicit foreshadowing is principally for the reader. The resurrection of Jesus is every bit as expected as his death. That observation will be important for interpreting the conclusion of the Gospel.

Peter serves as the spokesman for the circle of disciples in his confession. Now he acts on their behalf in rebuking Jesus. What Jesus has announced is intolerable, precisely in view of what Peter has confessed. Such treatment is unthinkable for "the Christ." There was no preparation in Jewish tradition for a Messiah who is **rejected** and is **killed,** despite the remarkable variety within eschatological tradition. Peter reacts as did Paul, who can say years after his conversion, "we preach Christ crucified, a scandal to Jews . . ." (1 Cor. 1:23).

Jesus then responds to the whole circle as well as to Peter in his rebuke: "**Get behind me, Satan!** For you do not have your mind set on God's things but on human things." The idea is not so much having taken sides (RSV, **You are not on the side of God, but of men**) as having one's eyes set in the right direction. There is a difference between "the things of God" and "human things," as the story intends to make clear. That is why Jesus' ministry as the divine means of establishing the kingdom has stirred such controversy. There must be a clash. The scandal of the cross is not due to slightly flawed scriptural interpretation but to the very nature of things. There must be a confrontation between God and the human race—and we are now told that the encounter will be marked by a cross. Someone must die, even if death will not have the final word.

Christian tradition has spun elaborate theories to explain this "necessity." Anselm's *Cur Deus Homo?* is probably the most famous example. There is a difference between such reflections and what is implied here in Mark. No speculations locate the "necessity" in a system of law to which God is bound. The need arises not from God's obligations but from the human plight. The narrative offers a sense of how things are between God and the human race. There is a barrier, manifested in a variety of ways, that has come to serve the race as a defense of "human things." Humans are powerless to break through that barrier; in fact, most are obliged to defend it. For God to reclaim a captive creation there must be a battle. And Jesus will be the casualty.

Satan is a reminder of Jesus' initial temptation. There is apparently an alternative road to the kingdom, but it is not God's. Jesus must go the appointed way: it is necessary. Peter, who has at least glimpsed the truth, has more to learn. That "more" will mean the difference between life and death, and the lesson will be unimaginably costly.

The disciples' lack of insight now becomes partial sight—and misunderstanding. The focus of that misunderstanding is the confession of Jesus as Christ. The title is correct; Jesus is the Christ. And yet he is nothing like the expected Messiah. The difference between the ways of God and human ways is captured in Peter's simple confession. "Understanding" all that the confession entails becomes the theme for subsequent chapters.

Taking Up the Cross (8:34—9:1)

Jesus now summons **the multitude**, who, **with his disciples**, are to receive the first in a series of lessons about what it will mean to follow. The instructions employ language appropriate to a post-Easter audience: **Take up** your **cross** would have made no sense to Jesus' contemporaries. Yet even to Mark's post-Easter audience, the reference to the cross would have been offensive. An instrument of torture developed by the Persians and used by the Romans for political criminals, it would seem ill-suited to serve as a symbol of discipleship. The imagery that follows illustrates the affront to common sense: those who wish **to save life** must **lose it.** It is not sacrifice for its own sake that is commended, however, but sacrifice **for my sake and the gospel's.** It would seem that nothing short of total devotion will suffice. Following will require abandonment of self—death. Though it is conceivable that Mark's readers would have to reckon with the possibility of martyrdom, subsequent chapters make it clear that this "death" signals a way of life as well as its end.

Jesus issues warnings: there is nothing that one can give in exchange for one's life; the attempt to preserve life will result only in destruction; therefore, self-abandonment for Jesus' sake is the only sensible course of action. The warnings include an eschatological dimension: those who are **ashamed** of Jesus and **his words** in this **generation** will be so regarded by **the Son of man** when he comes in his **glory.** From Mark's viewpoint, Jesus is speaking of himself (cf. the question of James and John about places of honor when Jesus is "in [his] glory" [10:37]). The imagery reflects the influence of Dan. 7:13 and the vision of the human-like figure, a passage to which Mark will allude later (13:26-27; 14:62). Jesus says forthrightly to his followers that they can expect his vindication and heavenly enthronement. He will eventually come "in his glory." Discipleship is lived in view of the cross but also in view of the coming glory. Jesus' threat is also a promise for those who are not ashamed of him and his words.

For centuries interpreters have been tantalized by Jesus' promise that some would **not taste death** until they saw **the kingdom of God** having come in **power.** Schweitzer used such passages to construct his history of Jesus as an apocalyptic fanatic who miscalculated God's timetable. Jesus meant, Schweitzer insisted, that the kingdom would come within his—and his disciples'—lifetime. He was wrong, and Christians have been offering apologies ever since. Other interpreters tend to view the passage as an undigested bit of tradition, whether authentic or not.

It seems likely either that Mark wrote with confidence that the kingdom would come "in power" in the very near future, or that in some sense the promise is fulfilled within the confines of the narrative.

Excursus: "The Christ"

Among the titles used of Jesus in Mark, "the Christ" occupies a prominent place. We know that the designation "the Christ" is a title because it appears as a predicate nominative in sentences (e.g., "You are the Christ"). It is an official designation whose meaning is largely taken for granted. As readers, we are expected to know what it means to be "the Christ."

If we exclude from the list of titular occurrences the initial "Christ" without a definite article in 1:1, the variant reading in 1:34, and the anarthrous "of Christ" in 9:41, the title appears five times in Mark. Peter is the first to use the title (8:31, "You are the Christ"), the mockers at the foot of the cross the last (15:32, "Let the Christ, the King of Israel, come down now from the cross. . . ."). Jesus uses the term twice, once in a dispute with the scribes about scriptural interpretation (12:35-37) and once in his glimpse of the future (13:21; see also 13:22, "false Christs"). The title appears in the question that marks the climax of the action in Mark 14:61-62: "Are you the Christ, the Son of the Blessed?" "I am. . . ." It appears for the last time in the taunts as Jesus hangs from the cross, "If you are the Christ, the King of Israel, come down . . ." (15:31).

Study of Jewish tradition in the last decades provides a context within which interpretive hunches can be explored and evaluated. The results of a conference on messianism at Princeton in 1988 tend to confirm the following exegetical proposals:

1. While there is not a single occurrence of the absolute "the Messiah" in the Old Testament, the term was familiar to postbiblical Jewish tradition by the Christian era. By New Testament times and in later rabbinic tradition, a particular figure can be designated as "*the* Messiah (Christ)."

2. While in the Old Testament both priests and kings were anointed—and even prophets could be described figuratively as "anointed" by God, by the first century "the Messiah (Christ)" refers to a particular royal figure, the offspring of David who would arise at the end of days to deliver Israel. In Mark's passion story, Jews refer to "the Christ, the King of Israel," while Romans refer simply to "the King of the Jews," aware that "the Christ" means "King" (of course, they were not interested in the religious dimensions of that kingship).

3. The claim that Jesus is "the Christ" does not ring true to "messianic" tradition, as the authoritative spokespersons of society make clear. To the Jewish leaders, Jesus' willingness to accept the designations "the Christ, the Son of the Blessed," constitutes blasphemy—and it deserves only mockery. To the Romans, Jesus' refusal to deny that he is "the King of the Jews" constitutes sedition and likewise deserves mockery. The designation "the Christ" makes sense to Mark's audience—and they are expected to know that in view of its place in Jewish tradition, its application to Jesus sounds wrong. In fact, one purpose of the narrative is to explore this tension between the tradition and the "facts" (Jesus is indeed the Christ, as God has demonstrated by raising him from the dead).

Attempts to understand "the Messiah (Christ)" as a generic term, encompassing aspects of various savior figures, thus must be called into question. Christians, of course, reinterpreted the title in view of the particulars of Jesus' career. In Mark, however, that reinterpretation does not obscure the shock: that the offspring of David should be invested and enthroned on a cross, a victim of those from whom he was expected to deliver Israel, is an offense (1 Cor. 1:23) (see bibliography, Dahl, Juel).

A Glimpse of Glory: Transfiguration (9:2-8)

Immediately after Jesus promises that some of those present would not die before seeing the kingdom of God having come in power, he withdraws with the inner circle of the Twelve, **Peter and James and John,** to offer them a glimpse of his "glory"—the glory with which the Son of man will return. What the disciples see and hear on the **mountain** are matters reserved for the last times. They are offered a preview, a foretaste of what is to come.

The persistent suggestion by commentators that the transfiguration account is a "displaced resurrection story" deserves at least brief comment. Such suggestions take as their point of departure not Mark but such works as the *Pistis Sophia* and the *Sophia Jesu Christi*, Gnostic writings in which the appearance of Jesus in a transfigured state (radiant, in dazzling apparel) is a typical feature of a post-resurrection revelation (in these two works, the appearance is located on the Mount of Olives, where Jesus appears to his disciples and discloses to them heavenly mysteries). The differences between these accounts and the transfiguration in Mark, however, are as striking as the similarities. In the Gnostic works, Jesus functions as a revealer of heavenly mysteries. There is no action, only speaking about celestial secrets in appropriately esoteric language. The only speaking Jesus does in Mark is with **Moses and Elijah**—not for the disciples' ears. In the Gnostic works, Jesus is first absent, then he appears. The only similarity is the depiction of Jesus as a heavenly being.

The transfiguration narrative in Mark is obviously not a resurrection story. It does serve as ultimate foreshadowing of Jesus' destiny, however. He is a heavenly being. He will eventually appear in his "glory" (8:38; 14:62). The inner group of disciples is given a preliminary glimpse of this glory. But it is only preliminary. There can be no final glory, no consummation until after the cross. That is the "necessity" which dominates Jesus' career.

It seems quite likely that in some respect the transfiguration is related to Jesus' promise in 9:1. It offers to the inner circle at least a foretaste of what is to come. They glimpse the future glory of Jesus associated with the consummation of the kingdom of God.

The transition, **after six days,** is unusually specific. Such detailed temporal references occur elsewhere only in the passion narrative. Given the similarities in this account to the Sinai theophany, it is possible that the **six days** is intended as an allusion to the six days of preparation for the appearance of God to Moses on Mount Sinai (Exod. 24:15-16). The transformation of Jesus, the presence of light, the voice from the cloud—all are reminiscent of God's appearance to Moses.

The precise location of this **mountain** is unspecified. However, that the location is a mountain is important.

The term **transfigured** is rare in the New Testament. Significant is the occurrence in 2 Cor. 3:18, where Paul speaks of being "transformed into the image" of Christ. The passage is an extended interpretation of Moses' veil and his glimpse of God's "glory"—dealing, in other words, with traditions about the theophany at Mount Sinai. The passage in Mark obviously speaks about transformation into a heavenly being characterized by glory. Jesus is thus transformed in the presence of the disciples. The extraordinary whiteness of **his garments** only confirms the unearthly character of his appearance. Elsewhere such imagery is reserved for the messenger (or angel) at the empty tomb (see Matt. 28:3). The language and imagery are familiar from scenes in apocalypses.

The simple comment that **Moses and Elijah** appear to speak with Jesus must presuppose considerable background on the part of Mark's readers. Both figures were granted an appearance by God on Mount Sinai (called Mount Horeb in 1 Kings). Both are likewise eschatological figures. The return of a "prophet like Moses" is predicted in Deuteronomy 18; Elijah's return is announced in Mal. 4:5-6. In intertestamental times, both those scriptural promises enjoyed a prominent place in Jewish visions and dreams of the future. The presence of these eschatological figures suggests that some important condition is being met, that some great moment has arrived. It is difficult not to see a connection with Jesus' promise about his return "in the glory of his Father" as well as with the prediction about some of his followers seeing the kingdom of God (8:38—9:1)—though this is by no means the "end" to which those predictions point.

Peter's comment, explained as a frightened response, refers to the construction of tents or **booths,** some form of temporary lodging. It is possible that some reference is intended to the Feast of Booths, one of the major pilgrimage festivals in the Jewish year. According to the prophet Zechariah, the climax of all the great wars and plagues will be the celebration of the Feast of Booths by the survivors of all the nations (Zech. 14:16-21). If Peter's remark alludes to some such tradition, however, it is too vague for much to be made of it. Until we know more about the eschatological traditions of postbiblical Judaism, we can only guess how Peter's words might have been heard by Mark's audience.

According to Mark, Peter was appropriately frightened in the presence of heavenly beings and **did not know what to say.** The offer to construct some simple housing suggests a desire to remain on the mountain and to savor the experience of heavenly visions. Remaining, however, is contrary to divine necessity. Other things must take place before Jesus comes in his glory with the holy angels.

The presence of the **cloud,** as in the accounts of Moses' and Elijah's visits to Sinai, symbolizes God's presence. The heavenly **voice** repeats the declaration made at Jesus' baptism, except that here the voice is intended not primarily for Jesus ("you are") but for the disciples: **This is my beloved Son.** The disclosure represents an important new stage in their "enlightenment." The heavenly affirmation of Jesus' filial status, playing on Ps. 2:7 and 2 Sam. 7:14, lends additional credibility to Peter's confession. Jesus is the Christ—the King whom God had promised to call **Son.** The voice also adds authority to Jesus' words: **Listen to him.** The command is reminiscent of the promise of a "prophet like Moses," to whom all Israel is obliged to listen (Deut. 18:16-20).

The transformation affords only a brief glimpse of Jesus' heavenly status—and destiny. The experience is over as quickly as it began. The disciples are left with Jesus—not the Jesus resplendent in his glory, but the one baptized in the Jordan by John, indistinguishable from sinners and tax collectors, the man with whom they ate and slept. They might have wished for more. But they do have Jesus with them—and he will accompany them to the valley where a different kind of reality awaits them.

Private Instructions (9:9-13)

Jesus' instruction to his disciples not to recount **what they had seen until the Son of man should have risen from the dead** for the first time offers a clue to his secrecy, or at least to the time when the secrecy will end. Jesus promised earlier that nothing is hidden except to be revealed. Now he suggests when the time of disclosure will come: after the Son of man has been raised **from the dead.** The disciples are to tell no one what has just transpired, for now. But the time to speak will come.

The disciples appear to understand little of what Jesus has just said. For the reader, his words offer a sense of anticipation. There will come a time for resolution of mysteries and the disclosure of secrets. Perhaps the disciples will even understand.

The disciples' question about **Elijah** suggests they have understood something of what has transpired. The academic tone (**Why do the scribes say . . .?**) indicates a traditional matter about which there is some dispute. The view of **the scribes** is not contrasted here with the will of God but is accepted as a valid reading of the Scriptures (Malachi 4). Elijah must come first (note again the use of *dei* to speak of divine necessity). **First** indicates that his coming is the prelude to further events. Elijah's task is **to restore all things,** a phrase reminiscent of Sir. 48:10:

> You [Elijah] who are ready at the appointed time, it is written, to calm the wrath of God before it breaks out in fury, to turn the heart of the father to the son, and to restore the tribes of Jacob.

Jesus accepts the view of **the scribes** and then offers an interpretation of what **is written: Elijah has** already **come,** and they **did to him whatever they pleased.** Jesus' reference to John the Baptist is patent. By including John's name, Matthew simply makes explicit what Mark implies.

The career of John/Elijah is bound up with the one for whom he prepares (1:7-8). If John's career proceeds according to some script, the same is true of Jesus, the one who refers to himself with the enigmatic "the Son of man." The career of the Son of man has also "been written." Like the one who has prepared the way, Jesus will prove to be a victim.

Precisely which biblical passages are implied here is unclear. The reference to suffering **many things** is usually taken as a reference to Isaiah 53. More likely is an allusion to Psalm 22, which figures so prominently in Mark's account of the passion. In Ps. 22:6, the phrase "despised by the people" translates the same Greek root as **treated with contempt** in Mark 9:12.

The passage bears the clear marks of Christian interpretive tradition. The Scriptures were mined for material that could help Jesus' followers understand how it could be that the Christ must suffer and be treated with contempt. This interpretive enterprise represents the beginning of Christian theologizing and was of fundamental significance for the development of the tradition. Jesus' words in Mark reflect that exegetical tradition.

John appears in the Gospel as a forerunner. He is only a prelude to the real drama. John's role has been understood in light of scribal traditions about Elijah. The surprise is not that Elijah must come first but that he has already come—and that he was killed. In that sense he is a true forerunner of the Son of man, who will share a similar fate—with the additional promise that he will rise from the dead.

The little interchange is important once again for Mark's readers. We are offered a biblical framework within which to locate the drama as it unfolds. The disciples seem to learn very little from their scriptural lesson.

The Healing of a Possessed Child (9:14-29)

When Jesus returns to his disciples, he finds them embroiled in a dispute with the **scribes** and **a crowd.** The reaction of the crowd upon seeing Jesus is reminiscent of the Israelites' reaction to Moses when he returned from Sinai. They are **amazed.**

The reason for the dispute is not a doctrinal abstraction but the disciples' inability to heal a young boy with a **dumb spirit.** The dispute introduces a miracle story, unusual only because of its placement in the narrative. With the exception of this story and the healing of blind Bartimaeus in chapter 10, healings and exorcisms are confined to the first eight chapters of the Gospel.

The special point of the story is the **disciples'** inability to perform a cure. Their success on the preaching tour earlier in the Gospel (chap. 6) contrasts with their failure here. Jesus attributes their inability to a lack of faith. The disciples' faith has still not matured. **How long?** Jesus asks again. When will the disciples be prepared to assume the ministries for which they have been called?

The story is in most respects typical of healings and exorcisms. The malady that is described sounds like epilepsy, here attributed to the work of a demon bent on the child's destruction. The symptoms are described in detail. The story offers one of the strongest statements yet about the power of faith. **If you can do anything,** the father begs, **help us.** Jesus picks up on the father's words: **If you can! All things are possible to** [one] **who believes.**

The father responds with faith—and a plea that Jesus will compensate for whatever is lacking in that faith.

Jesus' healing is typical of popular miracle stories—though unusual for Mark—in that he does not take the boy away from the crowd but heals him when he **saw that a crowd came running together.** The crowd has a role to play: they again testify to the desperate character of the malady. They believe the child is dead. As he did with the young girl, Jesus takes the boy **by the hand** and raises him up.

Though a crowd is present, nothing is said about a reaction. The reaction of the crowd is less important here than the lesson to be learned from the healing. The **disciples** do not understand why they were unable to effect the cure. Their question about that inability to heal the child elicits an interesting response from Jesus: **This kind cannot be driven out by anything but prayer.** Jesus' comment suggests there are varying degrees of possession and illness. The most potent weapon against the forces of darkness is **prayer.** The faith to which Jesus calls the child's father will find expression in petitions addressed to God. Jesus promises that prayer is efficacious. Later he will tell the disciples that confident prayer can move mountains (11:24). Ask, and it will be given to you. The disciples will have to learn about prayer if they are to carry on Jesus' ministry.

Second Prediction (9:30-32)

The second of Jesus' predictions of what is to come is provided a general setting: Jesus is traveling with his disciples **through Galilee**—incognito. The prediction is intended only for the **disciples.** The forecast of what is to come, the shortest of the three, speaks of betrayal, death, and resurrection. The disciples apparently do not yet understand what Jesus is announcing—but they know enough to be afraid.

Who Is the Greatest? (9:33-37)

When the group arrives in **Capernaum,** Jesus asks what his followers were discussing. Though the disciples do not respond,

Jesus already knows. The topic of conversation seems absurd: **they had discussed with one another who was the greatest.** Peter's response to Jesus' first prediction of his fate in Jerusalem was to rebuke the master. The disciples seem to have learned little. While Jesus speaks of being handed over and killed, his followers discuss their respective statuses. To the disciples' credit, they have apparently understood something about the glory Jesus has promised. But they have no sense whatever of what must precede—the rejection of Jesus and his death—and what are the implications for their behavior as disciples.

The contrast between Jesus' prediction and the disciples' topic of discussion provides an occasion to speak about true discipleship. While earlier "taking up your cross" meant "losing your life for my sake and the gospel's," here the issue is greatness. The contrast between "God's things" and "human things" can be understood in terms of status: anyone wishing to be **first** must be **last, and servant of all.** The **servant** here is a *diakonos*, one who waits on tables. The disciples do not think of themselves as waiters. They dream, as do ordinary partisans of a powerful leader, of position and rank. Divine standards run headlong into conventional measures.

In what follows, Mark records a series of instructions that explore what it means to follow the one who must die. Little effort is made to provide smooth transitions from one issue to the next. All the instructions are explications of the challenge to "human things" embodied in Jesus' cross, which turns the world upside down. The last are first and the first last.

One measure of the "service" Jesus describes relates to hospitality. Taking **a child,** Jesus tells his disciples that within his circle receiving children in his name will be a mark of faithfulness. While the image of a child or a "little one" may symbolize all those within the Christian family, we should not move too quickly to the symbolic. "Receiving children"—welcoming them, caring about them—means what it says (see Mark 10:13-16). Jesus' gesture is more potent than we sense. In ancient culture, children had no status. They were subject to the authority of their fathers, viewed as little more than property. Membership within the community of the faithful will involve giving status to those who have none. Accepting such an unimportant member of society in Jesus' name is equivalent to accepting Jesus. And accepting Jesus is equivalent to accepting God. Hospitality, a major aspect of life in the ancient world, is to be extended to the most unlikely, thus challenging traditional notions of status.

Hospitality to the unimportant will be a hallmark of the circle of Jesus' followers, as it was in Jesus' own ministry. And this has everything to do with faithfulness to the one whose rejection and death mark the way to glory.

For Us and Against Us (9:38-41)

Attitude toward "outsiders" is the concern of the next pronouncement of Jesus. **John** asks the leading question: What are we to think of an exorcist who speaks **in your name** but is not a member of our circle? Jesus' principle is that such exorcists should not be hindered. Those who work in Jesus' name are not enemies. They will not **speak evil of me.** Thus, those who are **not against us** are **for us.** The question probably presumes an early stage of "denominationalism" and the attendant suspicion of strangers outside the familiar circle.

Returning to the theme of hospitality, Jesus blesses those who will provide for his followers because they are **of Christ.** The setting is reminiscent of the mission charge in chapter 6, where Jesus' followers were sent out relying on the hospitality of those to whom they would preach. The movement will be totally dependent upon ordinary people for such support. Implied, perhaps, is that "apostles" temper their own self-importance by acknowledging the significance of those who are not preachers and teachers—their benefactors.

The phrase **of Christ** is as close as one comes to "Christian" in Mark (the label does not appear in Mark; it occurs only twice in Acts and once in 1 Peter). Elsewhere in Mark the title "Christ" is used sparingly, appearing with greatest frequency in the passion sequence (see below).

Warnings about Offense (9:42-50)

The promise of reward is paired with a warning against anyone causing **one of these little ones who believe in me** to stumble. The term **little ones** is not restricted to children, though they are not excluded. The term applies to followers of Jesus who are to think of themselves not as great but as small. The warning is perhaps best directed at leaders impressed with their status—those who relish the opportunity to exercise authority (see 10:42-45). With leadership comes great responsibility.

The reference to "stumbling" (RSV, **to sin**) leads to a series of sayings about causes of stumbling. The graphic warnings about **hand, foot,** or **eye** leading one into sin intend to speak about priorities. Even the faithful need to calculate what is important and what is not. Jesus is concerned with wholeness: he has healed a man with a withered hand (3:1-6), a paralytic (2:1-11), and a blind man (8:22-26). Some things are more important than physical wholeness, however. **Life,** which means here life in the kingdom of God, is worth considerable sacrifice, even the surrender of one's body (8:35-37). The alternative prospect is eternal punishment. The warnings are reminiscent of Jesus' saying about "treasure in heaven" in Matthew and Luke. Once again, the context—the disciples' inability to understand the implications of what lies ahead—might suggest that their concern for externals betrays a faith that will have to be tempered in the fire-storm to come.

The reference to the fires of Gehenna (RSV, **hell**), which is taken from Isaiah, leads to the strange saying—found only in Mark—about being salted with fire. It takes as its point of departure the quotation from Isaiah which speaks about destruction with **fire.** The numerous textual variants and the host of scholarly interpretations are eloquent testimony to the enigmatic character of the saying. One of the variants refers to Lev. 2:13, which speaks of using salt with sacrifices. Perhaps the best sense we can get is the promise of some purification by fire that is to come ("He will baptize you with the Holy Spirit and with fire" [Luke 3:16]). Jesus promises that **everyone *will* be salted with fire.** This is perhaps similar to his promise that James and John will drink the cup that he drinks and will share his baptism (10:39).

The reference to salt introduces an injunction about retaining **saltness.** There is to be something distinctive about Jesus' followers. If not, they will prove as worthless as **salt** that has lost its zest.

The concluding exhortation to **be at peace with one another** brings the instructions back to the initial setting. Bickering about status betrays a deep misunderstanding of what it means to follow Jesus. Much will transpire before the disciples learn what they must.

Care for the Weak: Marriage and Family (10:1-16)

Transition (10:1)

In 8:31, Jesus announces that he must go to Jerusalem. Through the subsequent episodes in chapters 8 and 9, his movements give little indication of a definite journey to Jerusalem. With the beginning of chapter 10, however, Jesus and his followers journey to the region of Judea and to the Transjordan, where his ministry had begun with his baptism at the hands of John. The third of his predictions and the ensuing instructions to his disciples are the last of such before his fateful arrival. The healing of blind Bartimaeus completes the sequence that began with the healing of a blind man and provides the transition to his grand entry to the city.

Family Matters (10:2-16)

Earlier in the story Jesus made a radical statement about family, defining as his "mother, brothers, and sisters" those who do the will of God. The ties that are most significant, he tells his followers, are those that unite teacher and student, leader and followers. Later, Jesus promises that families will be divided "because of my name" (Mark 13:12-13). In a society where family was the primary social unit, where religious and political life was bound up with the household, a threat to the family was a threat to the whole society. The major criticism aimed at Christians in the Roman world—and the reason for later persecutions—was that they were antisocial, threatening bonds that held together the human community from the family to the state.

It is perhaps not surprising, therefore, that the narrative must attend to matters of social utility. If these chapters are about discipleship, there must be some attention to questions about how followers of Jesus are to live. What about family matters? What will a "community" look like? The questions are important even to members of cults who are taught not only how to break ties with family and society but also how to form new ones. The conventional nature of much ethical advice in the New Testament indicates, however, that early Christianity did not intend to be perceived as a cult. It aimed at the transformation of the whole society. And while there would be radical social restructuring, the ultimate goal was the rebuilding of the human family, not its destruction. The question of the **Pharisees** about **divorce,** therefore, while contributing to the development of the conflict in the story, deals with a question of fundamental importance to Mark's audience. It provides Jesus an opportunity to speak about family matters from another perspective.

The question of **divorce** is asked **to test** Jesus. Such questions were discussed in detail within the learned community. According to Deut. 24:1-4, men were permitted to divorce their wives. The disputed matter was the meaning of the phrase, "if she finds no favor in his eyes because he has found some indecency in her." In the Mishnah, opinion is divided on how to read the phrase— and, according to the learned community, the difference of opinion was of long standing. One view, attributed to the followers of Shammai, was that divorce should be permitted only in extreme circumstances—such as in the case of adultery. The contrasting view, attributed to the followers of Hillel, permitted men to divorce their wives for virtually any reason. The account of the dispute in the Mishnah (*Gittin* 9:10) reads as follows:

> The School of Shammai say: A man may not divorce his wife unless he has found unchastity in her, for it is written, "Because he hath found in her *indecency* in anything." And the School of Hillel say: [He may divorce her] even if she spoiled a dish for him, for it is written, "Because he hath found in her indecency in *anything*." R. Akiba says: Even if he found another fairer than she, for it is written, "And it shall be if she find no favor in his eyes. . . ."

The elaborate discussions in the Mishnah deal principally with the circumstances under which a **certificate of divorce** can be written and in which it is valid. Divorce, of course, was permitted only to men.

Jesus' approach to the question differs radically from that of either of the two "houses." Following the principle that Scripture interprets Scripture, Jesus turns to Genesis as the fundamental text for understanding marriage. Building on the biblical phrase, **and the two shall become one flesh,** Jesus declares the union sacrosanct. In view of the verse in Genesis, the provision for **divorce** in Deuteronomy is seen as secondary. The reason for the command is **for your hardness of heart.**

The interpretive approach is similar to that of the rabbis. The Bible, according to Jewish views, could contain no contradictions. Where one encountered apparent conflicts, there were various ways to resolve them. The most common procedure was to identify one passage as primary and to explain the second as valid only in a narrow sphere. The discussion in Mark presumes there is a contradiction between "becoming one flesh," which no one is to separate, and rules permitting **divorce.** Here, Jesus accords Genesis priority. Deuteronomy is valid only in the sphere of human experience where **hardness of heart** is the basic fact of life. The nearness of the kingdom of God implies new possibilities; it means acknowledging God's will that a union between a man and a woman should be permanent and that divorce laws must be understood accordingly.

While the interpretive approach is similar to that of the rabbis, the conclusions are not. Jesus' radical views tend to relativize the whole Torah. Drawing a distinction between the real will of God and the written law offers a possible critique that can have devastating consequences. And Jesus offers this view on his own authority, without citing precedent. In the eyes of the Pharisees, Jesus' view on this matter, like his other legal pronouncements, is radical and dangerous.

We should not miss the significance of this social statement, however. While Jesus' preaching speaks of fidelity to God in a way that threatens the fabric of society, his ultimate goal is not the destruction of human community but the establishment of that community on a firmer foundation. Marriage is ordained by **God,** Jesus insists, as a basic feature of the law. While the way of the cross will break up family units, Jesus' movement is not antifamily. There may be dramatic social realignments, but orderly life together is what God intends for everyone. Jesus agrees with the Pharisees that family life should be structured according to the law. In these verses, however, his emphasis is on enlisting the Torah as a safeguard of marriage bonds—over against a use of the law which justifies breaking them. The dispute is reminiscent of an earlier contrast between *corban* vows and the commandment to honor mother and father (7:6-13).

The disciples' question provides an opportunity to emphasize the permanence of the marriage bond: Jesus interprets the commandment against **adultery** as applying even to remarriage (9:10-12). The warning is addressed to women as well as to men, though there are important textual variants which disagree. Codex D, for example, reads "if she *abandons* [not 'divorces'] her husband and marries another, she commits adultery." Since **divorce** was not permitted women in the Jewish law, the reading is probably an attempt to "correct" a passage that seemed too radical, and thus the reading should probably be viewed as secondary. If Jesus did grant women the possibility of divorce (as Paul does in 1 Cor. 7:10-12), his departure from Jewish tradition is the more radical. Roman law acknowledged in a limited way the right of women to divorce. Jesus apparently agrees. On this matter women are equal before the law of God—and thus potentially as culpable as men.

Unlike Matthew's version of the saying about **divorce**, which begins with the consideration of exceptions ("except for unchastity" [19:9]), Mark's does not intend to speak of specific instances. The discussion of divorce and remarriage is cast in the form of absolute pronouncements. That there was separation from families, in fact open hostility within households, is acknowledged later in the chapter and in the warnings Jesus addresses to his followers in chapter 13. Much of Paul's discussion of marriage in 1 Cor. 7 has to do with "mixed" marriages in which one member is a believer and the other is not. While citing the "word of the Lord" that there can be no divorce (1 Cor 7:10-11), Paul presumes that in the case of these mixed marriages divorce is a near certainty. Acknowledging that God does not will divorce does not settle specific cases. The "what if" questions must await another occasion. The point of the discussion in Mark is to be clear about the law's intent.

For both Jesus and **the Pharisees, divorce** is an issue of law. Laws governing marriage and divorce have always been crucial in structuring the life of the human family. The particular function of divorce laws has been to protect women and children. Particularly in ancient societies where women could not legally own property, survival meant being a member of a household. Properly understood, laws against easy divorce were meant to prevent irresponsible husbands from abandoning their families. In the debate with the Pharisees, Jesus takes an even more radical stance—on behalf of women. Women whose vocation is the raising of children require the protection of the law. It has always been thus. Jesus' attack on a tradition of law that granted divorce easily—however "realistic" that tradition may have seemed to those engaged in the practice of law—represented an attack on the social position of men. Jesus' position therefore seems to be that society has fundamental investments in the family that the law is intended to protect.

Not surprisingly, **children** are the next topic of discussion. Children were regarded largely as property, without rights. They could be sold by their parents. Laws preventing their exploitation were few. In the brief pronouncement story, **the disciples** mirror the attitude of society, keeping children at arm's length. Jesus' indignation arises from a different view of social structure; his is a community where children are welcomed. "Of such ones is the kingdom of God" (cf. RSV).

The discussion of **divorce** and the status of **children** thus reflects a larger concern about the nature of the "family" gathered about Jesus—the family of those who do the will of God.

The statement about receiving **the kingdom of God like a child** should be understood in the same light. In this setting, it has mostly to do with status. The disciples are portrayed as excessively concerned about position; they argue about who is the greater. A child has no status. Those who intend to save their lives must lose them; those who aspire to be first must become servants. Adults must be willing to become like children, without status, if they are to take their places in the kingdom of God. Hospitality toward those of little status is balanced by warnings addressed to those who aspire to positions of power and importance.

The Rich Man (10:17-22)

A community that intends to have a sustained existence must come to terms with certain basic aspects of life, one being the place and proper use of possessions. The occasion for considering wealth is a question asked by an unidentified man who comes to Jesus with a concern: **What must I do to inherit eternal life?** The man, who we learn is wealthy, kneels before Jesus and is thus not asking merely to trap Jesus into saying something dangerous, as is often the case in Mark.

The rich man addresses Jesus as **Good Teacher.** Jesus replies, **No one is good but God alone.** Jesus' insistence that God alone deserves the epithet **good** stamps him as a pious Jew concerned to safeguard the uniqueness of God. It is reminiscent of the hymn in Philippians which praises the one who "did not count equality with God a thing to be snatched at" (Phil. 2:6). It also anticipates

Jesus' statement that he came not to be served but to serve (Mark 10:45).

The man asks about "inheriting eternal life." **Eternal life** is obviously not a right but a gift. In asking how he must act in order to inherit eternal life (**What must I do?**), the rich man is not denying that it is God's to give, but is taking seriously the need to be a member of the family to whom inheritance is promised.

In response to the question, Jesus quotes from the "second table" of the law which deals with relations among the human family. His response is quite traditional. Not all the laws are quoted. In view of the preceding discussion of family matters, it is not surprising that the list includes respect for parents and prohibition of adultery. While Jesus critiques the tradition of the elders, he does not attack the commandments.

The response of the pious man, **All these I have observed from my youth,** does not earn a rebuke. Jesus does not question the man's integrity. The commandments can be kept. That is not enough, however. Jesus **loves** the man, and he offers him a place in the kingdom. The one thing needed is to surrender all his possessions, **give** the proceeds **to the poor,** and **follow.** The man is saddened by Jesus' words, **for he had great possessions.** He is unable to part with his possessions and thus goes away grieving. His disappointment at not meeting the conditions for "inheriting eternal life" is not sufficient motivation to force a total break with his past. He cannot lose his life in order to gain it.

Dangers of Wealth/Promises of Sacrifice (10:23-31)

The encounter of Jesus and the rich man provides an occasion to discuss the danger of wealth. Jesus' statement, **How hard it will be for those who have riches to enter the kingdom of God,** runs counter to popular piety, according to which **riches** were a sign of God's blessing. The attitudes among Jewish teachers varied. Some argued that one could expect the next life to be a reversal of this life. One who was poor in this life could expect to be well off in the next. Those who had been treated unjustly could finally be assured of justice. Of course, only Pharisees could hold such views. Sadducees did not believe in the resurrection and had to understand God's justice in terms of this lifetime only.

The disciples represent the view that riches are a sign of special blessing, and they are appropriately astonished at Jesus' saying. Jesus restates the warning with an image: **It is easier for a camel to go through the eye of a needle than for a rich man to enter the kingdom of God.** The disciples are all the more astounded: **Then who can be saved?** Jesus does not minimize the reality of bondage to this world; there are things which people like the rich man cannot do. But God is not bound by the rules: **All things are possible with God.**

It is clear, however, that wealth provides a special problem. It becomes an all-consuming passion from which the rich must be delivered. In human terms, deliverance is inconceivable. If the rich are to enter the kingdom, it will be because God has made possible what is otherwise impossible. If left to themselves, the "deceit of riches" will choke the seed planted in them, and their lives will prove fruitless.

Peter's statement, **We have left everything and followed you,** is often regarded as self-serving. That is to read too much into the text. Peter states a fact: Jesus' followers have left everything and followed. Jesus called his followers from home, careers, and even families (the reference to Peter's mother-in-law in the opening chapter must mean that Peter was married). What does it mean that they have abandoned everything to become disciples? Is the call to follow Jesus a call to abandon the world? Is there no way to follow Jesus and also live in the world in such a way that one can be involved with such ordinary and essential matters as property and possessions?

Jesus' response heads off any notion that discipleship requires absolute asceticism and abandonment of the world. It also affords a glimpse of community life among Jesus' followers, perhaps at Mark's time. To those who have suffered the losses attendant upon following him, Jesus promises, not simply rewards in the life to come, but concrete rewards in this life: **houses and brothers and sisters and mothers and children and lands.** The picture of early Christians as destitute does not square with these promises. For the homeless there will be homes; for those who have abandoned families there will be new families. New social units will take the place of the old. Jesus' words sketch a vision of a real community of believers prepared to live **in this time.** However radical the demands of discipleship, they include a promise of continued life which will require attention to such mundane matters as houses and fields.

Acts offers confirmation of the picture. In the opening chapters of Acts, dealing with possessions is an important facet of community life. Pooling of resources provides the means of caring for the poor. While the social experiment of surrendering all private property seems confined to the early days of the church, the use of wealth is stressed throughout Acts. The church does not abandon property precisely so that there are resources to care for those in need. The group for whom Mark writes did not anticipate abandonment of the world in view of the coming kingdom. People would continue to have need of friends, families, fields, and houses. God would continue to provide such necessities.

There is an important qualifier: **with persecutions.** The community of the faithful will not be completely at home in the world. Jesus offers more specific warnings later: families will be torn apart, people will be arrested and brought before magistrates and councils. The world will not prove to be a comfortable place. Yet the life of faith envisioned here is not characterized by poverty or misery; while a possibility, martyrdom is not the inevitable outcome of faith. The tension is critical and cannot be resolved either by escaping the world or by making peace with it. That is so because what God intends is the redemption of creation. The created order and all its material blessings are God's gifts. What is required is deliverance from bondage to sin so that all may enjoy those gifts.

Early Christian circles undoubtedly included many poor people. The church also included people with property who served

as benefactors. There are ample indications that Mark wrote for
Christians, some of whom who were quite at home in the world.
Jesus must still remind his followers that the world's standards
are an eternal temptation: **the last** shall be **first.** Possessions
continue to be important as the means of caring for those in need.

Third Prediction (10:32-34)

The image that introduces the scene is poignant: Jesus is preceding his followers on the way to **Jerusalem.** The same verb will
be used to speak of Jesus' "leadership" to Galilee after the resurrection (14:28 and 16:7). The amazement and fear of the disciples indicate they have not yet understood all that awaits them
on the road, but their sense of anticipation is growing. Jesus takes
the Twelve and, for the third and final time, offers a glimpse of
what awaits them in Jerusalem.

The forecast is the most explicit: it includes a prediction of
Jesus' betrayal to the **chief priests and the scribes,** his trial at
their hands, his being handed over to the Gentiles and their
maltreatment of him, which includes mockery, beating, spitting,
and execution—and his resurrection after three days.

Dispute about Status and the One Who Serves (10:35-45)

The detailed prediction makes little obvious impact on Jesus'
disciples—or rather, they appear to miss most of it. **James and
John** come immediately with a request that they be granted places
of honor at Jesus' left and right hand when he is **in** his **glory.**
They have understood something about Jesus' announcement that
the kingdom of God is at hand. They have apparently taken , the
King. They may even have heard something about resurrection.
They understand about **glory** and are anxious about securing a
place for themselves. Their picture of the kingdom may be either
a throne scene or a meal at which people are seated. There is
precedent for both: Jesus speaks later of "drinking anew in the
kingdom of God." In Matthew, the kingdom of God is compared

to a feast. Alternatively, both Matthew and Luke record a saying of Jesus according to which the Twelve will "sit on thrones judging the twelve tribes of Israel" (Luke 22:30; Matt. 19:28; the saying in LuAs inappropriate as the response of James and John seems, it does betray at least some sense of anticipation about what is to come. They are not completely without understanding. Yet they are no further along than after Jesus' first prediction of his impending death. Their response is strangely oblivious to the fate that awaits Jesus. Their response provides the final occasion for a discussion of discipleship.

Jesus' statement, **You do not know what you are asking**, is all the more ironic in light of the passion story, which narrates Jesus' death as "King of the Jews," and speaks of two bandits crucified with Jesus, "one at his right and one at his left" (15:27). James and John have no idea what they are asking. The **glory** of Jesus' kingship is of a sort they cannot imagine.

Jesus questions their ability to share his fate: **Are you able to drink the cup that I drink?** The image of the cup comes from Isaiah (51:17, 22). Jesus employs the same image in his prayer in the garden, where he asks that the "cup" be taken from him.

The second image is more unusual: [Are you able] **to be baptized with the baptism with which I am baptized?** While the term "baptism" could be employed in Greek literature to speak about being overwhelmed by catastrophe, the awkwardness of the phrase may suggest that it is chosen because of its place in the church's technical vocabulary. In Paul's letters, the rite of Christian Baptism is interpreted as sharing Christ's death (Rom. 6:1-5; in Ephesians 2 and Colossians 2, sharing in his resurrection as well).

It is tempting to speculate that the images of **cup** and **baptism** are chosen here in light of Christian ritual. Understanding Jesus' words to James and John does not require locating them within Christian tradition. The images of **cup** and **baptism** are sufficiently clear by themselves. In view of that tradition as it is known elsewhere in the New Testament, however, it is tempting to speculate that Jesus' words represent an effort to understand more deeply what is implied in the church's sacramental practices. In Baptism and the Lord's Supper, the faithful share Christ's destiny. That is precisely what James and John want—and it is precisely what they fail to understand. They know that the kingdom will come; what they do not grasp is how and at what cost.

It is a promise, however, that dominates the passage: **You will drink the cup.** . . . **You will be baptized.** . . . Jesus promises that the **We are able** of the two Zebedees is more than a naive and idle boast. They will prove faithful, perhaps in spite of themselves. If Mark's story ends without reporting the final emergence of Jesus' disciples as full-fledged apostles, it certainly prepares us for that eventuality. Jesus makes promises, and this is one: **You will drink.**

While Jesus can make promises about their eventual performance as disciples, he cannot speak about places in the heavenly court. Someone else has responsibility for such arrangements. The use of the passive **for whom it has been prepared** reflects the Jewish convention of using passives to avoid having to use the word "God," out of respect for God's holiness. One's place in the future kingdom is God's business.

The conversation moves the other **ten** disciples to indignation. This is not righteous indignation but jealousy. The reaction is consistent with their earlier performance when they were discussing their respective greatness. Their indignation provides an occasion for a final and climactic saying of Jesus that deals with their relations to one another.

What does it mean to follow Jesus? True discipleship requires a foil: the way things are done among **the Gentiles.** And how is it among the Gentiles? Rulers generally dominate (the root is *dominus*, Latin for "lord," which is the meaning of the Greek word here) those under them; those who aspire to greatness let others "feel the weight of their authority" (JB). The Greek gives the sense of position and authority being used against those below. The world is arranged hierarchically; there are masters and slaves, superiors and inferiors. That is how it is among the Gentiles.

The standards of the world are not those of the disciples. **It shall not be so among you.** Self-seeking, ambition, abuse of authority—all are ruled unacceptable. In keeping with the inversion of values in this community, leadership will involve the denial of familiar models. It is wrong to speak of "masters" and "slaves" in this community. It is the masters who must assume the role of slaves; it is the leaders who must wait on tables.

There is no doubt that the disciples will be given position and authority. But how will it be used? **For the Son of man also came not to be served but to serve, and to give his life as a ransom for many.** Becoming disciples of such a teacher will involve adopting a very different style of leadership.

Jesus is more than an example to be emulated, however. He will be a **ransom.** The bonds that hold captive the human race will not be loosed by an example. People, including the disciples, will require deliverance. They will need to be ransomed. The image is unusual in Mark. Long before the Gospel was written, Christians had come to understand Jesus' death in a wide variety of ways. Among them is the view of his death as a sacrifice. In one of the oldest fragments in the New Testament, the confession in 1 Cor. 15:3ff., Jesus' death is described as "for our sins in accordance with the scriptures." Though no specific biblical passages are mentioned, followers of Jesus had done their homework. Drawing on traditions about martyrs, Jesus followers came to understand his death as a **ransom,** a purchase price.

There is no effort to spell out the systematic implications of such imagery; that would await later theologians like Anselm. There is not just one dominant image in the New Testament by which to comprehend Jesus' death, but many. The phrase in Mark indicates that such reflection can be presupposed. It is possible, as some have suggested, that a biblical passage like Isaiah 53 lies behind the statement. Other scriptural passages are also likely candidates. It is important to note that the Scriptures furnished language that helped not only to define the liberating power of Jesus but also to suggest the implications of that power.

While Jesus' first comments about discipleship suggest that followers must be prepared to take up their crosses and follow even all the way to death, that does not seem to be the issue here. The question is not willingness to die but rather willingness to lead without flaunting authority. The whole passage has to do with status and leadership—hardly of interest or concern to a community of desperate, persecuted believers. Such comments would be of interest to a community that has tasted power and likes it, a community that is already experiencing the pressures of institutionalization. Most of chapter 10 has to do with social relations and organization. The disciples serve once again as examples of inadequate discipleship, and here their problem is self-seeking ambition.

Conformity to the crucified involves such matters as social organization and relations. In the shadow of the cross we get a brief glimpse of a new community in which relations are not governed by power and status but by service and hospitality for those without status—a community in which those who have been ransomed live for others.

Blind Bartimaeus (10:46-52)

The instructions are followed immediately by the second account of Jesus' healing of a **blind man.** On the way to Jerusalem, Jesus passes through **Jericho.** A blind man identified as **the son of Timaeus** hears that Jesus is passing and he cries out for help. His plea, **Jesus, Son of David, have mercy on me,** is the first messianic confession apart from Peter's. **Son of David** is a designation of the Davidic Messiah. The blind man can see the truth that is so completely hidden from others.

The unseeing crowd tries to silence the **beggar,** but without success. His persistence is rewarded when Jesus summons him. In this instance, the conversation serves as a further declaration of faith. The blind man believes Jesus can heal him. His faith is vindicated when Jesus cures his blindness with a word. No special touch or ointment is necessary, nor is privacy any longer required.

More important than the reaction of the crowd is the response of the son of Timaeus: he follows Jesus **on the way.** Unlike the disciples, and unlike the inhabitants of Jerusalem, the son of Timaeus sees the truth.

■ Jerusalem (11:1—16:8)

With Jesus' arrival in Jerusalem, the narrative slows and broadens out. Events in the first 10 chapters move with considerable haste. There is little to mark the passage of time. Jesus' ministry may have lasted for a matter of weeks or, perhaps, for a period of a year. Time indications are much more specific once he arrives in Jerusalem. He enters the city during daylight hours but must put off his temple incursion until the next morning. The narrative creates an impression that events occur within six days (11:1, 11, 12, 19; 14:1, 12, 17; 15:42). The closer to the crucifixion, the more the detail about time and place. Events are dated "two days before the Passover," "on the first day of Unleavened Bread," "at the third hour . . . the sixth hour . . . the ninth hour." Places suddenly are important: Bethany, the Garden of Gethsemane, the home of the chief priest, the praetorium, Golgotha. A full one-third of the narrative is devoted to a few days in Jesus' ministry; one-sixth is devoted to his last 24 hours. What happens in Jerusalem clearly overshadows everything that has taken place thus far.

The heightened interest in detail arises from a preoccupation reflected in the tradition and creeds of the church: the significance of Jesus' ministry is focused on his death and resurrection. "Suffered under Pontius Pilate, crucified, died, and was buried" gets to the heart of the matter. It would be wrong, however, to see in the precise detail only a measure of significance. The narrative makes specific claims: it is under Pontius Pilate and no one else that Jesus was crucified; the place of execution is Golgotha, not Galilee. The appropriate response to the parable of the sower is not to ask what the farmer's name was or where his field was located. The story of Jesus' last days is quite different. Historical particularity is an essential feature of the narrative. While such things can be said about earlier chapters as well, both the details of the passion sequence and the weight of church tradition make it imperative that as interpreters of these chapters in Mark we consider to what extent the historical claims are well founded.

One basic matter that deserves consideration is the sequence of events as Mark describes them. The narrative, as noted above, gives the impression that events encompass no more than a week. There is some reason to doubt that that was actually the case, and commentators have frequently raised such doubts. Mark does not state explicitly that Jesus' grand entrance into Jerusalem initiates a visit for Passover. The ensuing controversies grouped together in chapters 11–12, like the earlier groupings in chapters 2–3, contain few temporal links. Yet Mark intends to create the impression that the events lead up to a crisis at Passover. To what degree this is due to Markan or pre-Markan editing and to what degree it reflects the actual course of events are difficult to determine.

Questions of historical precision are of particular significance in correlating Jesus' last hours with the festival of Passover. Was Jesus last meal with his followers a commemoration of Passover? Did Jesus' trial occur on the high feast day or on the day of Preparation? There is basic disagreement on these questions between the Synoptic Gospels and John. While we can be clear about the viewpoint of the respective Gospels, there may be a need to make decisions between alternatives in reconstructing the actual events. In such cases, interpretation must involve wrestling with "creative historiography," in some cases taking seriously the possibility that Israel's Scriptures may in some cases have given birth to narratives or at least determined how stories were to be remembered.

Even more serious questions have to do with the circumstances of Jesus' trial and death. Who was ultimately responsible for that death? Are the Jews or the Romans to blame? Answers to such questions have had enormous consequences in the history of the church. While such matters as persecuting Jews as "Christ-killers" are in any case absurd, the emotional power of issues surrounding Jesus' death requires that interpreters be as clear as possible about historical as well as exegetical matters.

One final matter deserves a comment. The passion narrative, beginning with Jesus' entry into Jerusalem, is filled with scriptural allusions. Particular sections seem little more than mosaics formed of Old Testament material. There are remarkably few explicit quotations. Identifying scriptural allusions has to do with how the narrative is heard by a particular audience.

Speculation about possible scriptural allusions may, of course, lead to overinterpretation of details that perhaps intend only to lend concreteness and color to the narrative. The importance of scriptures, however, within Jewish and early Christian circles—as well as within Mark's Gospel—justifies attention to possible allusions that provide some interpretive framework for the events of the story.

Jerusalem and the Final Encounter (11:1—12:44)

Royal Entry (11:1-10)

If royal imagery is absent from the account of Jesus' Galilean ministry, it dominates the story of his last days in **Jerusalem.** His entrance into Jerusalem draws on imagery from Israel's royal tradition. In Matthew, the passage from Zech. 9:9 is quoted: "Behold your king is coming to you, humble, and mounted on an ass, and on a colt, the foal of an ass" (Matt. 21:5). While not cited in Mark, it is difficult to imagine that the passage is not in the background. The place of the donkey in the ritual installation of kings is noted in 1 Kings 1 with the anointing of Solomon. At least in its present form, the account of Jesus' entry to Jerusalem depicts it as a royal procession. The formative influence of Psalm

118 is also apparent, as we have already noted (see the comment on the first passion prediction, 8:31). The crowd's chant, **Blessed is he who comes in the name of the Lord!** is taken from Ps. 118:26.

While the account of Jesus' entry is quite specific about details, it also remains enigmatic. When Jesus sends his two disciples to fetch the donkey, do his instructions indicate elaborate preparation or prophetic foresight? Preparation seems more likely, particularly in view of the arrangements Jesus has made later for eating the Passover meal (14:12-15). Jesus not only understands the necessity of what is to come; he seems to have made certain plans—though we are given little insight into the specifics.

The interest in the details of securing **the colt** suggests there is more to the narrative than historical reminiscence. Twice we are told that the colt is bound and must be **untied.** Commentators have suggested here the formative influence of Jacob's oracle regarding Judah in Gen. 49:10-12 and its reference to a bound colt. The relevant verses read:

> The sceptre shall not depart from Judah,
>   nor the ruler's staff from between his feet,
> until he comes to whom it belongs;
>   and to him shall be the obedience of the peoples.
> Binding his foal to the vine,
>   and his ass's colt to the choice vine,
> he washes his garments in blood. . . .

There is much to commend the suggestion. The passage from Genesis was of considerable significance in early Christian tradition. It is likewise clear that the oracle from Jacob's testament was understood messianically in Jewish circles both before and after the Christian era. It is likely that the reference to "the one who comes" in Psalm 118, shouted by the crowd (Mark 11:9), is understood in light of the "coming one" in Gen. 49:11.

The phrase **on which no one has ever sat** likewise seems significant. What is apparently emphasized is the cultic fitness of the animal. The closest parallel is in the description of the animals selected to pull the ark in 1 Sam. 6:7: they are to be cows "upon which there has never come a yoke." Only such beasts are fit for their sacred task. The placing of **garments** in Jesus' path clearly signals respect (see 2 Kings 9:13 for a similar response, when Jehu is anointed as king by Elisha). The **leafy branches** are likewise a mark of honor.

The chanting of lines from Psalm 118 is highly significant. The psalm was appointed for use by pilgrims to Jerusalem, and it was used at the Feast of Tabernacles and Passover. The psalm was significant to Christians for other reasons: it provided insight into the career of the crucified and risen Christ. A verse from the psalm is quoted in Mark 12:11, at the conclusion of Jesus' parable about vineyard tenants. Acts 4:11 indicates the place of the psalm in reflection on Jesus' resurrection ("The stone which the builders rejected has become the head of the corner"). The reference to **the kingdom of our father David that is coming** is appropriate in light of Jesus' identity as "the son of David" (10:48, the confession of the blind man). The prayer for deliverance, **Hosanna,** is about to be answered—though hardly in the manner anyone expects. The story, at least in its present form, may well have been shaped by language from the psalm.

Jesus' entry is the beginning of his acclamation as the coming King. The crowd, we learn, proves fickle, and when Jesus disappoints their expectations, shouts of adoration turn to jeers. In their view, the veneration was misplaced and the acclamations addressed to the wrong candidate. As readers, however, we know what the crowd cannot: Jesus is the coming King. Though he will be rejected, humiliated, and executed, God will vindicate him on the third day. His grand entrance to the city is entirely appropriate—at least when viewed from the privileged position we share with the narrator. That vantage point becomes increasingly significant as the end nears and as the distance widens between readers and participants in the story.

The Cursing of the Temple (11:11-26)

Jesus' destination is **the temple,** which is one of the focal points for the narrative that follows. It is the site of a dramatic disturbance in the Court of the Gentiles (11:15-17). Jesus' provocative act introduces a polemic against the temple that carries through to the end of the Gospel. Jesus explicitly predicts that Jerusalem and the temple will be destroyed (13:1-2). His opponents, the scribes, chief priests, and elders who are officially responsible for the temple, regard him as a threat and plot to do away with him. False witnesses testify at his trial that Jesus threatened the temple (14:57-58). As he hangs on the cross, he is mocked as a would-be destroyer of the temple (15:29-30). And at the moment of his death, there is a dramatic portent in the temple as the curtain is torn in two (15:38). The temple and its impending demise are organizing themes throughout these last chapters.

The account of Jesus' first visit to the temple is remarkably vague. He simply arrives at the temple, surveys the scene, and returns **to Bethany, as it was already late.** We have the sense that some major event is about to take place, but nothing occurs.

It may be that his arrival at the temple is significant by itself in light of Mal. 3:1: "The Lord whom you seek will suddenly come to his temple." If so, the terse, cryptic account of his arrival is intended for readers who know the "script" for the drama.

A strange little story precedes Jesus' eventful visit to the temple on the following day. Approaching **a fig tree** in hopes of finding something to eat, Jesus is disappointed to find no **fruit**—and in response, he curses the tree. The tale is reminiscent of the miracle stories included in the apocryphal Infancy Gospels—little more than crude displays of power, sometimes performed out of anger. By itself, the story is taken up with a sheer display of power. The picture of Jesus is unflattering, and the miracle is devoid of religious significance. One can only with difficulty imagine why such a story would be told among the faithful.

In its present setting, however, the miracle story functions symbolically. One clue is the division of the story into two parts. It serves as an introduction and conclusion to the temple cleansing. As is the case with other such bracketing in Mark, the stories

155

are to be read together. The cursing of the fig tree interprets Jesus' visit to the temple.

Even a symbolic reading of the little story does not eliminate the problems. The account is implausible: Jesus sees the **fig tree in leaf** and yet seeks to find fruit on the tree. During the spring, only early green figs would be produced, and they would be unpalatable. The foliage would indicate what Mark explains in v. 13: **For it was not the season for figs.** If one could not expect fruit at this time, why is the tree cursed? There have been a host of creative suggestions, ranging from thoughtless editing to cryptic scriptural allusions. The most interesting of the suggested scriptural antecedents is Jer. 8:13: "When I would gather them, says the Lord, there are no grapes on the vine, nor figs on the fig tree." As yet, however, no one has been able to explain the strange statements to the satisfaction of other commentators. Such details may serve as reminders that we read as outsiders and there may be things that made sense to another audience that we will never understand.

There are, of course, things that are plain. The story implies that Jesus wanted to find fruit and did not. For that reason, he cursed the tree—with devastating results. The first part of the story ends with the imperfect: the disciples "were listening" to him (RSV: **his disciples heard it**). With the strong words still ringing, Jesus and his band enter the temple for a provocative act.

When Jesus arrives, **the temple** is the scene of buying and selling. The buying and selling of animals, like the changing of money, was a service provided for festival pilgrims. Passover was much like a party. When pilgrims came to Jerusalem, they were expected to celebrate; they were obliged to spend a portion of their income on the festivities. Foreign currency had to be exchanged. People needed to purchase animals for temple offerings and a lamb for the Passover meal. There is nothing to suggest that these services were themselves signs of a corrupt establishment. There is certainly no suggestion that Jesus became angry because merchants were dishonest (see below on the translation **den of robbers** [Greek, *lēstēs*]).

Because so little detail is provided, it is not surprising that Jesus' actions have been interpreted in a variety of ways. Some, like S. G. F. Brandon, have argued that Jesus' actions are tantamount to revolution. Pointing to the comment, **he would not allow any one to carry anything through the temple,** he argues that Jesus took over the whole temple mount. Because it was Passover time, Pilate would have been in the city with his army, stationed at the Fortress Antonia located adjacent to the temple mount. That must mean, argues Brandon, that Jesus' action required considerable force.

One major obstacle such interpretations must surmount is that the Gospels offer no such account—a fact that commentators like Brandon must attribute to a major rewriting of history by the authors of the Gospels. Further, while the author of Mark is allegedly interested in veiling the nature and scope of the takeover, he still includes potentially damaging details in his story ("would permit no vessel to be carried through the temple").

More plausible is the view that Jesus' action was modest and largely symbolic; otherwise he would have been arrested on the spot. Had Jesus been engaged in open rebellion with his followers, it is inconceivable that he alone would have been executed by Pilate—or that it would have taken the Romans more than a few hours to deal with him. His disruption of buying and selling, even enlisting the populace in an effort to prevent others from using the temple as a shortcut, need not have been a large-scale action.

The narrative offers little detail in recounting the incident, but it does offer an assessment. It reports tersely what Jesus taught: **Is it not written, "My house shall be called a house of prayer for all the** Gentiles [RSV, **nations]"? But you have made it a** bandits' lair [RSV, **den of robbers**]! Jesus interprets his actions in terms of what has been **written.** The scriptural passages can be expected to shed light on how the event is to be understood.

The first passage cited, "My house shall be called a house of prayer for all the Gentiles," is taken from Isaiah 56, a chapter devoted to promises that foreigners who "keep justice and do righteousness," and who "keep the sabbath, not profaning it," can count on a place on Mount Zion when God's salvation is revealed. Isaiah's expansive view of who will be included in God's salvation, contrasted with the more exclusive view of an Ezekiel, extends the promises to "all the Gentiles":

> These I will bring to my holy mountain,
>   and make them joyful in my house of prayer;
> their burnt offerings and their sacrifices
>   will be accepted on my altar;
> for my house shall be called a house of prayer
>   for all peoples.
> Thus says the Lord God,
>   who gathers the outcasts of Israel,
> I will gather yet others to him
>   besides those already gathered.
>
>   (56:7-8)

Readers are expected to know that the setting is the Court of the Gentiles, a large area in the temple complex which provided a place for non-Jews to worship—and the only area large enough to accommodate merchants and moneychangers. The temple complex was arranged into areas of heightened sanctity. Gentiles were not allowed into the inner courts. Israelite women could move further into the holy precincts into an area reserved for them; Israelite men had a place closer yet to the holy center. The sanctuary was reserved for priests, the Holy of Holies—the place where God was symbolically present in the temple behind a curtain—for the chief priest alone on the day of atonement.

On one level, Jesus' actions are a protest on behalf of Gentile participation in temple affairs. The presence of merchants in the Court of the Gentiles prevents the temple from serving as their house of prayer.

Jesus' protest has more far-reaching significance, however. The second allusion consists of two words: "bandits' lair." The translation **den of robbers** is unfortunate, since it seems to suggest the problem is dishonesty on the part of the merchants. The image comes from the prophet Jeremiah. The image appears in Jeremiah's denunciation of the temple and prophecy of its destruction:

> Do not trust in these deceptive words: "This is the temple of the Lord, the temple of the Lord, the temple of the Lord." . . . Behold, you trust in deceptive words to no avail. Will you steal, murder, commit adultery, swear falsely, burn incense to Baal, and go after other gods that you have not known, and then come and stand before me in this house, which is called by my name, and say, "We are delivered!"—only to go on doing all these abominations? Has this house, which is called by my name, become a den of robbers [bandits' lair] in your eyes?
>
> (Jer. 7:4-11)

The sermon goes on to promise that God will do to the "house which is called by my name" as he did to the temple at Shiloh, which was destroyed. Were it not for friends in high places, Jeremiah would have been executed for treason for preaching such a sermon. Jesus, it turns out, has no such advocates.

The expression "bandits' lair" gives the sense of a more fundamental corruption. While the occasion for Jesus' protest is desecration of the Court of the Gentiles, his attack is more basic. The temple is thoroughly corrupt, as was the case once before in the history of Jerusalem. Evidence of that corruption will be the refusal of its priestly leaders to accept Jesus. Jeremiah's sermon offers precedent for Jesus' attack on Israel's central religious institution—and even precedent for predicting its destruction. The reference to Jeremiah is a veiled threat that will become explicit shortly.

The familiar image of Jesus' "cleansing" the temple is far too weak an appraisal of what is occurring. Jesus' act is symbolic of something more serious: it is a sign that the temple will be destroyed. The story of the fig tree provides a more suitable image: this is the "cursing" of the temple. The house called by God's name has not served its appointed purpose. Like Jeremiah, Jesus declares that its days are numbered.

The temple was in fact destroyed when Jerusalem fell to Titus's legions in A.D. 70 at the conclusion of the four-year seige. Those familiar with the story would be struck by the aptness of the image Jesus borrows from Jeremiah. The temple served as the last bastion of defense for the Jewish rebels—whom Josephus contemptuously termed "bandits" (*lēstai*). Roman legions broke through its walls, slaughtered the defenders, and destroyed the temple, which would never be rebuilt. While dating Mark's Gospel is speculative, it is possible that Jesus' curse had even deeper significance for readers.

The reaction of the temple leadership is predictable: they fear Jesus' popularity with the crowds and want him out of the way. Jesus' provocative act sets in motion the machinery that will eventually bring him to trial and secure his execution.

The narrative returns to **the fig tree** Jesus cursed, which Peter observes has been **withered**. Peter's comment prompts a brief discussion of faith. The first pronouncement summarizes what miracle stories have made clear: **faith in God** can accomplish extraordinary things. So do not hesitate to pray, Jesus tells his followers—that is, to ask of God even what seems impossible.

In catchword fashion, the teaching about the power of **prayer** recalls another saying about prayer, this time about the importance of forgiveness. Jesus declares that before asking for God's forgiveness, you should **forgive** others against whom you may have something. The words recall the petition of the Lord's prayer: "Forgive us our sins, as we forgive those who sin against us."

While the various sayings about prayer seem artificially linked, it is hardly accidental that Jesus chooses precisely this occasion to teach the disciples about prayer. He has just cursed the temple, which was intended to be a "house of prayer for all the Gentiles," but which is not. If the temple is to be destroyed, will there be a new "house of prayer"? Will the disciples have any role to play at such a place of prayer? While the imagery is not fully developed, a reference made at Jesus' trial may offer some glimpse of what will take the temple's place after its destruction—that reference is to a "temple not made with hands" (see the discussion of the trial, below).

The Question of Authority (11:27-33)

Jesus' return to the city after his dramatic intrusion into the affairs of the temple initiates a series of controversies. The somewhat artificial framework and transitions only draw attention to the collection, much as in chapters 2–3. It remains to determine what distinguishes these controversies from those earlier in Jesus' ministry and what role they play in the unfolding of the passion narrative.

The first of the disputes has to do with Jesus' **authority,** a problem since early in the Gospel. The whole batallion of authorities—**the chief priests and the scribes and the elders**—pose the question, **Who gave you this authority to do** these things? Jesus speaks on his own authority, not citing precedent.

In the familiar style of a debater, Jesus answers with a counter-question: What do you think of **the baptism of John?** Was it a human enterprise or from God? His interrogators are unable to answer. Knowing John's reputation with the crowds, they cannot offer a negative evaluation; they have no desire to alienate the common **people.** On the other hand, they cannot offer a positive view of his ministry since they did not acknowledge John as **a prophet** or submit to baptism by him. Thus impaled on the horns of a dilemma, they are unable to answer. So Jesus refuses to answer their question.

The dispute deals with more than Jesus' silencing of his critics. John was introduced in Mark as Jesus' forerunner. It is with John's arrest that Jesus begins to preach. When Herod gets word of Jesus' activities, he fears John has been brought back to life. The same ambiguity attends Jesus as attended John. **The people** regard both as prophets, while the leaders fear their popularity. Just as John proved to be a threat to Herod, Jesus will threaten the Jerusalem authorities—and like John, Jesus will finally be "treated with contempt" and put to death.

Parable of the Wicked Tenants (12:1-12)

Jesus responds to the question about his authority with a parable about **a vineyard** and its **tenants.** The image of the vineyard as a symbol for Israel is familiar from tradition, particularly Isaiah. In its present form, the parable is a thinly veiled allegory which offers a preview of what to expect from the priestly leadership and how their actions are to be understood.

The situation the parable presumes is not as far-fetched as it may appear. Absentee ownership of land was common in Galilee and a cause of considerable resentment among the peasants. According to inheritance laws, if an owner of a piece of property died without an **heir,** the ownership was transferred to the first claimants—in this case, those already working the land. In the story, **the tenants** interpret the long absence of **the owner** as a sign that he might not return. Their refusal to pay amounts to a test of strength. When the heir comes, they view his arrival as a sign the owner is dead. By killing the **son,** they hope to secure ownership of the vineyard. Their hasty action is a gross miscalculation, however, which secures their destruction.

The allegorical features are rather obvious. Perhaps clearest is the reference to the **beloved son,** familiar from two passages where the words are used by God to speak of Jesus. The opening imagery is likewise allegorical. The reference to the **hedge, the wine press,** and the **tower** come from Isaiah 5—the "Song of the Vineyard," a prophetic indictment of Jerusalem that ends with a threat that God will tear up the vineyard that has yielded only wild grapes. Interestingly, that portion of Isaiah is interpreted image-for-image as a reference to the Jerusalem temple by the targumist in the Targum of Isaiah. In other words, the "Song of the Vineyard" served later generations of Jewish interpreters as a way of understanding the destruction of the temple. The details from Isaiah 5 may well serve the same function here in Mark.

The reference to the succession of **servants** who are maltreated may well refer to the prophets—though in view of the previous reference to John the Baptizer, the maltreatment of the emissaries seems particularly fitting as a description of John's fate. By the first century, Israel's rejection of the prophets had become a common preaching theme. Legends had grown up about the martyrdom of the prophets, such as the legend that Isaiah had been sawn in half. Stephen can assume such knowledge in his speech: "Which of the prophets did not your fathers persecute? And they killed those who announced beforehand the coming of the Righteous One . . ." (Acts 7:52). Such traditions are brought to bear as an interpretation of what will happen to Jesus. Like the prophets and like John, Jesus will be treated with contempt and cast out.

The criminal actions of the tenants secure their destruction. **What will the owner of the vineyard do? He will come and destroy the tenants, and give the vineyard to others.** Careful reading is required here. Who are the **others**? Christian interpreters have traditionally read the verse as announcing the rejection of Israel and the passing of the birthright to "Christians." There is no justification for such a reading. The words "Christian" and "church" are never used in Mark. There is no suggestion that a Christian church composed of Gentiles will displace Israel as God's elect. The **others** are not specified here. There will be rejection and replacement—in this context, the **tenants** must be understood as the temple leaders, the scribes, chief priests, and elders. However, **tenants** should not be understood as referring to Israel in general. Thus, while Gentiles will be included among the **others,** Mark gives no indication that the price will be the rejection of Israel. Jesus promises here that those who reject him will be rejected—and it is the aristocratic leadership that will condemn him to death. Their punishment is precisely specified in the announcement of the temple's impending demise.

The parable is concluded with a quotation of Ps. 118:22, a verse we have noted earlier (see the discussion of 8:31). The citation provided Jesus' followers with a way of understanding his death and resurrection as being "in accordance with the scriptures." According to the psalm, the **stone** will be **rejected** by **the builders** but vindicated by God. Here, the **builders** are the temple leadership—those who try **to arrest him,** because they know he is telling the parable against them.

Jesus' parable thus provides an explanation for what follows: he will be rejected by the corrupt leadership of the "Lord's vineyard." According to an earlier image, the temple has not borne the expected fruit. Here, the tenants are unwilling to pay what is due from the fruit they have gathered. They see the execution of the heir as an opportunity to secure their existence. Their miscalculation will result in their destruction.

We should not miss the political overtones in the parable. Historically, the priestly aristocracy was committed to peace. They were opposed to the leaders of sedition in the north (Galilee). The real unrest, with the formation of a particular political party, did not occur until after Jesus' death, perhaps in the 40s, but before Mark was written. The parable takes the unruly behavior of northern peasants and uses it to shed light on the actions of the priestly aristocracy in Jerusalem. The effect would have been highly ironic.

Taxes to Caesar (12:13-17)

The next controversies deal with issues of considerable interest not just to Jesus' contemporaries but to later generations of Jews and "Christians." The first has to do with the matter of **taxes.** In A.D. 6, Judea became a Roman province, administered by a procurator instead of Herod's family. Taxes were paid to Rome, in Roman coin—collected by Jewish tax farmers whom many viewed as collaborators with Rome. Some Jews were convinced that one could not be a Jew and honor **Caesar** as lord, a title reserved for God. Josephus, the Jewish historian, writes that Judas the Galilean protested the census under Quirinius on the grounds that "the assessment carried with it a status amounting to downright slavery" (*Antiquities* 18.4). Roman coins, with Caesar's image, were a religious offense—the more so after Jesus' day, when the inscription *dominus* (lord) was added.

The question put to Jesus is thus one of burning political significance: Can one be a Jew and still **pay taxes to Caesar?** Answering the question would put Jesus in a difficult position whatever his reply. If he denied that people should pay taxes, he could be arrested for sedition. Precisely that charge is made in Luke: "We found this man perverting our nation, and forbidding us to give tribute to Caesar . . ." (Luke 23:2). By permitting taxes, Jesus would alienate those who opposed Roman rule, thus undermining his popularity with the crowds.

Jesus' answer cleverly avoids the dilemma on which his opponents sought to impale him. However, the answer is not as ambiguous as some have suggested. While Jesus does not give an unambiguous endorsement to Roman rule and the legitimacy of taxes, he certainly does not endorse the religious position that regarded taxation as unacceptable. Jesus is no Zealot. His response leaves open the possibility of paying taxes to Caesar in Roman coin as rendering **to Caesar the things that are Caesar's**— while at the same time leaving open the possibility that one will be in conflict with Rome if one renders **to God the things that are God's.**

Jesus' words hold open the possibility that one may be a Jew and pay taxes to Caesar. What they do not offer is a blanket endorsement of secular authority as ruling by divine right. Jesus did not promise peaceful coexistence between Rome and those whose primary allegiance is to the Lord God. The Roman government certainly did not understand Jesus to be politically harmless. It is only a bit later that Jesus is executed as a threat to the state. The confession of Jesus as the Lord's Christ was still too politically dangerous.

The Question of Resurrection (12:18-27)

The second question put to Jesus is asked by **Sadducees.** Little is known about the group, since no Saducean writings have been preserved. The group was apparently small in number, made up largely of the priestly aristocracy. Josephus describes them as a "philosophy," a school characterized by a particular viewpoint. From the little information Josephus and the New Testament provide, we can gain at least an impression of Sadducees. They were "strict constructionists," insisting on a literal reading of their constitution, the Torah. Born out of the conflict over Hellenization during the time of the Hasmoneans, Sadducees were concerned to safeguard the sacred tradition from corruption. The center of the Scriptures was for them the Torah, the five books of Moses. They did not endorse the Pharisaic oral law (the tradition of the elders), regarding it as an innovation. According to Acts, "Sadducees say that there is no resurrection, nor angel, nor spirit" (Acts 23:8), presumably because such things cannot be found in the Torah.

The dispute with Jesus has to do with belief in the resurrection, a belief that separated Pharisee from Sadducee in Jesus' day. The question of the Sadducees, seemingly contrived, is a clever attempt to reduce belief in the **resurrection** to absurdity. The Sadducees begin by quoting the Scriptures—specifically, the law of levirate marriage from Deuteronomy 25. The law, designed to assure heirs to a family, provided that **brothers** were obliged to have children with sisters-in-law in the event a brother died without heirs.

The force of the question, **Whose wife will she be?** depends upon the absurd problem created by the law. If there is a resurrection, so the argument goes, why would God give a law that made for such an impossible situation? The implication is that the problem is due to the doctrine of the resurrection, not the Torah. There will be no complication for anyone following the law because the whole idea of resurrection and a world-to-come is a human invention. The elaborate question seeks to expose the absurdity in believing there will be a resurrection.

Jesus' response is thoroughly Pharisaic and learned in tone. The statement about "not knowing **the scriptures**" implies an academic setting in which there is dispute about what the Scriptures really say.

The first point arises from traditional Jewish angelology. The dead **neither marry nor are given in marriage, but are like angels in heaven.** The notion that the bonds of marriage do not extend to the next world is familiar from Jewish sources. The particular reason offered here—that people will become **like angels**—presumes some specific argument. What are angels like? While there is room for speculation, most likely the notion here is that angels are male. Names of angels in the Old Testament are male names: Michael, Uriel, Gabriel, etc. The mysterious "sons of God" in Genesis 6, angelic figures who have intercourse with women and give birth to the race of "giants," reveal a similar view (Luke uses the expression "sons of God" and "sons of the resurrection" to speak of the state of those after the resurrection [20:36]). The mythology is presumed in the Gospel of Thomas, in a saying attributed to Jesus that concludes the work:

Simon Peter said to them: Let Mary go away from us, for women are not worthy of life. Jesus said: Lo, I shall lead her, so that I may make her a male, that she too may become a living spirit, resembling you males. For every woman who makes herself a male will enter the kingdom of heaven.

(#114)

Few will find such words comforting or convincing. More likely, modern readers will take offense. We should remember that we are dealing here with mythic language—words taken from human experience that describe what is beyond experience. Further, mythic language is culture-bound, as is all language. We do not have the right to assume that our pictures of the age to come are naturally superior to others—but neither need we invest too much in first-century imagery depicting heavenly existence, even if the source is Jesus or the evangelist.

The second "proof" of the resurrection is cast in the form of an interpretation of Exod. 3:6. The interpretation is academic in form and outlook, much like proofs of the resurrection attributed to rabbinic sages. Pharisees could, of course, find reference to resurrection in late books like Daniel, but, because the Torah was regarded as the primary authority, proof of the resurrection from one of the five books was regarded as most convincing.

The "proof" in the verse from Exodus seems to lie in the absence of the past tense of the verb "to be." The passage could have said, "I was the God of Abraham. . . ." Because it does not— because the absence of a past tense implies a present tense—the passage does not view **Abraham, Isaac,** and **Jacob** as eternally

167

dead, according to Jesus. Thus the passage is a proof that there is life after death—and that there will be a resurrection.

Some are offended by the artificial character of the proof, believing that Jesus would not have employed such shaky argumentation. We may grant to those who hold this view that it is not clear that the passage should be attributed to Jesus. Much of the "schoolish" scriptural interpretation occurred within Christian circles, among those Matthew terms "scribes trained for the kingdom of heaven." Jesus was probably not a sage. His standard form of teaching was more popular, like the parable. That granted, we must also say that there are fundamental problems with the view of those who find fault with Jesus' method of argumentation here. Whether the argument is offered by Jesus or by later believers, the rules of argument are those of a particular culture. "Scientific" scriptural interpretation as practiced in Jewish and non-Jewish circles through the Middle Ages followed established procedures that are different from our own. Offense at such modes of argumentation is foolish. To expect post-Enlightenment arguments from first-century interpreters is a form of imperialism. We must appreciate the scriptural arguments of another age— then find appropriate ways to make our own for our own time.

In this passage, Jesus is depicted as a typical sage, capable of interpreting the Scriptures with the most adept. His "proof" of the resurrection is thoroughly Pharisaic. The point of the story is that one can believe in the resurrection while holding fast to the Scriptures. Sadducees are thus branded as unenlightened, understanding neither the Scriptures nor the power of God.

The Question of True Sacrifice (12:28-34)

The last of the questions put to Jesus seems more sympathetic. While the inquirer is identified as a **scribe,** we are not told that he intends to trap Jesus. The question is, in fact, a familiar one from Jewish tradition: Is there a way of summarizing the commandments?

Jesus' response is highly traditional. He recites the *Shema*, the prayer from Deut. 6:4 which Jews were obliged to pray daily: **Hear, O Israel: the Lord our God, the Lord is one.** The command to **love God** with all one's being is linked with a second, likewise traditional: **Love your neighbor as yourself** (see Lev. 19:18). The summary is in no sense radical. Jesus says nothing that a good Jew would not applaud.

The important shift occurs in the words of the **scribe.** After summarizing Jesus' response and pronouncing it satisfactory, the scribe adds a comment: to do these commandments **is much more than all whole burnt offerings and sacrifices.** Opposition between doing the commandments and temple sacrifices is certainly not part of Jewish tradition. Much of the law has to do with rules for proper sacrifice. The language of the temple did, however, provide Israel with ways of speaking about forms of worship, like prayer, that were more ordinary and therefore different from temple sacrifices. Particularly in the Psalms, temple language is used to speak of prayer as the "sacrifice of praise," the "sacrifice of the lips." Although this would certainly seem to endorse forms of worship different from sacrifices, such usage does not imply an opposition between prayer and sacrifices.

There were, however, branches of Jewish tradition in which such scriptural possibilities provided a means of opposition to the temple. The inhabitants at Qumran, for example, understood their communal worship as sacrificial, accomplishing atonement for Israel. Their interpretation did not arise from an opposition to bloody sacrifices but from a conviction that the priests in charge of the temple were corrupt and all their sacrifices invalid. Their substitution of devotion to the law for active participation in the sacrificial cult was a temporary strategy, valid only until they could secure control of the temple.

After the temple was destroyed by the Romans in 70, a similar task faced the rabbinic sages. On the one hand, they scrupulously preserved discussions of ritual matters as if the temple cult might once again be restored. On the other hand, they created a piety which substituted prayer and obedience to the Torah for bloody sacrifice.

Jesus' approval of the words of the scribe (Jesus tells him, **You are not far from the kingdom of God**) places Jesus squarely in the camp of those who believed it was possible to be a Jew without a temple. The passage again anticipates Jesus' prediction that the temple will be destroyed (13:2) and offers a glimpse of what will take its place: obedience to the law. Doing what Deuteronomy and Leviticus require is worth far more than what happens in the temple. The passage prepares for the time when the temple will be no more.

With Jesus' response, his critics are silenced. Unable to trap him in debate, they will have to find another way to silence him.

David's Son (12:35-37)

With the conclusion of the interrogation by opponents, Jesus poses a question of his own. The question is in the form of learned comment on scriptural passages and most probably reflects Christian exegetical tradition. Jesus is pictured here as a scriptural scholar capable of learned debate. His interpretation provides scriptural underpinnings for the confession of Jesus as the crucified and exalted Messiah.

The question is formulated as an academic debate: **How can the scribes say . . . ?** The question is reminiscent of the disciples' question on the way down from the Mount of Transfiguration. The issue here is messianic tradition, specifically the identity of the Messiah as **Son of David.** There is ample evidence that the term "Messiah" was in the first century a designation for the coming Davidic King. **Son of David** is a title; the substance, if not the title itself, is derived from such passages as 2 Sam. 7:10-14 and Psalm 89, which recall God's promise of an offspring to David who will sit on his throne. The title is used earlier in Mark. Blind Bartimaeus hails Jesus as "son of David."

Jesus' question identifies a potential conflict within the scriptural tradition. **The scribes** say that the Messiah will be David's son. Yet in Ps. 110:1—a passage which Jesus assumes all regard as "messianic," i.e. as David's words about the coming Messiah-King—David refers to the Messiah as **Lord** (the second "lord" in the verse). That is not the way a father generally refers to **his son.** Jesus' statement follows good rabbinic precedent in asking about an apparent contradiction in the Scriptures. How can passages like 2 Samuel 7 and Jeremiah 33 speak of the Messiah as David's son, while in Ps. 110:1 David calls this figure "lord"? Is there a contradiction within the Scriptures?

Jesus' audience would, of course, have rejected the possibility of scriptural contradictions. Contradictions were only apparent. Explaining the alleged contradictions often required ingenuity and sometimes provided the clever teacher an opportunity to score a point in an argument. Jesus plays the role of sage here, citing an alleged scriptural contradiction as a way of making a point with his argumentative audience. Cleverness is less important, however, than the argument made in support of faith in the crucified and risen Christ.

The answer to Jesus' question is not supplied. He ends with a challenge to his audience: **David himself calls him Lord. So how is he his** [David's] **son?** The solution must be implied—known in this case to Mark's reader. The Messiah must be David's son; the Scriptures say so. Yet David apparently **calls him Lord.** How can both be true? Only if the Son of David is exalted to the right hand of God—only if the Messiah, according to the Christian view, is raised from the dead. Jesus, the one who died as "King of the Jews," was raised from the dead and exalted to the right hand of God. He is thus both **Son of David** and the one David calls **Lord.** Only if Jesus is the crucified and risen Christ can the alleged scriptural contradiction be explained.

In Luke, the proof is taken one step further: the promise of eternal domain in 2 Samuel 7 ("I will establish the throne of his kingdom for ever") is fulfilled only by Jesus' exaltation to God's **right hand,** where he reigns forever (Luke 1:32-33; Acts 2:23-33, 13:32-37).

Many commentators have seen in this passage a rejection of Jewish messianism. They take Jesus' statement to be a rejection of the Davidic Messiah. That interpretation fails to understand both Jewish messianic tradition, according to which there is no other Messiah than the Davidic offspring, and the form of scriptural reflection current in learned circles within the Jewish and Christian community.

This passage offers evidence of creative reinterpretation of Jewish messianic tradition in view of the death and resurrection of Jesus the Messiah. It seems most likely, therefore, that this particular passage derives from the church rather than from Jesus' own scriptural reflection.

What is striking about the controversy section is how "Jewish" are the issues discussed. Can one be a member of God's people and pay taxes to Caesar? Can one hold to the Scriptures and still believe in the resurrection? Can one serve God without a temple in which sacrifices are offered? Can one believe in a Messiah who is both David's son and the "Lord" enthroned at God's right hand? The questions are precisely the sort that would be of interest to Pharisaic Jews who had witnessed the destruction of the temple and its aftermath—and who believed Jesus to be the promised Messiah.

The placement of these controversies within the framework of Jesus' last days as contributing factors in his eventual rejection seems to align Jesus and his movement with a particular segment of the Jewish community. Mark's audience has an investment in matters of concern to Jews. It is difficult, therefore, to regard Mark's implied audience as "Gentiles" with no investment in Israel's tradition or institutions. While the narrative presumes some among the readers who require technical information about certain Jewish customs, much of the story seems directed to people who regard themselves as part of Israel—people as much in need of clarification about the temple's demise as others among the people of God.

These controversies in particular rule out those interpretations that speak of Mark as recounting "the rejection of Israel." Some will be punished—Sadducees and priests in particular. The future of Israel is far from closed off, however.

Beware of Scribes (12:38-40)

Jesus follows with an attack on **the scribes**, by which he means religious authorities. His depiction of these authorities as enjoying public prominence is reminiscent of his earlier description of

"Gentiles" as loving authority and position (10:42-45). His attack on a piety that sees no opposition between "devouring" **widows' houses** and long prayers is reminiscent of the attacks against empty piety by Israel's great prophets. The **widow** was a good test of the community's resolve to protect the helpless. Deprived of a husband, a widow was dependent upon the charity of the community. The religious leaders demonstrate no care of widows. The injunction to "love your neighbor as yourself" has made no impact on their piety.

There is some question as to what Jesus means by "devouring widows' houses," since scribes were not allowed to charge for their services. It may be they are accused of abusing hospitality (see the *Didache*, where a false prophet can be recognized if he stays more than three days with one family), perhaps from those least able to provide it.

The Widow's Penny (12:41-44)

The example of false piety is followed by an example of true piety. While the scribes devour widows' houses, one destitute **widow** contributes all she has to the temple. **The treasury** was used to support the priesthood. Jews from all over were expected to pay an annual tax; contributions could be made at any time. What sets the widow apart is not the size of her gift but its totality: **She has put in everything she had.** She is able to part with her possessions—unlike the young man who comes to Jesus and "goes away sorrowing" because he cannot sell what he has. We can recall the promise of Jesus earlier: those who lose their lives will save them. This woman gives "her whole life" (RSV, **her whole living**), as Jesus will give himself away as a "ransom for many."

A Glimpse of the Future (13:1-37)

The section that follows is generally labeled "The Little Apocalypse." Titles can be helpful or misleading. This one is both. The designation "Little Apocalypse" derives from the parallels between the discourse and "apocalyptic" works, like the book of

Daniel or the Revelation (Apocalypse) of John. Such visionary works purport to disclose heavenly secrets, usually about the future, employing bizarre and highly conventionalized imagery.

While Jesus' discourse makes use of some conventional imagery (the "sacrilege that makes desolate" and the vision of the Son of man coming with the clouds, both from Daniel), neither his brief discourse nor Mark's Gospel can be termed apocalypses. Few of the standard conventions of apocalyptic literature are present; the cosmic imagery makes up only a small portion of warnings about what is to come; the seer is not some hero of the past who is told at the conclusion to seal the prophecy until some future date; and, most importantly, the glimpse into the future does not conclude Mark's Gospel but introduces the account of Jesus' trial and death. Overall, the title "Little Apocalypse" is probably more misleading than helpful.

Like the small collection of parables in chapter 4, Jesus' discourse is important as a way of understanding what is to occur. The chapter projects beyond the ending of Mark's Gospel and thus helps to place Jesus' story within a larger framework. The empty tomb will not mark the end of what God has determined "must" occur. Our concern should be how the immediate "tribulations" of Jesus and his band are to be understood against the backdrop of the future—and how the tribulations that lie ahead appear in view of Jesus' confrontation with the religious and political leadership.

It is probably impossible to read the chapter without recognizing the earmarks of editing. It seems likely that some of the material has had a history prior to its incorporation into Mark's Gospel. Such was the case, of course, with much apocalyptic imagery. While unearthing the prior history of the material that makes up the chapter is a legitimate task, the focus of our study is the present form of Jesus' predictions.

The Destruction of the Temple (13:1-2)

The warnings are set as Jesus leaves **the temple,** his public ministry now ended. The discourse marks a brief pause in the action. The **disciples'** admiration for the temple and its courts provides the occasion for Jesus' explicit prediction: Jerusalem will be totally destroyed. What has been implied since Jesus' arrival in Jerusalem is now stated explicitly.

The Birth-pangs (13:3-23)

The Mount of Olives is the setting for the predictions that follow. Jesus' audience is the inner circle of **Peter, James,** and **John,** with the addition of **Andrew.** Their question about when **these things** will take place occasions the lengthy warnings about what is to come. The temple's destruction signals the beginning of a series of events that lead inexorably to the end of all things.

While the horizons of Jesus' glimpse into the future are cosmic, the first trial about which he warns his followers relates to matters internal to the community of believers: **Take heed that no one leads you astray.** Acknowledging the dimensions of the troubles ahead should not blind the faithful to what is near at hand. There will be persecution from the outside, but there will also be temptations from within. Many will presume to speak **in my name,** Jesus warns. The formula, **I am he!** should be translated, "I am the one." The phrase **lead astray** is a technical term used of false prophets (Deuteronomy 13).

The history of the church is eloquent testimony to the havoc wrought by competing voices presuming to speak for God. It was not persecution as much as internal dissension that nearly tore the Christian movement to pieces in the second century. The development of the canon and the evolution of institutional structures did not solve the problem but at least provided ways to cope. It is unreasonable to expect a solution to a problem that will not be resolved until the end of time. Until the end, however, the faithful are to beware of those who presume to speak in Jesus' name.

The reference to **wars and rumors of wars** fits any period in history, though here it points forward to the troubled decade of the 60s, which ended with the war against Rome and the eventual destruction of the temple in A.D. 70. Wars will come, says Jesus; "it is necessary" (RSV, **this must take place**). The necessity is viewed here as due to the decision of God—the same necessity that stands over Jesus' career. Not accidentally, scriptural language—from Daniel and Isaiah—is used to speak of these wars to come, since it is in the Scriptures that God's will is disclosed. The necessity that governs the future is reason to take heart if God is to be trusted—which is the point of Jesus' instructions and of Mark's Gospel.

The wars do not mark **the end** of the age. The passage underscores the point: **the end is not yet.** These terrible events mark the beginning of a series that must occur prior to the close of the age. **Wars, earthquakes,** and **famines** are but **the beginning of the birth-pangs.**

The expression is important. The translation "sufferings" in early editions of the RSV seriously missed the point. The image of **birth-pangs** betrays an orientation. By characterizing the disasters to come as birth-pangs, the seer—Jesus in this case—testifies to God's control over history and to the essential hopefulness of the future. History is compared to natural processes. There is a certain rhythm in nature, with certain necessities. Birth is one such process. Prior to the birth of the child, as mothers know, pain becomes intense. The closer to the birth, the worse the pain. History is like that. The closer to the end, the worse the suffering.

The image of **birth-pangs** is essentially hopeful. It suggests there is a purpose to the suffering, a direction to all of history. Such hopefulness is in no sense naive; the reality of pain and suffering is taken with infinite seriousness. But even the pain and suffering are caught up in a movement that is headed somewhere. The goal is a new beginning. History's termination marks the birth of a new age. Paul uses the same imagery in Romans:

> The creation itself will be set free from its bondage to decay and obtain the glorious liberty of the children of God. We know that the whole creation has been groaning in travail together until now; and not only the creation, but we ourselves, who have the first fruits

of the Spirit, groan inwardly as we wait for adoption as sons, the redemption of our bodies.

(Rom. 8:21-23)

The terrible events that lie ahead are not the end; they are the beginning of the birth-pangs. God's kingdom cannot be far off.

The next warnings return to the more intimate dimensions of community life. The faithful will be persecuted. Jesus promises that his followers will be handed over to Sanhedrins (**councils**), **beaten in synagogues** (see Paul's list of his sufferings in 2 Corinthians 11, which includes beatings at the hands of synagogue authorities), and dragged before **governors and kings** to give **testimony**. Note that the terms "witness" and "testify" belong to the language of the court. The setting for such witnessing will be trials before courts of law.

Such predictions are more than vague possibilities. Their reality is confirmed when Jesus is handed over by Judas and must appear before the Jerusalem Sanhedrin and Pilate. In this sense, Jesus' own experience only confirms the picture he sketches of what his followers can expect of the future.

Among the warnings about persecution and testimony appears another feature of the history God has determined: **the gospel must first be preached** to all the Gentiles (RSV: **nations**). Preaching is one of the "necessities" ordained by God. **First** apparently means "before the end." Within this divine necessity is embedded a promise: the gospel *will* be preached. Persecutions will not silence the preachers. The word will be spread. This is not a command but a declaration of what God will make possible. Others—"all the Gentiles"—will hear of Jesus because God has willed it to be.

The verse is one of many in Mark that makes a promise about what will occur after Jesus' ministry—thus after the conclusion of Mark's story. The end of Jesus' story will not mark the end of the gospel ministry. Promises create a momentum that must carry readers beyond the frightened silence at the empty tomb.

And how will God accomplish the preaching and testimony? The story has thus far given little reason to invest confidence in

those selected for the task. **Do not be anxious beforehand what
you are to say,** Jesus instructs his disciples. You will be "inspired."
The book of Acts takes up that promise as one of its themes. In
Mark, it remains a promise. The disciples, who have thus far
understood little and do not know what to say, will one day speak
the right words. That will be the work of the **Spirit.**

The image behind this notion of inspired speech is prophecy.
One of the distinctive features of the Christian movement was
the conviction that the prophetic spirit had again been poured
out. Paul lists prophecy as one of the church's spiritual endow-
ments (Rom. 12:6; 1 Corinthians 12). Peter's speech in Acts 2
employs a quotation from Joel to argue that the spirit of prophecy
has now been poured out as a sign that the "last days" are at
hand. In Acts the appearance of the apostles before authorities
develops the theme that unlearned men can offer such compelling
testimony (Acts 4:13). The *Didache*, among other works, indicates
that at the turn of the century there were such "inspired" speakers
in early Christian circles. Such promises of inspiration are tempered by warnings of false prophets (see below on 13:21-22). The
early church was to learn, as did ancient Israel, that inspiration
is a mixed blessing.

The gospel will find ready hearers; the testimony will be effective. But faith in Jesus will mean division as well as unity.
Families will be divided by the preached word. We have already
observed that division in the case of Jesus' own family. His followers "left everything and followed" him. Jesus has promised
that those who leave families for the sake of the gospel will find
new brothers and sisters. Here, he reiterates his warnings about
the cost of discipleship. We know from Paul's letters that this
division was a reality. Families were broken over the issue of faith
in Jesus. Eventually the Jewish community itself was fractured,
leading to the birth of a movement that understood itself as
"Christian" rather than "Jewish." Faith will prove to be costly,
Jesus warns.

You will be hated by all. The little band of followers cannot expect instant popularity when their leader is rejected by everyone, ending his career on a cross. In the immediate future, disciples will be perceived as members of a countercultural movement and will receive appropriate treatment from the world. There will be an end to the troubles, but not yet. What is required is endurance: **He who endures to the end will be saved.**

The passage that follows might qualify as "apocalyptic." It draws on cryptic imagery from the book of Daniel. In Daniel, the **desolating sacrilege** probably refers to the desecration of the Jerusalem temple by Antiochus Epiphanes, the Syrian ruler who sacrificed swine on the altar in his effort to Hellenize Judea (the story is recounted in 1 Maccabees). The mysterious image in Daniel invites the reader to decipher it (**let the reader understand**). Such language better suits the motif of heavenly disclosure than ordinary prose.

The same is true in Mark: the image refers to something the reader is expected to know. Readers are addressed directly by the narrator. Two suggestions have been made from the historical environment of Mark's Gospel. The first locates the image within the middle decade of the first century, when Gaius Caligula, the Roman Emperor, commanded that a statue of himself be erected in the temple. Irritated that Jews refused to revere him as god, the unbalanced emperor gave orders that could have easily led to open revolt. The legate of Syria, Petronius, yielded to the petitions of Jews, fearing rebellion, and delayed erecting the statue. The assasination of Gaius prevented a crisis (Josephus, *Jewish Wars* 2.184–203; *Antiquities* 18.257–309).

The problem with reading the **desolating sacrilege** as a reference to the statue of Gaius is that it never arrived in Jerusalem and the temple was not desecrated. It is possible that the image at some point served as a warning of the impending crisis, but the crisis was averted and could hardly serve Mark's readers as a credible reference to an event past or future.

A second alternative, perhaps more plausible, is that the image is employed as a reference to Titus, the Roman general who stood in the Holy of Holies when the temple was finally captured in the war of 66–70. That would explain an interesting grammatical irregularity in Mark: while the noun *bdelygma* is neuter, the participle that describes it, "standing," is masculine. The **desolating sacrilege** is understood as a reference to a person. The imagery from Daniel is employed to speak of some disaster, probably the destruction of the temple by the Romans in A.D. 70. That suggests that the words of this section are probably derived from Christian interpretation of events and are not those of the historical Jesus.

The warnings anticipate the terrible sufferings that will attend the destruction of Jerusalem. People are to make haste to **flee** the city. There will be no time to take anything. It will be especially difficult for pregnant women who are slowed by their additional burden. The times ahead will be worse than anything known previously. If the warnings anticipate the destruction of Jerusalem, the sufferings were terrible, as Josephus describes in detail in his *History of the Jewish Wars.*

The term **tribulation** is another technical expression, referring to the predetermined time of trial preceding the end of the ages. Such tribulation will "necessarily" come, since God has determined it. The trials and suffering will be so terrible, however, that no one would be able to endure them for long. So God has **shortened the days** of trouble. **For the sake of the elect,** God has appointed only limited trials so that at least some will be able to endure.

Jesus tells the faithful of what is to come beforehand so that they can be prepared. His warnings will also serve as comfort in the times to come because the faithful will know that nothing is outside the will of God.

From the larger context of national calamities, Jesus returns to temptations within. Before the end there will be pretenders claiming that **the Christ** is at hand. **False Christs and false prophets will arise . . . to lead astray the elect.** The language here is borrowed from Deuteronomy 13. The problem with **false prophets** is that they perform **signs and wonders,** as do true prophets—

but with the intention of deceiving the faithful. Jesus warns his followers to be on guard.

False prophets were a particular problem in Israel and in early Christianity. Deuteronomy 13 offers a glimpse of the problem, as does chapter 11 in the *Didache*. Prophets speak with the absolute authority of God ("Thus says the Lord"). Their authority arises from inspired visions. Yet prophets can disagree. The "true" prophets in Israel were always in the minority. In retrospect it is not difficult to determine who were the true and who the false prophets. Those listening to the words of prophets and witnessing their signs did not have the luxury of hindsight. Inspiration did not always lead the Corinthian congregation to the truth. Paul urged his charges to discriminate among the spirits, and he sought to identify standards by which prophetic pronouncements can be measured. Toward the middle of the second century, Montanus and his followers brought the crisis to a head by grounding their distinctive preaching in direct inspiration, bypassing church offices and tradition. The movement nearly destroyed the church and has led many to view charismatic authority with suspicion.

Jesus does not temper the promise of inspiration in view of its ambiguity. His followers are told to trust the guidance of the Spirit. They are also warned about false prophets. What is implied is trust in the common sense of the church and its scriptural heritage.

The Coming of the Man (13:24-31)

What follows the **tribulation** (note the indefinite **those days**) will be the end of all things. Internal strife, persecutions, warfare, even natural catastrophes are caught up in a cosmic drama. History is moving inexorably toward its end. Nature itself will offer testimony to the impending consummation with signs graphically depicted in prophetic visions: **the sun will be darkened, and the moon will not give its light, and the stars will be falling from heaven.** We may wonder whether the darkness at Jesus' crucifixion is not an initial fulfillment of Jesus' prediction about the days to come and a sign that the end is at hand. If so, Mark's Gospel closes in anticipation of that end.

The heavenly signs are an immediate prelude to the arrival of **the Son of man** with the **clouds** of heaven. The imagery derives from Daniel's vision of the humanlike figure who comes to the "Ancient of Days" to take his place on a throne appointed for him (Daniel 7). The vision has been interpreted by Christians as a reference to the risen Christ who "comes" from God to earth. It is here that all will glimpse Jesus' **glory** (note the use of the term in 10:37 in the request of James and John, "in your glory"). Crucial is the reference to seeing. The secret about Jesus will finally become visible to everyone. The end will provide a final, public vindication of those who have remained faithful. **Angels** will be sent to **gather** the faithful from all corners of the world.

The passage reflects Christian interpretation of the Scriptures. Jesus comes from God's right hand, where he is enthroned at his resurrection (Ps. 110:1). The reference to "seeing" may well reflect Zech. 12:10: "when they look on him whom they have pierced, they shall mourn for him" (see Rev. 1:7 and Matt. 24:30). The same images appear in Jesus' promise to the high priest at his trial: "You will see the Son of man sitting at the right hand of Power, and coming with the clouds of heaven" (14:62).

The signs of the end will be as obvious as the signs of **summer.** Once again nature furnishes the imagery. When trees begin to put out foliage, it is obvious that summer is at hand. Likewise when the tribulations Jesus has predicted begin to occur, the end is near. The signs will be unambiguous. And like other natural images Jesus has employed—seedtime and harvest, small seeds and large shrubs, birth-pangs and delivery—there is an inevitability about what "must" occur. However oppressive the times, deliverance is certain.

The promise that follows has intrigued commentators since earliest times: **This generation will not pass away before all these things take place,** Jesus says. What can be meant by the words? Albert Schweitzer insisted that Jesus meant what he said: he believed the end of history was imminent. He went to Jerusalem convinced that God would bring the age to an end—and he died disappointed. Christians who believe that Jesus was raised from the dead might at least concede that Jesus was surprised by the details of what God had in mind.

There is some evidence to suggest that Jesus' followers understood his words to mean that the end of all things was imminent. Paul, for example, believed the end of history was not far off; it would certainly occur within his own lifetime. John, the seer who wrote Revelation, certainly did not believe the world would continue for long. It is possible that Paul and other Christians misunderstood Jesus. It is reasonable to wonder exactly what Jesus had in mind, but the fact is we probably cannot know.

We can ask how these words are to be understood in Mark. Did the evangelist understand himself and his contemporaries to be part of **this generation** that would witness the termination of history? There is an indication in our chapter that Mark believed the end to be near at hand—that the destruction of Jerusalem would signal the beginning of the end. There are other indications that the chapter intends to dampen enthusiasm, preparing for a time of tribulations prior to the coming of the end. "The end is not yet"; these things are "but the beginning of the birth-pangs."

Whether or not Mark believed the end was imminent, the fulfillment of Jesus' promise that some in this generation will see "these things taking place" is located in part in what follows. Jesus himself appears before the Sanhedrin and the governor. Judas, an insider and "brother," hands Jesus over to death. The sun is turned to darkness while Jesus hangs on the cross. These fulfillments do not mark the end, but they demonstrate that Jesus' words are to be trusted. While **heaven and earth** will disintegrate, Jesus' promises will stand forever.

Mark has taken great pains to stress Jesus' foreknowledge of what will happen to him and his disciples. Three times he predicts his suffering and death. On five occasions he speaks of his resurrection. The detailed fulfillment of those prophecies provides a basis for trusting Jesus' predictions about the more distant future—predictions that hold promise for the faithful.

In this regard, the discourse in chapter 13 is much like the parables in chapter 4 in offering hope in the face of disappointment. While there will be many tribulations that threaten the faithful, those who endure will be saved, just as the seed, though threatened by hazards, will produce an abundant harvest.

Stay Awake! (13:32-37)

Verse 32 is a major qualification: the precise **day** and **hour** of the end is known only to God. While the chapter emphasizes Jesus' foreknowledge, and the preceding verses stress the nearness of the end, this verse adds a disclaimer: though he is **Son,** there are matters he does not know, just as there are decisions he cannot make (see 10:40, where only God can decide who will sit at Jesus' left and right). The exact time of the end is a mystery. The faithful can be confident that there will be an end to the tribulation, that the sufferings are part of the great birth-pangs preceding the glorious return of Jesus. They must be prepared for what is to come, however. If Jesus is uncertain of God's timing, there is good reason to be suspicious of other forecasters boasting knowledge of matters reserved for God alone. History is strewn with the wreckage of groups who heeded some false prophet claiming to have deciphered the secret code. The yearning to know what God knows is great; the temptation to "be like God" seems to be inherent in humankind. Jesus urges patience and endurance. Faith produces hope. It is enough to know that the day will come.

Jesus' words about what is to come can be heard in different ways. For those in danger of losing their nerve in the face of the darkness, they provide light. If Mark wrote for a beleaguered group of believers whose sufferings had tested their endurance to the breaking point, Jesus' words about what lies ahead would afford comfort and strengthen resolve.

For others who have found faith in Jesus compatible with human experience and for whom the world is a comfortable place, the warnings are heard differently. The world is a dangerous place, Jesus warns his disciples—and that is precisely what the last days of his ministry demonstrate. There are powers at work rightly to be feared. A world that had no room for Jesus cannot be expected to welcome his followers with open arms. Peace is a great gift and eagerly to be sought. Yet believers ought not be naive about what to expect from a world bound by sin that hung Jesus on a cross.

The little parable that concludes the chapter takes the warnings more in the latter direction than the former. What does it mean to be vigilant because **you do not know when the time will come**? The little parable Jesus tells emphasizes not the desperate plight of his followers but rather their indifference to the crisis at hand. **It is like a man going on a journey.** It seems clearly to refer to the situation in which Jesus will leave his followers. Once again he uses the image of the householder. As master of the house, he gives to his slaves authority to run the estate. The imagery is significant: we have already learned that Jesus is the stronger one who has bound Satan and is despoiling his house. Apparently having secured control, he now leaves his slaves in charge. They are given authority and specific tasks to perform. **The doorkeeper** is commanded to remain watchful.

The contrast on which the parable plays is between watching and sleeping. We might well translate, "Stay awake, then, for you do not know when the master of the house is coming." The danger, according to the parable, is that no one will be watching and that all will be asleep when **the master** arrives. The worst situation is that no one will be awake to greet the master. Not knowing when he is to return, they will lose interest and fall asleep.

The little parable first of all introduces what happens in the ensuing narrative. The listing of the various times when the master might return are suggestive of a structure of events: **evening** (the meal); **midnight** (the garden and arrest); **cockcrow** (Peter's denial); **in the morning** (the final gathering of the Sanhedrin and Jesus' trial before Pilate). The clearest connection, of course, is between the warning to "stay awake" and the disciples' sleep while Jesus prays in Gethsemane.

The danger, according to Jesus, is that those in charge of the household will be **asleep,** unaware of the crises ahead, and will be caught unprepared. That is precisely what happens to the disciples. They are asleep when the crisis comes. When Jesus is arrested, they run away, completely unprepared for what must occur.

Jesus' warnings about the future conclude with an injunction addressed not only to the disciples but **to all:** stay awake (RSV: **Watch**). The danger of falling asleep exists for those who read the story. The warning seems more appropriate for the indifferent than for the desperate. Mark seems directed to believers, perhaps especially those in authority, who have experienced some success and are tempted not so much to lose heart as to drift off into indifference, unaware of the tests that lie ahead. It is precisely in this sense that Jesus' followers embody inadequate discipleship. Their fault is a complete lack of understanding of what the future holds. To the very end they hope for positions of glory. When the test comes, they are asleep, unprepared, and they crumble under the pressure.

What I say to you I say to all, Jesus says. "Stay awake!"

It may well be these words were addressed to a sleepy church—one in which believers had tasted success and liked it, a church in which there were already positions of authority to which people aspired, perhaps even competing for power. "Stay awake," Jesus warns them. The world is a dangerous place for the elect. The future holds trials, worse than anything since the foundation of creation. There is hope in the end—but the faithful must be prepared for what is to come. Naiveté is the prelude to disaster. "Stay awake."

With that, the account of Jesus' last 24 hours begins.

The Passion of Jesus (14:1—15:47)

The Setting (14:1-2)

While Jesus is warning his little band of what lies ahead, events are moving quickly toward his own inevitable demise. The religious leaders—**the scribes, the chief priests,** and the elders—

are now intent upon arrest and execution. Their problem is still Jesus' popularity. They do not wish to cause a riot by arresting someone for whom the common people have such high hopes. **Not during the feast** is the sage advice of the professionals. **The feast** is **Passover,** a commemoration of Israel's deliverance from bondage to foreign powers at the hands of a savior whom God had raised up. The celebration of that pivotal event in Israel's history serves as the backdrop for the drama that is about to unfold. The leaders have decided Jesus must go. He poses too great a threat. Yet to make a martyr of one whom the common people regard as their champion would be suicidal—particularly at Passover. So they must await their chance.

The temporal reference, **two days before the Passover and the feast of Unleavened Bread,** locates these events firmly within Israel's commemoration of its past and its hopes for the future. The literal "after two days" could be read in the same way as "after three days rise again" (8:31)—the latter meaning two days later. (In the system of reckoning, the first day is counted in the series, whereas in our present system the first day is not counted.) Therefore, the phrase translated **two days before** may mean simply the day before Passover. It is possible, in other words, that Mark compresses all the subsequent action into a period of less than 48 hours. That would, however, make the phrase in 14:12, "On the first day of Unleavened Bread," redundant. More likely that action is divided as follows:

Wednesday: Jesus' "anointing" at Simon's house
　　　　　 Judas's conference with the authorities
Thursday: Preparation for Passover
Friday (beginning at sundown on Thursday and ending with
　　 sundown 24 hours later; the actual festival of Passover):
　　　　　 The Last Supper
　　　　　 Jesus' arrest and trial before the Sanhedrin
　　　　　 Jesus' trial before Pilate and execution
　　　　　 The burial

Anointing for Burial: "In Memory of Her" (14:3-9)

While the **priests** plot the death of Jesus, he is visiting **Simon the leper,** one of several characters in the last chapters about whom we know nothing. That he is known as **the leper** (certainly cured) suits the pattern of Jesus' association with outcasts.

At first glance, this episode seems the only one not dominated by Jesus' impending death. It is only apparent, however. The action of an unnamed **woman** is to be seen, according to Jesus, as anointing **my body beforehand for burying.** As we have come to expect, the declaration makes little impact on Jesus' immediate audience, who seem preoccupied only with more ordinary matters. As readers, we are given to know what this act really means.

Mark's version of the story makes nothing of the woman's character. There is no indication she is a sinner. We are not told whether or not she is a member of the household, which would at least explain her presence at the meal. All we learn is that she pours expensive oil over Jesus' head as an act of devotion.

The response of **some** at the meal is to take offense. The act of devotion was a waste, they insist. The **ointment** might have been used for something important. Had it been sold, the money might have been **given to the poor.** In the Fourth Gospel, the complaint is issued by Judas, who, we are told, kept the money box and was interested only in his own gain, not the poor (John 12:4-6). No such motives are attributed to the woman's detractors here. They simply resent the lavish display of devotion. Interest in the poor is commendable, but here it arises from a suffocating piety that prevents spontaneity and life. Even a "virtuous" concern about money can choke off growth of the seed, resulting in a barren piety (4:18-19).

Jesus' response to his **indignant** table companions is to point out they will never lack opportunity to aid **the poor:** there will **always** be poor people, and devoting oneself to their care will continue to be a worthy vocation. There is something special about Jesus' presence, however. When the bridegroom is present, celebration—even careless, lavish celebration—is the only thing to do. It is the presence of Jesus that gives life, as the woman's joyful act testifies. For those devoted to virtue and moderation, that presence is a threat that will soon be eliminated.

The woman's act has a deeper significance in its present setting: it is the "anointing" that prepares Jesus for burial. Even so joyful an act cannot escape the shadow the cross casts over everything. Jesus must die.

In view of the narrative that follows, dominated by the image of Jesus as the anointed King, it would be tempting to view this act as Jesus' "anointing" as King. The word play works only in English, however. The Greek word translated **anointed** in this passage is not the same as the word used to speak of "anointing" as installation to office. Jesus has already been anointed by the Spirit. He will be invested as King by his enemies.

An apparently insignificant act by a statusless member of society assumes cosmic proportions as part of Jesus' story. The joyous, reckless act of an anonymous woman in an obscure corner of the world has not been forgotten. Jesus promised that wherever the gospel was preached, this story would **be told in memory of her.** And so it has been.

Betrayal (14:10-11)

The woman's act contrasts sharply with another unforgettable deed: Judas's betrayal. The terse reference to Judas's action raises a host of questions. The cryptic comment provides no information about motives. Nor is the reference a surprise: we have known since the beginning that **Judas** would **betray him** (3:19). Filling in gaps has proved an irresistible temptation to later generations. What kind of person was Judas? Was he disillusioned with Jesus? Was he trying to force Jesus' hand? While novelists and filmmakers have taken the liberty to invest Judas with a personality and motives for his action, it must all remain speculation. Mark affords no insight into the mysterious figure without which a crucial link in the psychodrama is lacking. The author apparently feels we do not need to understand Judas to appreciate his action and the consequences.

The need to satisfy curiosity is great. Speculation about Judas began almost at once. Each of the later evangelists adds a bit to the growing legend, including reference to the number of silver pieces Judas received (Matthew and Luke), a possible motive (greed—the Fourth Gospel), and the circumstances of his death. Contributions to the legend continue to flow in; *Jesus Christ Superstar* and *The Last Temptation of Christ* are but two modern examples.

Passover is celebrated in the shadow of the impending crisis. Judas is already at work seeking a time when Jesus is vulnerable to arrest.

Preparations for Passover (14:12-16)

The first day of Unleavened Bread would normally designate the first day of Passover. The qualifying clause, **when they sacrificed the passover [lamb]**, indicates that what is meant is the day of preparation. In this context, *pascha* means **the passover lamb.** The verb translated **sacrificed** may be read more generally as "slaughter." It is not clear from Jewish sources that the killing of the lambs was regarded as a sacrifice, though that seems to be presumed in the New Testament (see 1 Cor. 5:7, where the same verb is used).

The dating of the final events in Jesus' life differs in crucial respects between John and the Synoptic Gospels. Passover was celebrated on the 15th day of the month of Nissan. The lamb was killed and preparations made on the 14th. When the sun had set on the 14th—thus when the new day had begun—the Passover meal was to be eaten. According to the Synoptic Gospels, Jesus' last meal with his followers was a Passover meal. His last 24 hours begin with a meal at sundown, include his prayer in the garden, his arrest, trial, and death—all concluded before sundown on the 15th.

According to John, Jesus' last meal, his arrest, trial, and death all took place on the day of Preparation; thus Jesus was dead prior to the beginning of Passover. All the Gospels are agreed that Jesus died on Friday and that the next day was the Sabbath. They disagree on the Jewish calendar.

None of the Gospel accounts is a neutral source of information. It is crucial to Mark that the last meal is a Passover celebration. It is likewise critical to John that Jesus' death occurs on the day the lamb was slaughtered. In his commentary on John, Raymond Brown carefully sifts the evidence for dating and concludes that probability favors John's chronology. It is highly unlikely, he argues, that the Jewish hierarchy would have taken action against Jesus on the actual festival day, which would have been totally contrary to the law. Some will be convinced by his arguments, others will not. Lacking a consensus, we can at least determine how Mark wishes Jesus' last day to be understood. The dating is of obvious importance for our understanding of the meal.

The question of Jesus' **disciples** indicates that the meal is to be a celebration of Passover. Jesus' response seems to indicate elaborate preparation—perhaps some secret preparation regarded as necessary in view of the plotting against him. His instructions are reminiscent of those with regard to the donkey on which he rode into the city. The disciples find the mysterious man carrying **a jar of water** (women's work) and are led to the **room** which will be the site of Jesus' last supper.

The Last Supper (14:17-25)

The meal begins **when it was evening.** Dinner was customarily eaten in the late afternoon. The late hour indicates that the meal is a Passover supper which must be eaten after the sun has set. Jesus begins by indicating that **one** of the **twelve** will betray him. Judas's name is never mentioned. Jesus' reference to his betrayer as one who **is dipping bread into the dish with me** indicates that Judas is present. No mention is made of Judas's reaction or his departure, so he is presumably present during the words of institution and the actual eating and drinking.

The importance of the detail may arise from the Scriptures. Jesus speaks of **one who is eating with me.** The reference may be an allusion to Ps. 41:9, where the speaker laments:

Even my bosom friend in whom I trusted,
　who ate of my bread, has lifted his heel against me.

The psalm verse is not quoted, and the wording in Mark is not an exact parallel. There are reasons to suspect the narrator was aware of the verse, however. When in the following verses Jesus speaks of **the Son of man** going **as it is written of him,** we are to think of such passages as these. Here, as throughout the passion story, allusions to Old Testament texts add depth to the story—though only for those who know the Scriptures. Allusions indicate something about Mark's audience as well as about the history of the narrative material. "Proof from prophecy" is not the point of the allusions. The scriptural references indicate that it was impossible to tell the story of Jesus' last days without using the language of the Scriptures. The events made sense, even from earliest times, only within a scriptural framework. The conviction that Christ died "in accordance with the Scriptures" is basic—more basic perhaps than individual scriptural arguments.

Jesus' woe anticipates Judas's demise, though it is never reported in Mark. The author sees no unfairness in the declaration that Judas is responsible for his action—and that the script has been **written.** That Jesus "must" die does not detract from the historical particularity or from human culpability. Actual human beings make real decisions with earth-shaking consequences. Only in retrospect can we see that the reality of what is occurring is not exhausted within the realm of human intention. In, with, and under the human acts, God is at work.

While Mark intends to depict Jesus' last meal as a celebration of Passover, few remnants of the traditional meal remain. By Mark's day, the account of Jesus' last supper was firmly established in Christian ritual. In writing to the Corinthians, Paul can recall words he "received from the Lord," handed on to him by an earlier generation of Christians, that bear the marks of liturgical action. In the Passover meal, the blessing of the **bread** which opens the actual meal and the blessing of the (third) **cup** of wine are separated in time, and both are preceded by significant words and actions. The present wording reflects usage at the Christian "Lord's Supper."

What difference does it make if Mark's account of Jesus' last meal is to be understood against the background of the Passover ritual? The question is complex. Most who study it are interested to work back through the tradition to what Jesus had in mind. Our primary interest is Mark's investment in the issue. What would Mark's readers have been expected to know about the Passover? To what degree do the instructions in the Mishnah offer a fair glimpse of what went on a century and a half earlier?

The host of studies have raised interesting possibilities. One significant factor is the prominent place of the Hallel Psalms (113–118) in the Passover ritual. Psalm 118 in particular was of considerable importance in the evolution of Christian tradition and furnishes imagery for Mark as well ("the stone which the builders rejected" [Mark 12:11]). If it was customary for the last psalm to be sung at the table (**And when they had sung a hymn, they went out to the Mount of Olives**), it is tempting to read through Psalm 118 in the context of Jesus' prayer in Gethsemane. The prominence of the psalm in Christian tradition may be related to its ritual function.

Another critical factor is the relationship between God's deliverance of Israel and the salvation to be accomplished in the death and resurrection of Christ. That Jesus uses for his own purposes bread and wine with a rich traditional heritage must suggest continuity as well as a break with the old. The God who will raise Jesus from the dead is the same God who delivered Israel from bondage in Egypt. In particular, Jesus' reference to **the blood of the covenant** ties his fate to God's action in the past.

At least that much may be said about links with Passover traditions. Detailed arguments must remain speculative.

Jesus blesses the bread, breaks, and distributes it—actions reminiscent of the accounts of his feeding of 5000 and 4000. The blessing is probably the familiar prayer:

Blessed are you, O Lord our God, King of the Universe,
  Who has caused bread to sprout forth from the earth.

Whatever significance the bread has in the Passover service is now decisively stamped with Jesus' interpretation that focuses God's deliverance on his own impending suffering and death: **This is my body.** The same is true of the cup: **This is my blood of the covenant, which is poured out for many.** Bread and cup will be henceforth bound to Jesus' act of deliverance. Israel's past and future are to be viewed in light of what is to happen to God's Christ.

The blood of the covenant recalls the language of Exodus 24, where Moses concludes his reading of the law by sprinkling the people with blood: "Behold the blood of the covenant which the Lord has made with you in accordance with all these words." **The blood** by which the new **covenant** will be ratified is Jesus' own. The idea of atonement is not developed in Mark. It is taken over from earlier Christian tradition, of which we likewise see glimpses in Paul's letters. Jesus' death is a "ransom"; his blood is efficacious. It is striking that in view of the inordinate space Mark devotes to Jesus' death so little effort is made to develop theories about it. Spinning such theories would be left to later generations.

The Christian church has invested considerable time and effort in reflecting on this brief account of Jesus' last meal with his followers. The words, accompanying the eating of bread and drinking of wine, have become an established feature of Christian traditions. Interpretations differ, however, in ways that have transformed the Lord's Supper into a sectarian ritual. The brevity of Mark's account is perhaps exemplary. While efforts to understand the language of ritual are necessary, there is something about the actual performance that outstrips our ability to articulate a theory of what occurs.

Perhaps it is enough to say that Jesus promises his presence, and that the promise is bound to bread, wine, and specific words. When the promises are declared and the bread and wine eaten, Jesus' body and blood are effectively present. They accomplish the deliverance he intended. No explanation can replace the eating and drinking, and no specific theory about "presence" should limit the **many** for whom Jesus' body and blood are intended.

Jesus' oath not to drink **until that day when I drink it new in the kingdom of God** is reassurance that the day will come—and a sober reminder of what lies ahead. There is another cup from which Jesus must drink before the banquet begins.

Predictions (14:26-31)

When they had sung (presumably the psalms), the group sets out for **the Mount of Olives.** The scene includes a significant set of predictions. Quoting the Scriptures—here, Zech. 13:7—Jesus predicts that his followers will scatter with his arrest. He also predicts that after he has been raised from the dead, he will **go before you into Galilee.** The words will recur on the lips of a heavenly messenger at the empty tomb as a reminder of what "he told you." Jesus' predictions play a critical role in the Gospel. For the fifth time, Jesus explicitly predicts his resurrection. There can be little doubt the author intends to prepare us not simply for Jesus' death but also his resurrection.

Peter's boast that he will not stumble elicits another prophecy from Jesus: **Before the cock crows twice, you will thrice deny me** (RSV: **three times**). His words will be fulfilled to the letter. Peter's insistence that he is prepared to **die** rather than deny Jesus only readies us for the depth of his fall. If there is to be any future for Jesus' movement, it will not be because Jesus' followers demonstrate nobility. Peter will crumble, as will all the disciples.

Jesus' predictions have two functions. Their fulfillment focuses again on the disciples' shortcomings and their total lack of preparation. Only a few verses later, the inner circle, asked to watch with Jesus, falls asleep. They will prove unable to meet the test, despite their intentions. On the other hand, the predictions characterize what is to occur as part of the divine necessity. Jesus knows what is to come; it has all "been written." And however bleak things may seem, there will be a new beginning—**after I am raised up.** Jesus' words will not pass away.

Gethsemane (14:32-42)

> For we have not a high priest who is unable to sympathize with our
> weaknesses, but one who in every respect has been tempted as we
> are, yet without sin.
>
> (Heb. 4:15)

The famous words from the letter to the Hebrews find remarkably little echo in the Gospels. The evangelists spend little
time trying to probe Jesus' mind. One place where we glimpse
Jesus' agony, however, is in the account of his prayer in the
garden. Jesus has successfully endured Satan's testing before the
beginning of his public ministry. He has resisted Peter's suggestion
that there is a way around the cross. Now he must finally embrace
his destiny and drink the cup God has prepared.

For this last test, Jesus brings with him the inner circle of the
disciples, **Peter, James,** and **John.** The language is remarkably
candid and unrestrained: Jesus **began to be greatly distressed
and troubled.** Borrowing the language of the Psalms, Jesus speaks
of his soul as troubled to the point of **death.** He asks only that
his close friends **watch** (remain awake).

Jesus' prayer employs the unusual Aramaic form **Abba.** The
use of Aramaic for color is familiar; the particular Aramaic term
is not. Joachim Jeremias has invested considerable energy in a
study of the word **Abba,** the intimate term for **Father.** While
there may be some precedent for calling God **Father** in the
Scriptures and Jewish tradition, Jesus' use of the familiar term
in prayer seems singular. The term of address is far more intimate
than is customary in prayer and would probably have seemed
disrespectful. The usage made an impact on Christian prayer, as
is clear from Paul's letters as well as the Gospels. That usage is
at least one component in Christian use of father/son language
to speak about Jesus and God (see excursus, above, pp. 59–60).

The image of drinking the **cup** as submission to God's will recalls
Jesus' question of James and John in 10:38-40. The image itself
derives from the Old Testament (such passages as Ps. 60:3; Isa.
51:17-22; see also Jer. 49:12). It is possible that Paul alludes to
such imagery when he speaks of the Lord's Supper principally in

terms of Jesus' death: "For as often as you eat this bread and drink this cup, you proclaim the Lord's death until he comes" (1 Cor. 11:26).

Jesus once again faces temptation and passes the test. It is finally the will of God that will determine his course. And, as we know, "the Son of man goes as it has been written of him." Death is inevitable.

That is not true of the **disciples.** The passage contrasts Jesus' agonized submission to God's will and the disciples' inability to remain watchful. When Jesus returns to find them **sleeping, Peter** is the first addressed, though Jesus' warnings are intended for the whole group. **Peter** is again the symbolic representative of the group—the one who insisted that he would remain steadfast regardless of the consequences. He is unable to remain awake even **one hour.** What will happen when the real test comes?

The phrase, **the spirit indeed is willing, but the flesh is weak** provides some insight into the problem. Performance is not simply a matter of will, as we have seen. The disciples' problem cannot be reduced to a lack of effort. The problem is **the flesh.** The usage here does not signify the lower nature but the whole being— over which the disciples cannot exercise control. The sense that the disciples are not in control is emphasized again when Mark says **their eyes were very heavy.** The verb is passive ("were weighed down"), just as in "their hearts were hardened." The problem is something beyond their strength. The disciples, like others, require redemption and liberation. They cannot help themselves.

The threefold repetition of Jesus' questions focuses attention not so much on Jesus' agony as on the disciples' failure. Despite their bravado, they cannot remain watchful. The crisis will find them totally unprepared, asleep. The threefold repetition, like Peter's threefold denial, indicates the totality of their bondage.

Jesus prays that the cup may pass from him. In a sense, the disciples' sleep is an answer to his request. God is silent—and the **sleeping** disciples provide a graphic demonstration that there remains no alternative to the cross. Nothing less than an act of deliverance will solve their problem—and the problem of the human race.

Jesus concludes with an announcement that the hour has come. **The Son of man is betrayed into the hands of sinners—and his betrayer is at hand.**

The Arrest (14:43-50)

The account of the arrest is cryptic. Once again, no motivation for Judas's action is offered. The narrator simply indicates that he had made an agreement with the temple authorities to hand Jesus over when it was safe. There is cruel irony in the choice of a sign of betrayal: the intimate sign of affection provides the mark of death ("the **kiss** of death"). With that intimate gesture, one of Jesus' inner circle hands him over to the authorities. The collapse begins that will end with Jesus abandoned by everyone—even by God.

The little detail about the high priest's **slave** losing **his ear** is tantalizing but enigmatic. The person who draws his **sword** is identified only as **one of those who stood by.** The story invites creative enlargement, and each of the other evangelists offers additional comment. In Matthew, Jesus gives a brief discourse about the inappropriateness of using weapons. In Luke, a whole group of the disciples appears ready to fight. We are told that the slave loses his right ear. Jesus rebukes his followers—and heals the ear of the slave. John, like Luke, indicates that the slave lost his right ear—and he goes so far as to name the assailant as Simon Peter and the slave as Malchus. In John's account of Peter's denial, one of those who identifies Peter is named as a relative of the slave. It is evident that tradition continued to grow even after written accounts had been produced.

Mark's terse narration is the sort that has given generations of interpreters the sense that his Gospel was written by an eye-witness. While that seems unlikely for other reasons, it is true that the narrative has the feel of authenticity. The terseness may well suggest that the story was told for people who knew the facts already and could fill in some of the gaps. The expansion of the story by Matthew, Luke, and John indicates how such narratives work on later readers.

Have you come out as against a bandit [RSV: **robber**]? Jesus asks. The term translated **robber** should be understood in a broader sense. It does not mean "thief" but "bandit." It was a term of contempt used by the historian Josephus to speak of the guerrillas who carried on a campaign of violence against Romans and Roman sympathizers. The presence of soldiers (we are to think here of the temple police, not Roman soldiers) suggests that Jesus is a dangerous criminal. His protest—**Day after day I was with you in the temple teaching**—suggests that he does not fit the image of someone plotting criminal actions in secret. In context, particularly in light of the trial before Pilate, Jesus' protest should be understood as a denial of political intrigue. He is arrested as a revolutionary—yet there is nothing secret about his mission and nothing that could justify his arrest as a "bandit" (insurrectionist).

And you did not seize me. The reason, of course, is that the leaders feared the people and Jesus' popularity. His arrest in the relative safety and privacy of the garden is due to the information Judas provided.

But let the scriptures be fulfilled. Here again, we learn that the events being played out have been scripted. They are not accidental but ordained. Judas has now played his fateful role. Though nothing is said about his demise, Jesus hinted at it earlier ("It would have been better if he had not been born" [14:21]).

Particularly striking is the terse reference to the disciples' response: **And they all forsook him, and fled.** Despite the elaborate preparation, a successful preaching mission, and Jesus' repeated warnings about what lay ahead, the disciples are totally unprepared for what occurs. Though they all insisted they would never abandon Jesus, they run. Interestingly, this is the last we hear of the disciples in Mark—apart from the instructions to the women at the empty tomb that they are to "tell the disciples and Peter." They have no further role to play—except for the role Jesus has predicted after he is raised from the dead.

The Flight of a Young Man (14:51-52)

Perhaps the most cryptic—and enticing—account in the Gospel now follows. We are told about an unnamed **young man** who is **seized** by the guards and runs away **naked,** leaving his **linen** garment behind. Numerous questions arise: What is meant by **with nothing but a linen cloth about his** naked **body?** Why is he not named? Is there any particular significance in his fleeing **naked?** The story invites imaginative response—and, not surprisingly, there have been imaginative responders.

One of the traditional interpretations of the passage is that it is the author's signature. The details lend a flavor of authenticity to the account. Perhaps the story was told to people who already knew the facts and who recognized that the unnamed **youth** was none other than the author of the Gospel, who—given the traditional ascription of the writing to John Mark—would have been a young man at this point. There is nothing in particular to commend this reading apart from its persistence in popular Christian lore.

There have been other interpretations as well. Austin Farrer, fascinated with images, observes that the story presently speaks of another "young man" at the tomb. There, the narrator observes that the "young man" is clothed in a white robe. Is there any relationship between the fearful young man who runs away naked and the clothed, confident youth who testifies to the resurrection? Perhaps.

A more sinister interpretation was proposed by Morton Smith in his work *The Secret Gospel.* The reference to the garb of the young man—a **linen** garment over a **naked** body—indicates the boy was headed for some unsavory rites, Smith argues, perhaps associated with forbidden forms of worship. Jesus was caught in the act and thus arrested. Jewish tradition does suggest Jesus was put to death as a magician, though there is no way to date the tradition and no supporting evidence. The Gospel writers, according to this interpretation, did their best to conceal the truth about Jesus. That would likewise presuppose that Mark, while trying to conceal the truth, was so inept as to preserve an accurate report of incriminating evidence.

Smith's reconstruction seems less motivated by historical concern than antipathy to Christian tradition—but it does indicate that the cryptic story is capable of more than one interpretation. None of the three noted here is particularly compelling. Smith's interpretation must presume ineptitude not only on the part of Mark but of the church that left untouched such potentially damaging evidence. The purely symbolic reading is out of character with the rest of the Gospel narrative. That the tale refers to someone known to the readers seems more plausible, though there is little reason to believe that person is the Gospel's author. Perhaps we will never know the "truth" about the story. It may well stand as a reminder that however successful we are at penetrating the secrets of Mark's Gospel, there will always be those dimensions we cannot probe. We still read as outsiders.

Two Trials (14:53-72)

The sequence that follows is a masterful composition. Nowhere is expectant reading more amply rewarded—and nowhere is the source-critical perspective so devastating to appreciation and understanding. The primary task of interpretation is to comprehend the whole narrative. Questions about the history of the passion tradition and the reliability of the Gospel as a historical source are important but secondary matters.

Stories are told not simply to provide information but to capture and communicate the "reality" of the events they narrate. As Mark's readers, we already know the facts. Jesus has predicted what will occur when he appears before the Jewish court: he will be "rejected" and condemned to death. The question for the interpreter is how the author has chosen to capture Jesus' appearance before the Jewish court and what we are to learn about the "reality" of the event.

A first observation is the shifting back and forth from **Jesus** to **Peter.** Jesus is arrested, we are told. Attention then focuses on Peter, who follows as far as the **courtyard** of the high priest's residence. Then the scene shifts inside to Jesus' trial, after which the narrative recounts Peter's "interrogation" in the courtyard. Other ways of telling the story were available to the narrator. The shifting back and forth is to depict simultaneity. Two trials are in progress, not one—the first, the trial of Jesus before the high council; the second, the trial of Peter in the courtyard in the presence of the high priest's household staff. The two trials are related; one must be understood in light of the other.

After Jesus' arrest, he is brought to the house of **the high priest,** where his enemies are **assembled.** Peter follows **at a distance**— the only one of the disciples courageous enough to follow. Association with Jesus will mean arrest and certain death. The trial opens, then, with Peter outside, **sitting with the guards** and servants. The little detail that Peter was **warming himself at the fire** is a gentle reminder that Peter is still concerned about himself. He is cold—perhaps even "out in the cold." While Jesus is on trial for his life, Peter is concerned about staying warm.

Jesus' trial then unfolds. According to the Mishnah, the second-century codification of rabbinic oral law, trials must begin with testimony for the defense. Jesus' trial begins with the court already committed to a guilty verdict. The only witnesses called are by the prosecution. The trial, in fact, violates virtually every precept laid down in the Mishnah about trials (Mishnah, *Sanhedrin*). A trial could not be held on a festival day; according to Mark, Passover has begun. The court cannot vote a death sentence without allowing a night between trial and sentencing, in order to give the judges every chance to change their minds. According to to Mark, the sentence was passed immediately. While the rules in the Mishnah are from another time and place, their consistent violation is hardly an accident. Mark intends to portray the hearing before the council as a miscarriage of justice.

While the court is committed to a guilty verdict, it seems remarkably clumsy: it is unable to secure consistent testimony. According to the Law (Num. 35:30 and Deut. 19:15), two witnesses were required to agree on testimony before it could be used to secure a guilty verdict. While supposedly in control, the court seems strangely powerless to work its will.

While **many bore false witness,** Mark chooses to report only one specific instance. **Some** spoke of an alleged threat Jesus had made against the **temple** and a subsequent boast. Their accusation is precisely formulated: **We heard him say, "I will destroy this temple that is made with hands, and in three days I will build another, not made with hands."** While this precise formulation is attributed to **some,** the narrator comments that even so the witnesses were unable to agree and thus could not secure a condemnation. The comment would seem to require some explanation—which the evangelist does not provide. The report of the ineffectual false testimony does, however, highlight the charge itself. Among the **many** false accusations, it alone bears repeating.

We are aware, of course, that Jesus has threatened **the temple**—both in somewhat veiled form at the "cleansing" and specifically in the presence of a few disciples in chapter 13. He predicted there would not be left one stone on another in Jerusalem. There is a sense, then, in which the accusation is correct.

On the other hand, Jesus has never spoken these precise words—at least not in the story Mark tells. He never threatened that he would himself destroy the temple, and he never spoke of building **another** temple, **not made with hands.** What, then, are we to make of the charge?

We can observe that a version of this charge is attested in the other Gospels, even John. There are significant differences in the formulation, however, as well as in the interpretation. Matthew's version is the closest to Mark's—though in Matthew, the "boast" is that Jesus could ("I am able" instead of **I will**) destroy and rebuild the temple in three days (Matt. 26:61). Mark's distinction of a temple **made with hands** and a temple **not made with hands** is unique. In Luke, the charge is omitted from the account of Jesus' trial, but a version appears in Stephen's trial. The "false witnesses" testify against Stephen: "We have heard him say that this Jesus of Nazareth will destroy this place" (Acts 6:14). Nothing is said of rebuilding. In John, Jesus says, "Destroy this temple, and in three days I will raise it up" (John 2:19). The narrator interprets the prediction in a singular way: "But he spoke of the temple of his body" (John 2:21). None of the synoptic Gospels understands the saying in this way.

The rather complex history of the temple saying suggests that some version of the testimony of the false witnesses circulated in pre-Gospel tradition. None of the Gospel writers can dismiss the saying; all feel obliged to offer an interpretation. The interpretations differ, however, so that simply reconstructing a history of this particular tradition does not account for any one of the four evangelist's interpretation.

The unique feature of Mark's account is the distinction between two temples—the present Jerusalem temple, one **made with hands;** the other, a temple of a different order, **not made with hands.** Mark alone is interested in the alleged prediction of a rebuilt temple of a different order. The phrase **made with hands** is customarily reserved for idols (see Acts 7:41, where it is used to refer to the Golden Calf). **Not made with hands** appears several times in the New Testament (e.g., Colossians 2—circumcision not made with hands) as a way of contrasting internal and external piety. And in 1 Peter, 1 Corinthians, and Ephesians, the image of the temple is employed to speak about the religious community—a feature common to the Dead Sea Scrolls as well.

There are several reasons to be interested in the charge in Mark. First, the temple and its impending destruction have been an issue since Jesus' arrival in Jerusalem. Second, the charge at the trial is picked up in the account of Jesus' death and repeated in taunts at the foot of the cross (see below). Third, in light of Jesus' earlier predictions, **in three days** can only be heard as an allusion to the resurrection. Finally, at the moment of Jesus' death the temple curtain is torn from top to bottom. In an important sense the testimony of the false witnesses is true—but in a way they cannot appreciate. Jesus' death will spell the end of the old temple. As the risen Christ, he will build a new temple "within three days"—a community that will take up the functions of the old temple, such as serving as a "house of prayer for all the Gentiles."

As important as the charge is, it does not secure Jesus' condemnation. The witnesses cannot **agree**. The fact is more important than the precise reasons. It means the trial must continue—that Jesus must finally have an opportunity to speak. Though the defendant and victim, Jesus is still in control. His enemies are unable to do anything until he opens his mouth.

The **high priest** seeks to get Jesus to speak, but he is silent. Some have seen here an allusion to the line from Isaiah 53 about the lamb who "opened not his mouth." That is possible, though in general the importance of Isaiah 53 for the passion tradition has been overestimated. The silence of Jesus leaves the truth of the accusation open to question. He neither confirms nor denies the allegations.

The trial now reaches its climax: **Again** the high priest asks Jesus, **Are you the Christ, the Son of the Blessed?** Though the **again** may simply refer to his interrogation, it may also imply the question was asked earlier. It may suggest that the question about the temple involved Jesus' identity as Messiah. Traditions about the coming Messiah varied widely among Jews. In 2 Sam. 7:10-14, an oracle regarded as messianic in pre-Christian Jewish circles, building the temple is one of the tasks assigned the coming Son of David (see also Zech. 6:12). There are good reasons to see some association between the temple charge and the climactic question of the high priest.

The formulation **the Christ, the Son of the Blessed** is unique in the New Testament. **The Son of the Blessed** is a reverential way of saying "the Son of God." While pronouncing the sacred name of God was strictly forbidden, Jews avoided using even the word "God" whenever possible. The question of the high priest represents the first time in the story that the title "the Son of God" appears on human lips. Otherwise, "Son" is used to address Jesus only by God and demons. The only other occurrence of the two titles together (Christ and Son of God) is in 1:1 (depending on one's assessment of the textual evidence for "Son of God").

In the high priest's question, the two titles are in apposition. Earlier generations of commentators, basing their views on extant evidence of post-Old Testament Jewish tradition, could insist that the use of "Son of God" of the Messiah was un-Jewish and must represent a highly Hellenized form of Christianity. The most recent discoveries from the Dead Sea, while not providing evidence of the use of the title for the Messiah, clearly indicate that such passages as Psalm 2 and 2 Samuel 7 were read as messianic oracles. In these passages God addresses the coming Messiah-King as "Son." Evidence from later Jewish tradition—partially, perhaps, a reaction to Christianity—indicates a growing discomfort with the scriptural possibilities and a conscious effort to avoid the application of such exalted language to the Messiah.

The decisive question has now been posed. The titles appear on the lips of the high priest himself. And for the first and only time in the story, Jesus gives an unambiguous response: **I am; and you will see. . . .** An important textual variant deserves at least some comment. Some authorities read, "You have said that I am." Though not well attested, the reading would explain the parallel readings in Matthew and Luke (Matthew: "You have said so"; Luke: "You [all] say that I am"). If the reading is accepted, it would in no sense imply a qualification. The response of the high priest indicates that he understands Jesus to have accepted the designations. The response "You said that I am" would parallel Jesus' retort to Pilate, which emphasizes above all the irony that it is precisely Jesus' enemies who have "said it." They have spoken the truth; they have made a good confession, though they have no idea what they are saying.

Jesus accepts the designations without qualification. While some commentators have seen the reference to **the Son of man** as a qualification, it must be understood here as a promise of vindication: **You will see the Son of man seated at the right hand of Power, and coming with the clouds of heaven.** His response includes a promise that he will be vindicated. The promise is couched appropriately in the language of the Scriptures: the image of sitting at the right hand of God is from Ps. 110:1, a verse of considerable importance to the early church as an interpretation of Jesus' enthronement; the image of the Son of man coming with the clouds is from Dan. 7:13. The allusion to Daniel in chapter 13 is further evidence that the verse was an important one to Mark's audience.

There may be a great deal beneath the surface of Jesus' response. Some have rightly asked how the narrator knows what is going on at the trial since none of Jesus' followers is present. It is perhaps not accidental that when Jesus speaks these climactic words, they come from the Scriptures. The Old Testament passages that furnish the imagery, particularly the verse from Daniel, played an important role both in Christian tradition and in controversies about heavenly intermediaries in later Jewish circles. During the first century, there was lively speculation about such heavenly beings, from Wisdom to a principal angelic figure. Philo of Alexandria, writing in the middle decades of the first century, could speak of this figure as the Logos or the "Second God." Later rabbinic sages became suspicious of all speculation about such heavenly beings and surpressed it forcefully.

Controversy about such passages may well date from a period before Mark's Gospel. By identifying himself as the "Lord" referred to in Ps. 110:1 and as the humanlike figure referred to in Daniel 7, Jesus thrusts himself further into controversy. The passages, employed by Christians to speak about Jesus' vindication "after three days," serve here as promises of a vindication that is "in accordance with the scriptures"—and, as Mark's readers would know, these promises had been fulfilled at least in part when Jesus was raised from the dead.

The secret, so carefully guarded throughout the story, is finally out in the open. The result is not conversions and a coronation, but condemnation. The response of the **high priest**—tearing his robes—conforms to the appropriate legal requirements when a court heard blasphemy uttered. Jesus is condemned for **blasphemy**, a capital offense.

There is some question about the charge, at least as measured by second- and third-century standards of blasphemy. In the

Mishnah, the lawbook of rabbinic Judaism written at about the end of the second century of the common era, blasphemy is described exclusively as pronouncing the sacred name of God. The prescribed response to hearing blasphemy in the court is tearing one's robes—but blasphemy is a restricted term. In Mark's version of the trial, Jesus is as scrupulous as the high priest about avoiding even the term "God": he uses at least one paraphrase for God (**right hand of Power**), perhaps two (**the clouds of heaven**).

The matter has been discussed at length by students of first-century Jewish jurisprudence. Measured by later rabbinic standards, nothing Jesus says at the trial constitutes blasphemy in the narrow sense. In all likelihood, however, blasphemy was a far wider concept in the first century, understood in the broadest sense as transgressing the prerogatives of God. And in any case, that is surely how the term is to be understood in Mark, whose author is not necessarily interested in all the intricacies of the law. In Mark blasphemy should be understood broadly. The accusation that Jesus' claim to forgive sins constitutes blasphemy (2:7) means the charge implies infringing on God's prerogatives. Jesus' statements are "blasphemous" in this sense.

But what is the precise offense in Jesus' response? Is the problem the acceptance of the titles, **the Christ, the Son of the Blessed,** or is it Jesus' statement about the **Son of man** seated at God's **right hand**? As we have noted, Jesus' response alludes to at least two Old Testament texts: Psalm 110 and Daniel 7. Both passages, particularly the verses from Daniel, provided the basis of controversy within later Jewish circles. The image of the humanlike figure seated on a throne in God's presence suggested to rabbinic sages implications about heavenly figures that threatened the sovereignty of God. At least one prominent rabbi was banned from the rabbinic academy for insisting that in a visionary journey to the throne-room of God he saw a principal angel seated in God's presence. It may well be that the verse in Mark and the response of the court give evidence that the passage had already become a basis for controversy within the Jewish community. The claim that Jesus was that figure seated in the presence of God seemed to some a clear violation of God's oneness—and would thus constitute blasphemy. Later Jewish opponents of Christianity regarded Christians as di-theists, people who believed in "two powers in heaven."

The whole passion narrative, however, indicates that the offense leading to Jesus' crucifixion is the assertion that Jesus is the Christ. Before Pilate, he is tried as "the King of the Jews." And as Jesus hangs on the cross, the chief priests and elders mock him as an alleged "Christ, the King of Israel." They do not use the expression "Son of man," and they say nothing about heavenly enthronement. Royal imagery dominates the story. The basis for Jesus' rejection by both religious and political authorities is the claim he is the King. The "offense," as Paul well knew, was "Christ crucified" (1 Cor. 1:23).

The trial of Jesus concludes abruptly after his testimony. The court agrees that he deserves **death**; **the high priest** tears his robes as a sign he has heard **blasphemy**. Strangely, nothing is said about why Jesus is not immediately stoned. The penalty for blasphemy, as stipulated in the Torah, is stoning. Yet Jesus is simply bound over to Pilate on political charges—for claiming to be "the King of the Jews"—and is executed on those grounds.

The lack of information about the court's reasoning has been the subject of much study, without any clear-cut results. Did the Jewish court have the right to execute capital criminals? The evidence is ambiguous, and without further data the matter cannot be decided. The author of John's Gospel insists that the Jewish court did not have the right (John 18:31), which explains why although Jesus is executed for religious reasons, he must die on a Roman cross. Mark makes no effort to explain why the Jewish court does not put Jesus to death in a manner prescribed by the law. The most we can say is that according to Mark, Jesus was condemned to death by the Jewish authorities. There are questions Mark does not feel obliged to answer.

What is important is that Jesus is "rejected" by the religious authorities—the "builders" of Psalm 118. The trial provides the basis for that rejection: the claim that Jesus is **the Christ, the Son**

of the Blessed. The psalm also promises that Jesus will be vindicated by God—as other Scriptures promise (Psalm 110; Daniel 7).

At the conclusion of Jesus' trial, he is mocked and maltreated by the servants of the court. The Gospel emphasizes the enormous distance between Jesus and traditional messianic expectations. While accepting the exalted designations and promising heavenly vindication, Jesus appears completely powerless. In the eyes of the court, his claims are pretentious and absurd. His movement has collapsed, his followers have fled. He makes claims he cannot sustain. In terms of Greek tragedy he is guilty of hubris—overstepping his bounds as a mortal in a way that brings about his undoing.

Some have suggested the mockery is intended to conjure up images from Isaiah 50. While that is possible, such views depend upon an interpretation of the servant passages in Isaiah that is probably untenable. The mockery—taunts, spitting, beating—are of a general sort and do not necessarily allude to any scriptural passage. There are numerous psalms that would fit the general pattern, but again there are few specific terms that require such an explanation.

The taunt, **Prophesy!** calls attention to Jesus' prediction that the court "will see." While his claims are blasphemous as measured by the law, they are simply absurd when measured by reality and common sense. "Let's hear some more prophecies," they taunt.

At that point, the narrator shifts to the courtyard where Peter's denial is played out. Alone among the disciples, **Peter** has risked his life by following Jesus—as he promised he would. Yet he too collapses, and his fall is all the more pronounced. Eric Auerbach, in his study of Peter's denial in *Mimesis*, calls the effect "pendulation": Peter comes closest to genuine heroism, so that he has farther to fall. Mark recounts with considerable detail Peter's disintegration. He must finally **swear** an oath that he does not know Jesus.

Peter provides a foil for Jesus. Much like the comic scenes in Shakespeare's dramas, what transpires outside the circles of power sheds light on what occurs inside. Jesus is on trial for his life. When asked to tell the truth, he does, though it seals his fate. Peter is also on trial. His interrogator, however, is a female servant in the household of the high priest—she is very low on the social ladder. Even in the presence of so unimportant a person, however, Peter lies—and thus saves his life. Jesus' courage is illumined by comparison—and Peter's cowardice all the more emphasized.

Several earlier themes are replayed here. We are reminded of Jesus' statement: "Whoever seeks to save his life will lose it." We are also reminded of his rejoinder to the religious authorities early in the story: "Those who are well have no need of a physician but those who are sick. I came not to call the righteous but sinners." Every vestige of heroism is stripped from the disciples. Like other sinners, they need deliverance and healing. If there is to be anything beyond Jesus' ministry, it will not be because of Peter's nobility.

Perhaps the most interesting feature of the account, however, is the inconclusive ending. It does not occur to Mark to tell us whether or not Peter escapes. The account of his collapse ends with the **second** crow of the **cock** (the textual evidence for the mention of the first crow is weak) and Peter's recalling of Jesus' prediction: **Before the cock crows twice you will deny me** thrice. [RSV: **three times**]. Then we are told: **He broke down and wept.** We are not told where that will lead. Will Peter hang himself? Will he escape arrest? Will he find the rest of the disciples who have already fled? The author does not tell us. The only subsequent mention of Peter is in the words of the young man at the tomb who instructs the women to "tell the disciples and Peter that he is going before you to Galilee. There you will see him, as he told you." But the women flee and say nothing to anyone.

The narrator is obviously not interested in producing a narrative that fills in every detail. No narrator can, of course, but the gaps in Mark's story are very obvious. Important questions are unresolved. Yet there is far more to the story than meets the eye. The account of Peter's denial ends with his recalling Jesus' prediction that this would happen. We too are reminded that however bleak things may appear, they have been foreseen—even "written." Things happen precisely as Jesus said they would.

That makes for a particular irony in view of what is occurring within the courtroom. Jesus is being mocked for his predictions; "Prophesy!" they taunt. Yet at that very moment one of Jesus' prophecies is being fulfilled in detail: **Before the cock crows twice you will deny me three times.** Unknown to his judges, Jesus is indeed a prophet. All will occur precisely as he predicted. There is more going on than any of the participants in the drama can appreciate. As readers, we are offered a glimpse of the inside of the story—the deeper dimensions where Jesus' predictions and God's will are being fulfilled. Even so apparently disastrous an event as the collapse of Peter, "the rock," is encompassed within the plan.

And because we understand that, the taunts of the court take on a new light. They assume an ironic tone in a sense quite different from what the taunters intend. They remind us of the truth: Jesus does prophesy, and what he says can be trusted. He will be vindicated after three days; he will take his place "at the right hand of power." There is more to come. Of course the members of the court have no way of knowing that. They judge by appearances, and in their view the notion that Jesus is the Messiah, the Son of God who will take his place at God's right hand, is absurd, even blasphemous. Yet their very taunt serves only to highlight the truth for the reader—and to confirm how great a chasm separates us and the characters in the story, how blind they are to the truth that we are now in a position to appreciate.

Mark offers us a glimpse of how it is with us and God—of how it is in the world where leaders are bound by traditions that cannot deliver what they promise, where those entrusted with safeguarding the public good are blind to the truth, where people are unable to see beyond appearances. The story also promises there are other forces at work, that God's will is done even by unwitting agents.

The Trial before Pilate (15:1-15)

As the narrative continues, the fate of Peter is ignored. The morning gathering of **the council** does not seem to presume the evening session. No mention is made of the capital sentence already passed. We learn only that the council gathers and binds Jesus over **to Pilate** for trial.

Pilate's question, **Are you the King of the Jews?** presumes that is the accusation on the basis of which Jesus has been handed over: he is accused of claiming to be a king. The phrase **King of the Jews** is appropriate on the lips of Pilate, a Gentile. The religious components of the Jewish "Christ" are unimportant to him; what matters is that Jesus claims to be a king. Further, Gentiles referred to Israelites as "Jews." "King of the Jews" is thus the appropriate Roman formulation. If Jesus claims to be a king in Caesar's domain, he is guilty of treason.

Mark is consistent in distinguishing Jewish and Gentile speakers. When the high priest speaks, he refers to the royal office as "the Christ, the Son of the Blessed." Those Jews who taunt Jesus at the foot of the cross use the expression, "the Christ, the King of Israel" (15:32). Israelites did not use the term "Jew" as a self-reference except in the Diaspora; "Jew" is a term employed by Gentiles. And when Israelites referred to their coming King, the term was "the Messiah."

The point is that it is Jesus' identity as King that is the issue throughout.

Jesus' response to Pilate's question needs tone of voice to be heard properly. In translating, "It is as you say," the New International Version has attempted to make clear what the words imply: Jesus does not deny that he is the King. Pilate understands Jesus' response—literally "you say so"—as an acceptance of the designation. The precise wording, however, is ironic. It is in fact Pilate who uses the words. Jesus acknowledges that the words are true, but it is equally important that they appear on Pilate's lips: It is as *you* say. Here, as throughout the passion sequence, it is Jesus' enemies who unwittingly testify to the truth about him. They speak the correct words and hail him as King, though they have no idea that they are speaking the truth. One of the greatest ironies may be that Pilate's formulation of the charge against Jesus assured for all time that Jesus would be confessed as the crucified and risen Messiah-King.

The chief priests, presumably present at the initial hearing, accuse Jesus of **many things.** While Luke specifies some of the "many things" Jesus was charged with, Mark does not. The only issue of importance is the messianic claim. Jesus' silence before Pilate, as at his trial, evokes amazement. Again, it is possible that the statement alludes to Isaiah 53 and the silence of the servant of God before his accusers, though that is by no means certain. Jesus makes no effort at self-defense.

The "custom" of releasing a prisoner at Passover to which Mark alludes remains a problem. Historical research has turned up no evidence of a regular release of prisoners on Passover. The gesture of good will is not impossible, but there is no way of confirming Mark's statement that it was a regular procedure under Pilate's administration.

The episode contrasts Jesus' fate with that of a criminal named **Barabbas,** from the Aramaic, meaning literally "son of the father." While it is tempting to see a play on words here (Jesus, who is "the Son of God," and someone named "the son of the father"), we cannot assume such knowledge of Aramaic on the part of Mark's audience. Barabbas is identified as an insurrectionist, arrested as part of an uprising in which **murder** was **committed.** The passage says only that Barabbas was among the insurrectionists who committed murder, not that he was himself the murderer. While Josephus provides numerous examples of small uprisings from the period of Judas the Galilean until the war against Rome in 66, he mentions neither an uprising during this period nor anyone named Barabbas. We should perhaps think of a small rebellion, a guerrilla action, that would become more common during the next several decades.

Pilate asks the crowd if they want him to release Jesus **the King of the Jews** as his gesture of good will. The question is somewhat sarcastic. **The King of the Jews** is Pilate's formulation. In the Fourth Gospel, the priests object to the use of the term as an inscription. They prefer "He said he was the King of the Jews." Even in Mark, it is clear that Pilate's use of the title is an insult, particularly biting at the time of Passover when Israel celebrated deliverance from foreign domination.

Pilate's knowledge that **it was out of envy that the chief priests had delivered him up** is somewhat strange. Pilate, of course, may have good reason to suspect that the Sanhedrin's handing over of Jesus is not motivated solely by allegiance to Caesar. Elsewhere, however, Mark comments that the priests "fear" Jesus and his popularity. The priests are not depicted as a petty group motivated by jealousy. Read in the context of the larger narrative, the comment probably means the priests envy Jesus' popularity with the crowds, which makes him dangerous. The comment ought not obscure the good reasons both Jewish and Roman leaders had for taking action against Jesus. He was dangerous. His popularity with the crowds and the mere suggestion that he was the promised Messiah-King marked him as a potential troublemaker against whom some action was required. The religious leaders rightly feared that some firebrand could spark a revolt that would bring Roman legions down on their heads. History proved them correct, for in A.D. 70 Jerusalem was captured by Titus and his soldiers and the temple was destroyed.

Some have seen in Pilate's actions an interest in justice and a genuine concern for Jesus. That seems unlikely. His suggestion that Jesus be released should be understood more as a desire to provoke the priests than as an expression of his interest in the fate of a lone Jew. And from the perspective of the law, Pilate's behavior is hardly exemplary. The greatness of the Roman system was its adherence to the rule of law. If he believed Jesus to be innocent, he should have released him. The story may suggest that Pilate hoped all along to release Jesus and simply miscalculated the resolve of the common people. That seems unlikely, however, and reads too much into the story. Pilate's reticence to release Jesus provides an occasion for everyone to participate in the death sentence. Pilate's question gives the mob an opportunity to demand Jesus' death. And according to Mark, Pilate capitulates to the will of the mob—the behavior of an incompetent administrator. Pilate is not really a sympathetic figure at all.

The crowd (or mob) proves to be fickle, easily manipulated by the priestly group. They are encouraged to ask for the release of **Barabbas,** the sort of freedom-fighter who could capture the imagination of the common people. Those who only days earlier hailed Jesus as a deliverer upon his entry to Jerusalem now demand his execution. It is not only that the crowd is manipulated by the priests. Jesus is a disappointment. His royal entrance to Jerusalem encouraged hopes that are now dashed. Barabbas at least took action; Jesus has done nothing. His movement is in shambles. The crowd's readiness to demand Jesus' death is their bitter response to shattered dreams. Jesus conforms to popular expectations of a deliverer as little as he conforms to other hopes and dreams.

There is considerable irony in the release of Barabbas and the condemnation of Jesus. Barabbas is a convicted revolutionary, precisely the sort the chief priests had to fear. They had everything to lose from popular uprisings. When war was finally declared against Rome, the priestly group was thrown out by the revolutionary leaders. At the conclusion of the war, the temple was destroyed, never to be rebuilt. In their opposition to Jesus, the aristocratic leaders make strange alliances, offering support even to such as Barabbas. Further, in demanding that Jesus be crucified, the crowds insist that the penalty for sedition be imposed on Jesus, who is innocent of such crimes. The guilty are set free, the innocent condemned. And this is how it "must" be.

Pilate, **wishing to satisfy the crowd,** releases Barabbas and sends Jesus to his death.

The Mockery of the King (15:16-20)

It is perhaps useful to observe what the Gospel does not do in narrating the account of Jesus' death. It focuses very little on Jesus' physical suffering. It stresses rather the total collapse of his movement and his complete isolation. When he dies, he has been deserted by disciples and crowds, ridiculed by religious and political leaders, mocked by those who hang with him, and abandoned finally even by God. He dies absolutely alone.

Further, the Gospel makes little effort to narrate the story so as to help the reader understand Jesus' death as a "ransom" or atoning sacrifice. While such imagery had become an established part of Christian tradition long before Mark wrote, it is virtually absent from the lengthy account of Jesus' death. The author presumes that "Christ died for our sins." The story is told less to explicate a theory about atonement than to see the world from the perspective of the cross. What does Jesus' death disclose about us and our world—and about God?

Pilate orders that Jesus be flogged, then hung on a cross. The penalty of crucifixion was reserved for criminals of lower classes accused of sedition. The unusually cruel form of death was to make a public spectacle of those who dared challenge the power of the emperor. Flogging could be a separate punishment, but it was also common as a prelude to crucifixion. The whip was fashioned of leather thongs with pieces of metal or bone affixed. Victims could easily be beaten to death, their flesh literally flayed from their bones. Such a beating weakened the victim and made crucifixion the more excruciating.

The mockery that follows offers another glimpse of how the confession of Jesus as King sounds to the participants in the drama. To the Roman **soldiers,** the claim that Jesus is **the King of the Jews** seems laughable. **The whole batallion** comes together to pay mock **homage** to the would-be King who dares to challenge the authority of Caesar. Mark says they dressed him in **a purple cloak.** Matthew uses the more correct "scarlet," the actual color of the soldier's garb. Mark is less interested in historical precision than in the symbolism: **purple** is the color of royalty. The **crown** of acanthus (**thorns**) is to be understood less as an instrument of torture than ridicule. The victor's crown was prominently displayed on statues of heroes and rulers. Jesus is dressed in a manner befitting royalty—only to be mocked and humiliated. The stick with which Jesus is beaten is presumably his staff. Philo offers an account of a similar mockery of a Jew who, during the riots in Alexandria, was dressed as a king and hounded through the streets in a mock procession.

The scene demonstrates the total contempt the soldiers hold for Jesus (and presumably for their Jewish subjects). For the reader, the scene provides ironic testimony to the truth. Jesus is invested as King—clothed in royal garb and hailed by the soldiers. They understand their horseplay as mockery. Unknown to them, they speak the truth and provide for Jesus' investiture. There is a dimension of truth quite obscured from them to which only readers have access.

When they have finished their mockery, they clothe Jesus in **his own clothes** and lead him off to be crucified.

The Crucifixion (15:21-27)

The little details about **Simon of Cyrene** carrying Jesus' **cross** undoubtedly lend to the narrative the feel of authenticity. The details also suggest that the story is told for people who are familiar with at least the names of the participants. Simon is **the father of Alexander and Rufus.** The names, omitted in Matthew and Luke, were obviously familiar to Mark's audience. We can only guess at these persons' identity, since no further record of them exists. The little details serve as graphic reminders that we read the story as outsiders and that there are matters we will probably never know.

The execution site is identified as **Golgotha,** translated as **the place of the skull.** The site, outside the city walls, was apparently a small hill that was shaped somewhat like a skull. There is still debate about the precise location of the site.

The offer of **wine** mixed with the drug **myrrh** is a humanitarian gesture. It is attested as a Jewish and not as a Roman practice. Jesus refuses the drug.

The crucifixion is not described in gory detail. Such a description would have been unnecessary, since people would have known about the practice. The absence of such details is likewise a good indication that Mark seeks to emphasize Jesus' utter loneliness rather than his physical pain.

The comment that the soldiers cast **lots** for Jesus' possessions conveys accurately what took place at executions. The words, however, are borrowed from Psalm 22. They are not introduced with a formula like, "Then, in order that the Scriptures might be fulfilled. . . ." Those unfamiliar with the Scriptures need notice nothing more than the facts. For those who know the psalm, the scriptural wording points to the deeper dimensions of the story. Jesus' fate has "been written." All is proceeding according to God's plan. Like the tormentors of the sufferer in the psalm, Jesus' enemies cast lots for **his garments.** They will also mock him (Ps. 22:8). Jesus' last, desperate cry is taken from the opening line of the same psalm. There is a script for what is occurring. These are not unplanned events. "It is necessary." Despite appearances, the "King of the Jews" is "going as it has been written of him."

While Mark's narrative earlier proceeds breathlessly from event to event, here the story slows. Specific times and places are important. The time of Jesus' crucifixion is **the third hour,** or 9:00 A.M. That does not fit with John's insistence that Pilate announces his verdict at noon. The temporal structure in the Fourth Gospel is not without theological significance, of course. Twelve noon on the day of Preparation is when leavened products are removed from the house and burned—when the hymn is sung praising God as Israel's King. At this very moment, according to John, the Jewish leaders seal Jesus' fate when they declare to Pilate, "We have no king but Caesar." The temporal reference in Mark probably has no such significance, except as a way of framing the story and marking the importance of what is occurring.

The inscription of the charge reads: **The King of the Jews.** Again, Pilate's sarcasm is evident. On the occasion of Passover, he provides for the Jewish populace a graphic illustration of what awaits enemies of Caesar. Jews would have to witness the death of one identified as their King.

There is probably no more certain historical remnant in the Gospel accounts than the inscription of the charge: Jesus was executed by Pilate as **The King of the Jews.** For this reason, when God raised Jesus from the dead he was hailed as the crucified and risen Messiah-King. It is Pilate who made Jesus' royalty the issue. We might well see Pilate as the most creative force in the development of New Testament "Christ"-ology.

It is uncertain whether the inscription was affixed to the cross, as Matthew, Luke, and John suggest, or hung around the neck of the victim. Historical evidence is sparse.

Two others are crucified with Jesus. They are identified as "bandits" (not **robbers**). Again, the term is the same used by Josephus to refer contemptuously to freedom-fighters whom he regarded as no better than common criminals. We are perhaps to think of the two as members of the group arrested with Barabbas in the insurrection. The emphasis is less on their status as common criminals than on their being men accused of political crimes.

The reference to the **right** and the **left** recalls the question of James and John, who sought places of honor when Jesus appeared in his glory. "You do not know what you are asking," he responded to them. Indeed! This is what it means to be associated with the "King of the Jews."

Mockery (15:29-32)

Two groups of Jewish bystanders taunt Jesus as he hangs on the cross, recalling the two charges at his trial. The description once again betrays the influence of the Psalms. "Those who pass by wag their heads, they make mouths at me," wrote the psalmist. Even the mockery is scriptural.

In describing the mockery, the narrative uses a particular word that is not found in the Psalms; it is the verb "blaspheme." The verse should be translated, "And the passers-by blasphemed [RSV: **derided**] him." The verb does not mean simply "mock," and it should be understood as parallel to the charge at Jesus' trial. From early in Mark's narrative the issue of blasphemy has been important. Jesus is charged by the scribes with blasphemy for claiming the authority to forgive sins (2:7). Yet we learn that in attributing Jesus' power to demonic possession, it is the religious leaders who are guilty of blasphemy (3:28-30). At his trial, Jesus is condemned to death for blasphemy. Yet it is really his enemies who are guilty; in their opposition to Jesus they are the blasphemers whom God will punish.

The taunt of the passers-by recalls the "false testimony" at Jesus' trial. The wording of their taunt differs slightly from the testimony at the trial. While the quotation at the trial distinguishes between "this temple made with hands" that Jesus will destroy and "another temple not made with hands" that he will build, the taunt refers to the destruction and rebuilding of the same **temple.** They have not understood fully what the statement promises and have heard only a boast that now seems pretentious. On the one hand, the taunt offers another glimpse of how Jesus appears to his contemporaries. He is alone and abandoned by everyone, powerless to carry out a threat against the temple, and so the claims made about him seem groundless and pretentious, fit only for ridicule. On the other hand, recalling the statement about the temple keeps the issue before the reader—so that the tearing of the temple curtain becomes all the more significant. Jesus' tormenters say more than they know. The execution of Jesus will have dire consequences for the temple, however unlikely that may now appear.

The taunt of the **chief priests** and **scribes, "He saved others; he cannot save himself,"** involves first a play on Jesus' name: Jesus, Jeshua, means "savior." It is hardly a likely name in this situation. Jesus seems quite incapable of saving anyone. In the view of the religious authorities, this incapability is a clear disqualification from office. We know, however, that Jesus has come to "give his life as a ransom for many." It is precisely by not saving himself that he will save others.

The mockery likewise picks up the second charge at Jesus' trial: "So you are **the Christ, the King of Israel,** are you?" The taunt emphasizes the incongruity between the title and Jesus' condition. Cross and messiahship do not fit together. Paul says in 1 Corinthians 1, "We preach Christ crucified, a scandal to Jews." The verse in Mark offers the same view. Only if Jesus **comes down from the cross** will his enemies be convinced that the title "King" is apt. Yet it is precisely the cross which is "necessary." Jesus does not come down, and in his death is hidden his identity as "the Christ, the King of Israel." Jesus has promised, however, that his judges "will see," as will the whole created order. His death will not be the end of the encounter.

According to Luke, one of the two executed with Jesus repents and is promised a place in paradise. In Mark, there is no dramatic repentance, nothing at all to brighten the somber tones. Jesus is a disappointment even to the bandits with whom he is executed. They too make fun of him.

A Last Word (15:33-34)

At noon, when the sun is at its highest, the sky is darkened. The created order itself provides an appropriate setting for Jesus' death. The reference may allude to Jesus' prediction that "the sun will be darkened and the moon will not give its light" (Mark 13:24). Some have suggested an allusion to one of Amos's oracles of doom:

> And on that day, says the Lord God,
>   I will make the sun go down at noon,
>   and darken the earth in broad daylight.
>   (Amos 8:9)

While that is possible, the image itself requires no hidden scriptural significance: the death of Jesus is a cosmic event. This is a time of **darkness.**

At three o'clock, Jesus cries out: **My God, my God, why hast thou forsaken me?** While Mark says little about Jesus' physical anguish, the narrative emphasizes his total isolation. Deserted by his close friends, mocked and tormented by the Jewish and Roman leaders, ridiculed by those who hang with him, Jesus now gives voice to his sense of abandonment even by God. He is overcome by darkness and the silence of God: "My God, my God, why have you abandoned me?"

The words, of course, come from Psalm 22. C. H. Dodd was the first to propose that the allusion to part of the psalm implied knowledge of the whole on the part of Mark's audience. The whole psalm should be read as an interpretation of the cross, says Dodd. While Dodd's argument that the quotation of part of a Scripture implies the larger context is not true of Jewish or Christian scriptural interpretation in general, it is possible that Mark presumed knowledge of the psalm on the part of his audience. The psalm ends with the vindication of the sufferer. Jesus has already promised his vindication—several times. Knowledge of the psalm does not make Jesus' agonized cry any less agonizing; it can hardly be viewed as a simple prayer of trust. The impact of the words is quite different, for example, from Luke's "Father, into your hands I commit my spirit," also from a psalm. However, the allusion does suggest to those who know Psalm 22 that even this abandonment is comprehended within the scriptural "necessity" and thus willed by God. Abandonment cannot mark the end of the story.

A Final Misunderstanding (15:35-37)

Jesus' cry is recounted in Aramaic, then translated into Greek. The reason is clear in what follows: Jesus' words are misunderstood by the crowd. **Behold, he is calling Elijah.** Matthew seeks to make the misunderstanding more intelligible by giving the initial words in Hebrew (*Eli, Eli,* rather than **Eloi, Eloi**), while still preserving the Aramaic for the rest. Commentators make too much of the difference in sound between **Eloi** and **Elijah.** Mark wrote in Greek, and his readers could hardly be expected to appreciate the intricacies of Aramaic pronunciation. The sounds are close enough. Jesus' words are misunderstood. The reaction of the bystanders is a fitting conclusion to Jesus' ministry: abandoned by everyone, including God, even his last agonized cry is misunderstood.

The passage is complex, for the precise character of the misunderstanding is significant in light of the rest of the story. The crowd believes Jesus is calling **Elijah,** probably attesting traditions according to which Elijah was expected to appear to aid the afflicted. The reader has been told, however, that "Elijah has come, and they did to him whatever they pleased, as it is written of him" (Mark 9:13). In his role as Elijah, John the Baptist came first—and as the appointed preparer of the way he was put to death by Herod. Jesus must suffer the same fate. The reference to Elijah only underscores for the reader how clearly events are proceeding according to plan—and how completely the crowd fails to understand.

A few, still interested in a spectacle, wait to see if Elijah appears **to take** Jesus **down.** The offer of **vinegar** to drink, whatever the motivation, alludes to Ps. 69:22. Once again, participants in the drama unwittingly play the role assigned them in the Scriptures.

There will be no spectacle, no escape from death. With one final **cry,** Jesus breathes out his spirit. The would-be King is dead, his movement in shambles. He committed his cause to God, and God abandoned him. At least that is how it seems. The narrative has prepared us for more to come—but Mark chooses to stress the incongruity, the scandal. His story relentlessly follows Jesus' career from the world's perspective. If truth is visible at all, it is visible only to the reader who knows things the characters in the story cannot. Even for the reader, the truth seems to be in danger.

The only means of providing insight into the "reality" of such a story is by means of irony. Mark constructs a world in which a chasm separates reality from appearance and then plays on that contrast. Like Paul and the author of the Fourth Gospel, Mark is impressed with the scandal of the cross. He attempts in narrative form a "theology of the cross"—a glimpse of reality that takes as its point of departure the execution of the King of the

Jews. If Jesus is the promised Messiah, this is how the world must be—and this is the only way the story can be told!

Portents (15:38-39)

Two seemingly insignificant events signal the reader that despite appearances something significant has occurred. The first is the tearing of **the curtain of the temple . . . from top to bottom.** The event is reported by the narrator. We are given no insight into the reaction of characters in the story. That the event occurs is all we need to know. The tearing provides a great *inclusio*, completing what began with the tearing of the heavens at Jesus' baptism. The event, reported without interpretation, is an invitation to the reader's imagination.

Imagination requires some direction. Information about the imagery is helpful. **The curtain** which is torn may be the one which separated the Holy of Holies, the place where God was symbolically present, from the rest of the sanctuary. The sacred precinct where the Ark of the Covenant was kept was out of bounds for all mortals except the high priest, who was allowed to enter it only once a year, on the day of atonement. The curtain provided protection from God's holy presence, for that presence could mean death for any who encountered it. The tearing of the curtain implies the end of that protection.

In the letter to the Hebrews there is a lengthy reflection on the meaning of Jesus' death, and that reflection plays on precisely this imagery. In chapters 9–10 of the letter, the death of Jesus is understood as his entering into the Holy of Holies once for all, providing his own blood as the required sacrifice. As a result, believers are encouraged to "enter the sanctuary by the blood of Jesus, by the new and living way which he opened for us through the curtain" (Heb. 10:19-20). In Hebrews, Jesus' self-offering is understood as the end of sacrifice and the beginning of a new order. While Mark offers no such explanation of the image, such reflection fits well with Mark's narrative, which plays regularly on the theme of old and new: "new skins for new wine" (Mark 2:22). The relationship between God and the created order will never be the same. A barrier has been removed because of Jesus' death.

The image likewise anticipates the end of **the temple.** Since Jesus' arrival in Jerusalem, Mark's narrative has pointed to the impending destruction of the temple. Jesus explicitly predicts that not one stone will be left on another. The confused testimony of false witnesses at Jesus' trial links the destruction of the old temple and the construction of the new with his death and resurrection. And at the moment of his death there is dramatic confirmation that the old order is in fact doomed.

The use of such an image as a portent of the temple's destruction becomes more plausible in view of an intriguing parallel found in two forms in the writings of Josephus (*Jewish Wars* 6, 293–96) and in the Talmud (b*Yoma* 39b). The passage from the Talmud reads:

> Our Rabbis taught: During the last forty years before the destruction of the Temple the lot ["For the Lord"] did not come up in the right hand; nor did the crimson-coloured strap become white; nor did the western-most light shine; and the doors of the *Hekal* [temple] would open by themselves, until R. Johanan b. Zakkai rebuked them, saying: *Hekal, Hekal,* why wilt thou be the alarmer thyself? I know about thee that thou wilt be destroyed, for Zechariah ben Ido has already prophesied concerning thee: "Open thy doors, O Lebanon, that the fire may devour thy cedars." (Zech. 11:1)

In addition to the inner veil before the Holy of Holies, the temple was fitted with a large veil that served as a door in the summer when the massive gates were left open. The large veil was embroidered with cosmic imagery, symbolizing an association with the heavens as a cosmic veil. It seems natural to link the tearing of this veil and the tearing of the heavens at Jesus' baptism.

Such historical work only underscores the significance of the image of the "curtains" as an imaginative interpretation of Jesus' death and its consequences. Something is finished with Jesus' last breath—here, the temple itself, which will be destroyed, giving way to another order, a "temple not made with hands" that the risen Christ himself will build. No one knows that yet, however, besides the narrator and the reader. Only subsequent events will make clear what is hidden.

The second event which occurs at the moment of Jesus' death is the "confession" of **the centurion.** The verse makes no attempt to forge a connection with the tearing of the veil. Knowledge of the earlier account of Jesus' baptism provides all the connection needed between the images, which now bring the story full circle. The centurion, standing opposite Jesus and witnessing his death, makes his statement as a counterpart to God's opening declaration. The centurion says: **Truly this man was the Son** [or a son] **of God.**

The grammatical ambiguity of the Greek *huios theou* provides an intriguing possibility for interpreters. Most English versions choose **the Son of God** for the text and "a son of God" for the footnote. Grammar cannot settle the matter. If the variant in Mark 1:1 is read as part of the text, there is precedent for reading the anarthrous *huios theou* as "the Son of God." On the other hand, the more common grammatical form of the title with definite articles appears in Mark as well (Mark 3:11).

Translation here requires attention to the logic of the text. Many who choose to render the Greek with the full-blown title, "the Son of God," regard the statement of the centurion as the first "Christian" confession. A Gentile sees what Jews cannot, so the interpretation proposes—and the secret is finally out in the open.

Though that is possible, in view of the rest of the narrative it is unlikely. The reasons for such translation probably derive more from Christian piety than from sensitive interpretation. Elsewhere in the narrative, the role of Jesus' enemies, Jews and Romans alike, is to speak the truth without understanding what they say. "You are the Christ, the Son of the Blessed?" says the high priest. "You are the King of the Jews?" asks Pilate. "Hail, King of the Jews," the soldiers taunt. "So, you are the Christ, the King of Israel, are you?" say the bystanders at the cross.

It would seem more appropriate to read the statement of the centurion in such light. The grammatical ambiguity makes it possible to hear the statement in two ways. The first would be to regard the "confession" as a purely human estimate. The centurion, impressed perhaps by Jesus' utter collapse, offers an estimate: "Truly this man was [note the past tense!] a son of God." That might mean "a religious man," i.e., hardly a criminal. Luke takes the statement in that sense: the centurion says, "He was innocent." The statement might also be read sarcastically in line with the earlier cynicism of the Roman soldiers who mock Jesus as "King of the Jews."

For the reader, who knows what the centurion cannot, the statement becomes a "confession," another testimony to the truth at the most unlikely moment in the story. Jesus is "the Christ, the Son of the Blessed," as the high priest put it. Testimony is offered, but by people who say more than they know. And only by means of this last piece of irony—the unwitting confession of Jesus' executor—can Mark adequately capture how the "gospel of Jesus Christ, the Son of God" must feel.

Those who regard such an interpretation as attributing too much sophistication to Mark need only read John's Gospel for an example of artful use of irony at precisely this point in the story. We have become so accustomed to expecting nothing from the "simple" evangelists that we miss the depths of their stories. "Sophistication" is perhaps the wrong term for Mark; it conjures up images of the school. The story is artful. The use of irony need not imply that the author is highly educated. Indeed, it is often the simple who have an eye for what is "real."

Burial (15:40-47)

With the words of the centurion, the career of Jesus is over—at least in the eyes of the bystanders. Nothing is left of Jesus' movement but a small group of **women.** The men have long since fled. The list of women's names appears here for the first time in Mark. All we learn about these women is that they traveled with Jesus from **Galilee** and served him (taking care of physical needs).

They alone remain. Their presence will become important in light of unexpected events soon to occur.

Unlike John the Baptist's disciples who came to get his body after learning of his death (Mark 6:29), Jesus' followers do nothing. Burial falls to an unknown figure identified as **Joseph of Arimathea.** Mark says only that he was a **respected member of the council, who was also himself looking for the kingdom of God.** Like Simon of Cyrene and his sons Alexander and Rufus, Joseph emerges briefly to play an important role, then disappears into the shadows. Here as well the name may have been familiar to Mark's audience.

When he hears of Jesus' death, **Pilate wondered.** He is surprised that Jesus did not last longer. Sometimes victims hung for several days before finally dying of exhaustion. There is nothing heroic at all about Jesus' death. When Pilate is satisfied that Jesus is indeed dead, he grants the corpse to Joseph.

The preparation for burial is hasty. Normally the body would have been anointed with spices, a task the women would seek to perform early Sunday morning. The reason for the haste is the advent of Sabbath. Jesus dies at 3:00 P.M. With sundown at 6:00, the Sabbath begins. Rather than have Jesus hang on the cross, Joseph is anxious to place him in **a tomb** before the sun sets.

Two of the women who remained to watch until the end also see where Jesus is buried. This little note prepares for what is to follow when the Sabbath concludes.

The Empty Tomb (16:1-8)

Excursus: A Textual Problem (16:1-8 [20])

Before interpreting the last chapter, it is important to know what verses should be included. Mark's Gospel has appeared with four separate endings throughout the history of the church. Deciding among those alternatives is the task of textual critics whose opinions are readily available elsewhere (see bibliography, Lincoln). While the evidence now favors printing a Gospel that ends with v. 8, the Mark known to most generations of Christians ends with v. 20, "Amen" (see KJV). The book we know as the Gospel according to Mark is thus quite different from the one known to earlier generations.

While there is little question in the minds of textual critics about the "alternative endings," there is still a reluctance to accept 16:1-8 as the conclusion to the Gospel. Typical are the comments in the *Oxford Annotated Bible* (pp. 1238f.):

> Certain important witnesses to the text, including some ancient ones, end the Gospel with v. 8. Though it is possible that the compiler of the Gospel intended this abrupt ending, one can find hints that he intended to describe events after the resurrection: for example, Mark 14:28 looks forward to an account of at least one experience of the disciples with Jesus in Galilee after the resurrection, while the friendly reference to Peter (16:7) may anticipate the recounting of the otherwise unrecorded moment of reconciliation between Peter and his Lord (compare Luke 24:34; 1 Cor. 15:5). If such accounts as these were originally part of Mark's Gospel, the loss of them took place very shortly after the Gospel was written. . . .

We are, of course, completely dependent upon copyists and earlier generations of Christians who handed on the text of Mark. We can work only with the manuscript evidence they have provided. Measuring the evidence we have by all the canons of textual criticism, verse 8 seems the earliest ending available to us. All the alternative endings must be judged later, intentional additions to the Gospel. The suggestion that there must have been a lost ending is thus complete fantasy and offers more evidence about interpreters than about Mark. The hypothesis is useful, however. It may in fact indicate why unknown scribes felt obliged to "improve" Mark's Gospel: readers cannot tolerate the unfinished and somewhat disappointing ending. Human needs and inclinations dictate how the story must end. Those needs ought not serve as ultimate criteria by which to measure everything, however, particularly if they arise from a will in bondage to sin. This is one place where the Bible deserves a chance to be heard, however uncomfortable it may feel. Because the various alternative endings seem clearly later additions, they are not considered in this commentary on "Mark." They belong properly to the later history of interpretation.

Part of the difficulty in dealing with the eight verses is their place within ecclesiastical tradition. The little episode is categorized as an Easter text. The verses are removed from their literary setting and placed within a liturgical context and furnished with hymns and prayers. The story may then feel wrong; it may seem out of accord with the hymns and the prayers of the day. One might of course ask if it is not the biblical passage that ought to dictate the mood of the service and not simply the liturgy of the church, but that exploration might take us too far afield.

The verses must first be read as an ending. They conclude Mark's Gospel. Endings are important for what they do. Understanding the meaning of these verses must involve a sense of their function in Mark. Do they, like some endings, tie up loose ends? Do they resolve some tension the story has generated? Do they finally reveal a mystery concealed from the reader throughout? Or are the verses intended to disappoint a reader who has been lured into believing that something good will come of Jesus' death? Readers of stories by Kafka or plays by Beckett will be aware of how endings can be used to devastate the naive.

If 16:8 is the last verse in Mark's Gospel—and that, to the best of our knowledge, is the case—it establishes a vantage point from which the whole story must be read. How can the "good news about Jesus Christ" have led to this—frightened women who say nothing to anyone? If this is the vantage point from which to view the Gospel, some appraisals of the work can be ruled out. Mark can hardly be classed as "missionary literature," for example. The events that serve as the punch line in ancient confessions—"that he was raised on the third day, and that he appeared to Cephas, then to the twelve . . ." (1 Cor 15:3-7)—are omitted. Most likely the book was written to people who already knew Jesus had been raised. In that case, the question becomes why the Gospel would be ended before reaching a more satisfying conclusion—why did the author not include at least one or two appearance stories to bring the narrative into the post-Easter world where his readers lived?

Even asking questions in this way sets interpreters on a far more promising course.

After **the Sabbath was past,** the women **bought spices** for preparing Jesus' body. The law did not forbid preparing the dead for burial on the Sabbath, but the women had obviously made no preparation and had to wait until after sunset on the Sabbath to purchase the necessary materials. Then they had to wait until first light to visit **the tomb.**

The list of names is slightly different from that in 15:40. **Mary the mother of James** replaces Mary the mother of James the younger and Joses. While the narrator is interested in such specifics, there is no attempt to reconcile the various lists.

The women are not deterred by the fact that Jesus' body would have begun to decompose. They are determined to do their duty. Nor do they recall that Jesus was already "anointed . . . for burying" (14:8). They certainly do not expect that Jesus will be raised from the dead.

The strange redundancy, **very early** and **when the sun had risen,** must mean "the moment the sun had risen, they set out for the tomb."

Their concern about **the stone** sealing **the tomb,** expressed only after they have set out, points ahead to the declaration that **the stone** has been **rolled back.** The comment that the stone was large only emphasizes the miraculous nature of what has occurred.

Inside the tomb the women are confronted by **a young man sitting on the right side, dressed in a white robe.** The white robe is probably sufficient to indicate that the young man is a heavenly messenger. Matthew speaks of the messenger as an "angel"; in Luke, there are two men in dazzling apparel. The women's response is appropriate to the heavenly figure: they are terrified.

The messenger seeks to dispel their terror by offering testimony that Jesus has been raised from the dead. **He is not here; see the place where they laid him.** There is no sense, as in Matthew, that anyone might understand the empty tomb to imply some theft of the body. Jesus' absence is proof that the crucified one has been raised—precisely as he said.

For the first time in the story, Jesus' followers are told to tell the great secrets about Jesus entrusted to them. There has been preparation for this moment. Coming down from the Mount of Transfiguration, Jesus instructs his intimates not to report what has occurred "until the Son of man should have risen from the dead" (9:9). The moment has now come; the time of secrecy is finally past: **Go, tell his disciples and Peter.** The women, who alone have remained with Jesus and have come to do their duty, are now offered the opportunity to be the first evangelists. They have the chance to herald the good news that Jesus has been raised.

They are instructed to tell **his disciples and Peter.** Peter is singled out, perhaps as an indication that he will require some special encouragement after his total collapse and denial of Jesus. And they are to remind the disciples of what Jesus promised: "After I am raised up, I will precede you to Galilee" (14:28). The last words of the heavenly messenger play one final time on a theme that echoes through the Gospel: **as he told you.** There is reason to trust what Jesus promised.

If the news is intended to dispel their terror, it does not succeed. The women do not do as they are instructed. Like the disciples, they flee, overcome by fear and astonishment. **And they said nothing to anyone, for they were afraid.** Mark ends with one last collapse. The story concludes with the world much as it has always been—shrouded in darkness and disappointment.

Yet the world is not the same. The tomb is empty. Jesus is out, beyond death's reach, on the loose. Readers know this cannot be the end of the story. There has been too much preparation for the next chapter. Someone must have spoken, since the Gospel has been written.

Interpretation must respect the two impressions with which the story concludes: disappointment and anticipation. The temptation is to resolve the tension and choose one or the other mood. A few bold interpreters have compared Mark to modern existentialist writers whose point is that life is endlessly disappointing. Mark's conclusion is "realistic," they insist, because it does not resolve tensions. Loose ends are infrequently tied up in real life; disappointment is the universal human experience. There may be some point to life, but we will never know it. The most we can hope for, as one author so eloquently puts it, is a "glimpse . . . before the door of disappointment closes on us."

While the ending in Mark does not attempt to conceal that aspect of life, it does not collapse human experience into disappointment. The story has generated momentum that carries beyond the ending. Jesus will precede his disciples into Galilee, **as he told you.** The Gospel has given us every reason to believe that what Jesus promises will take place. He died and was raised precisely as he announced. His followers scattered, as he said they would; before the cock crowed twice, Peter denied him three times. There is every reason to believe that the rest of his promises will be fulfilled: James and John will drink from the cup; the disciples will give testimony; the gospel will be preached to all the Gentiles. Jesus will be enthroned at God's right hand

and will one day come with the clouds of heaven so that "all will see" and will send his angels to gather the elect from the four winds.

That hope is realistic because it is lived constantly in the face of disappointment. The resurrection is not "the end" in the final sense. The women who followed Jesus, no less than the men, require redemption. Their eyes must be opened, their ears un-stopped and their tongues loosened. There is reason to be hopeful about the future—but not because any of Jesus' followers dem-onstrated heroism. Readers can only anticipate that like the first blind man Jesus healed, the women and the rest of the disciples will finally see things clearly. Somehow the disciples will make it to Galilee and will be prepared finally to do what they were called to do.

The story is not over and will not be until Jesus returns. The surprise for the reader is that the resolution of critical tensions in the story is left for the future. The life of faith is lived between the resurrection and the consummation, "between the times." Some interpreters have proposed that the ending leaves the con-clusion to the reader—to an act of faith that accomplishes what the disciples could not. The story hardly provides a basis for confidence in the performance of any "insiders," however. Making the successful conclusion of the story dependent upon human performance would seem as naive as the boast of the disciples to remain faithful even to death. Turning the completion of the story into an act of human will makes the same mistake as turning the parable of the sower into a statement about a task to be achieved: it turns a gift into a demand. There is hope only because Jesus is no longer imprisoned in the tomb—and because God can be trusted to finish what has been begun.

None of the Gospels can really end the story of Jesus. The whole point is that it continues—and that its significance contin-ues. Mark ends, however, with a greater sense of the mystery yet to be resolved and a deeper appreciation of the gulf that still separates "God's things" and "human things"—or, to use Paul's language, the wisdom of this age and the wisdom of the cross.

Jesus is full of surprises. Old skins cannot contain the new wine. The world's uneasiness in the presence of Jesus is fully justified. He will not be bound by tradition that defines human life; even death has no final power over him. The end only marks a new beginning—a beginning of the good news that Jesus, the one who is the ultimate threat to our autonomy, now becomes our source of life.

It is only fitting that just as the tomb will not contain Jesus, neither can Mark's story. Jesus is not bound by its ending; he continues into the future God has in store for the creation. In the meantime there is only the Word, the bread, and the wine, and the promise that "you will see him." We walk by faith and not by sight. We can only trust that God will one day finish the story, as God has promised.

SELECTED BIBLIOGRAPHY

I. Standard Commentaries

Achtemeier, Paul J. *Mark*. Philadelphia: Fortress Press, 1986.

Nineham, Dennis. *The Gospel of St. Mark*. Baltimore: Penguin Books, 1964.

Taylor, Vincent. *The Gospel According to St. Mark*. London: Macmillan, 1952.

Williamson, Lamar. *Mark*. Atlanta: John Knox, 1983.

II. Parables

Jeremias, Joachim. *The Parables of Jesus*. 2nd revised edition. New York: Charles Scribner's Sons, 1972.

Tolbert, Mary Ann. *Sowing the Gospel: Mark's World in Literary-Historical Perspective*. Minneapolis: Fortress Press, 1989.

III. Miracles

Best, E. *Disciples and Discipleship: Studies in the Gospel According to Mark*. Edinburgh: T. & T. Clark, 1986.

Brown, Raymond. "The Gospel Miracles." *New Testament Essays*. *Semeia* 12.

IV. Chapter 13

Hartman, Lars. *Prophecy Interpreted*. Lund: Gleerup, 1966.

V. Passion

Dahl, Nils A. *Jesus the Christ: The Historical Origins of Christological Doctrine*. Minneapolis: Fortress Press, 1990.

Danker, F. W. "The Demonic Secret in Mark: A Reexamination of the Cry of Dereliction (15:34)." ZNW 61 (1970): 48–69.

Juel, Donald. *Messiah and Temple: The Trial of Jesus in the Gospel of Mark*. Missoula, Mont.; Scholars Press, 1977.

———. *Messianic Exegesis*. Philadelphia: Fortress Press, 1988.

VI. The Ending

Kermode, Frank. *The Genesis of Secrecy*. Cambridge, Mass.: Harvard University Press, 1979.

Lincoln, Andrew. "The Promise and the Failure—Mark 16:7, 8." JBL 108 (1989): 283–300.

VII. Background Studies

Hengel, Martin. *Son of God*. Philadelphia: Fortress Press, 1976.

Lindars, Barnabas. *Jesus Son of Man*. London: SPCK, 1983.

Segal, Alan. *Rebecca's Children: Judaism and Christianity in the Roman World*. Cambridge, Mass.: Harvard Univ. Press, 1986.

———. *Two Powers in Heaven*. Leiden: Brill, 1978.

Vermes, Geza. *Jesus and the World of Judaism*. Philadelphia: Fortress Press, 1983.

ABOUT THE AUTHOR

Donald H. Juel is Professor of New Testament at Luther North-western Theological Seminary. He has taught also at Indiana University and Princeton Theological Seminary. A popular lecturer to clergy and lay groups, he is the author of several books, among them *Luke-Acts: The Premise of History* and *Messianic Exegesis: Christological Interpretation of the Old Testament in Early Christianity.*